Lutheran Spirituality

LUTHERAN SPIRITUALITY

Life as God's Child

GENERAL EDITOR
Robert C. Baker

CONTRIBUTING EDITOR
Charles P. Schaum

WRITERS
John T. Pless • John Kleinig • Holger Sonntag
• Klaus Detlev Schulz • Chad E. Hoover
• Naomichi Masaki • William M. Cwirla

CONCORDIA PUBLISHING HOUSE • SAINT LOUIS

Library of Congress Cataloging-in-Publication Data

   Lutheran spirituality : life as God's child / general editor, Robert C. Baker ; contributing
editor, Charles P. Schaum ; writers, John T. Pless . . . [et al.].
     p. cm.
   Includes bibliographic references and index.
   ISBN-13: 978-0-7586-2734-6
   ISBN-10: 0-7586-2734-3
   1. Lutheran Church—Missouri Synod—Doctrines. 2. Spiritual life—Lutheran Church—
Missouri Synod. I. Baker, Robert C. II. Schaum, Charles P. III. Pless, John T., 1953–. IV.
Title.
   BX8061.M7L88 2010
   248.4'841—dc22   201004791

1 2 3 4 5 6 7 8 9 10   19 18 17 16 15 14 13 12 11 10

CONTENTS

Preface

In the West, spirituality is as nebulous as it is popular. Having succumbed to humanism, rationalism, and Darwinism, communities once known for a genuine Christian piety now provide a fertile breeding ground for self-made theologies, Eastern religions, the worship of science and technology, or even a resuscitation of the old pagan gods. In a highly competitive environment, each of these spiritual philosophies seeks to fill the vacuum left by the seemingly departed Christian spirit.

Even among faithful Christians, and at other times and places, spirituality has run the gamut from the mystical to the almost sterile. From the emotional to the pragmatic, the experiential to the cerebral, the all-too-human desire to experience (and control!) the divine has proven to be especially resilient. Influenced by modernism, postmodernism, and whatever comes next, even those who try faithfully to follow Jesus Christ may find defining *spirituality*, or at least what is distinctively Christian about their own beliefs and practices, a significant challenge.

Do Lutheran Christians have a spirituality? Indeed they do! This book, adapted from the popular Bible study series of the same name, explores the rich depths of a distinctively Lutheran spirituality that begins in Baptism and is founded upon God's Word. There, the incarnate, crucified, and resurrected Lord proclaims His victory over sin, death, and the devil, and from there flows the proclamation of His Gospel and the administration of His Sacraments. It is through these means presented within the liturgy of His Church that Christ communicates not merely spiritual energies, an emotional high, a method of reasoning, or a stringent morality, but He truly communicates Himself—God in human flesh.

Written by respected Lutheran scholars in the United States and Australia, this book emphasizes the Bible, Luther's catechism, and the

Lutheran hymnal as concrete and integral resources for a truly Lutheran spirituality. May God richly bless those who study His Word, and through His Word may they experience the genuinely enlightening and life-giving spirituality found only in the life, death, and resurrection of our Lord and Savior, Jesus Christ.

Rev. Robert C. Baker
Senior Editor, Adult Bible Studies
Concordia Publishing House

ABBREVIATIONS

AC	Augsburg Confession
AE	Luther's Works, American Edition
Ap	Apology of the Augsburg Confession
FC Ep	Epitome of the Formula of Concord
FC SD	Solid Declaration of the Formula of Concord
ESV	English Standard Version
LC	Large Catechism
LSB	*Lutheran Service Book*
NASB	New American Standard Bible
NIV	New International Version
NKJV	New King James Version
SA	Smalcald Articles
SC	Small Catechism
Tr	Treatise on the Power and Primacy of the Pope

WORD

God Speaks to Us[1]

O ur God is a speaking God. Unlike idols made of mute stone or crafted by the imaginations of the faithless heart, the living God has a voice. He speaks and His words are "spirit and life" (John 6:63). By speaking His divine Word, one God—the Father, Son, and Holy Spirit—brought creation into existence (Genesis 1:1–2; John 1:1–3). The Word made flesh is the revelation of the Father (John 14:9–11) and the author of our salvation, for He was sent to suffer and die as our Savior. The Word of our Savior's cross, the message of reconciliation in the forgiveness of sins, is preached for the creation of faith, because "faith comes from hearing, and hearing through the word of Christ" (Romans 10:17). The same Spirit given by Jesus to His apostles on Easter evening (see John 20:22) inspired them to put the Word into writing "so that you may believe that Jesus is the Christ, the Son of God, and that by believing you may have life in His name" (John 20:31).

Lutheran spirituality is a spirituality of the Word. God's Spirit ties Himself to His Word. We do not look behind or above the Scriptures to find the Spirit; rather, we listen to the Spirit who speaks to us in Christ Jesus. There is no other Jesus than the one proclaimed by the prophets and the apostles. A nineteenth-century hymn of non-Lutheran origin says: "Beyond the sacred page I seek You, Lord." However, believers do not look beyond the sacred page of the Scriptures to find the Lord.

---

1   Adapted from *The Lutheran Spirituality Series: Word*, written by John T. Pless, edited by Robert C. Baker. Copyright © 2006 Concordia Publishing House.

The Lord Jesus is wrapped up in the words of Holy Scripture. To hear its words is to hear Him, for He is the very heart and core of the Bible.

This chapter will assist you not only in understanding what God's Word is and how it functions, but it also will sharpen your skills in listening to our Lord as He speaks in His Scriptures and in preaching that is governed by the Scriptures. To understand the Scriptures is to stand under the Scriptures. It is not so much that we interpret the Scriptures but that the Scriptures interpret our lives. With God's Law, they convict us of sin, that is, of unbelief. They interpret the story of our inborn failure to fear, love, and trust in God above all things as the root of all sin. But the ultimate message of the Bible is the Gospel, God's own declaration that He is for us in every way, bestowing on us the forgiveness of sins achieved by His Son's death on the cross. Any reading of the Bible that does not end up with Jesus Christ crucified and raised for our justification misses the mark, for God's Scriptures were given "to make you wise for salvation through faith in Christ Jesus" (2 Timothy 3:15). Keep your copy of Luther's Small Catechism and your hymnal close at hand as you read this chapter, for they are the two most important tools that you have to help you stand sure-footed under the Holy Scriptures.

In these pages you will see the footprints of Martin Luther. He charted a course for us to follow in learning how to listen to the Scriptures. The cloistered monks of the Middle Ages engaged in prayer, meditation, and the reading and copying of Scripture. From Psalm 119, however, Luther the Augustinian friar, amid the struggles that life in the world brings, drew three rules for the study of the Bible: prayer, meditation, and suffering (Latin: *oratio, meditatio, tentatio*). Scripture is prayerfully read (*oratio*) as that book "which turns the wisdom of all other books into foolishness,"[2] meditated upon in faith (*meditatio*), and held on to for dear life in the face of all that threatens us with physical or spiritual death (*tentatio*). That is how students of the Scriptures are made. Let Luther's three rules guide your reading of God's Word as well, for such a reading promises to yield rich fruit as God's truth is implanted in ear and heart and lives are tested and made strong under the cross.[3]

---

2   AE 34:285.

3   For a more thorough discussion of the Lutheran confession of God's gift of Holy Scriptures, see Robert Preus, *The Inspiration of Scripture* (St. Louis: Concordia, 2003), and Armin Wenz, "Justification and Holy Scripture: *Sola fide et sola Scriptura,*" *Logia* 14, no. 2 (Eastertide 2005): 5–15.

The God Who Speaks

Blessed Jesus, at Your Word
We are gathered all to hear You.
Let our hearts and souls be stirred
Now to seek and love and fear You,
By Your teachings, sweet and holy,
Drawn from earth to love You solely.
Tobias Clausnitzer [4]

As noted in the introduction to this chapter, God is a speaking God; He is not silent. In the beginning, God spoke and creation came into being. God spoke to Adam and Eve, telling them how to remain alive in Him. But the deafening clamor of our sinful nature and the subtle accents of the devil's beguiling speech may drown out the voice of the Good Shepherd for us, just as Adam and Eve grew deaf to their Creator. But the Holy Scriptures testify to Jesus Christ and to His saving work of declaring righteous the ungodly by faith alone for His sake. Certainly we hear this message as we read the Bible, but Christian sermons that are focused on the words of Scripture are the living voice of Christ Jesus. As we develop a regular pattern of the study of Holy Scripture in light of weekly worship with the congregation gathered around preaching and the Lord's Supper, our faith and trust in our Savior is strengthened.

What stands in the way of establishing this regular pattern of hearing God's Word? For some it may be a perceived lack of time. For others it may be boredom or a lack of discipline. But Jesus points out in the parable of the sower (Matthew 13:1–9, 18–23) that all these excuses come from Satan, the world, and our sinful flesh, which seek constantly to obstruct the hearing of God's Word. When distractions and duties overwhelm, Jesus reminds us, as He did Martha, that listening to Him is the only truly necessary thing (see Luke 10:38–42)—and we hear our Savior clearly in His Word.

BY THE PROPHETS

God speaks, but it is no random, unattested voice out of nature or out of nowhere. In the Nicene Creed, we confess that the Holy Spirit "spoke by the prophets." Here the creed echoes such texts as Hebrews 1:1–2 and Luke 24:25–48. These passages testify that the Old Testament writings are the Word of God and that they point to and are fulfilled in

---

4   *LSB* 904:1.

Jesus, who came in our flesh to suffer and die for the sins of the world. After our Lord's resurrection from the dead, He opens the minds of His disciples to understand the Scriptures.

In the Old Testament, God spoke to His people in various ways, including visions (Genesis 15:1), the burning bush (Exodus 3:1–12), and a low whisper (1 Kings 19:9–18). Nevertheless, these instances of God speaking were written down, witnessed in the books of the prophets. In other instances, we are simply told that God spoke (Genesis 12:1–3) or that the Word of the Lord came to the prophet (Jeremiah 1:1–10). For the prophet Samuel, God dramatically called him to service, even though he was still a young man (see 1 Samuel 3:1–18). Although Samuel was initially confused by the voice that he heard in the night, after direction by the priest Eli, Samuel answered the Lord's call: "Speak, for Your servant hears" (1 Samuel 3:10).

As we have observed in several Old Testament texts, God often used visions as the instrument of His voice to the prophets. According to the opening of the Epistle to the Hebrews, though God at one time used prophets to speak to His people, now He speaks to us by Jesus Christ, "His Son, whom He appointed the heir of all things, through whom also He created the world" (1:2). Jesus is God's ultimate Word to us. We do not rely on dreams or charismatic experiences to discover God's will for our lives. We listen to the Son, who speaks to us in and through His Gospel. No matter how spiritual the experience may seem or how angelic the messenger may appear, if it contradicts the Gospel, it is to be rejected (see Galatians 1:8).

After His resurrection, Jesus opened the minds of His followers to understand clearly the Old Testament message concerning the Messiah. Jesus had come not to overthrow political powers or to reestablish the temple worship, but because it was necessary that the Messiah should suffer and on the third day rise from the dead and that repentance and forgiveness of sins should be preached in His name to all the nations, beginning in Jerusalem (Luke 24:45–47; Acts 10:43). The author of Hebrews describes God's Son as the heir of all things and the one through whom the Father created the world (1:2). And the evangelist John makes the connection between Jesus and His participation in the creation by calling Him "the Word" by whom "all things were made" (John 1:1–3; see also Colossians 1:15–17; Genesis 1:3–4).

LISTENING TO THE SON

The transfiguration of Jesus (Luke 9:28–36) demonstrates Jesus' identity and shows Him to be the fulfillment of the Law and the Prophets. This event in the life of our Lord comes to a climax as the Father speaks out of the cloud: "This is My Son, My Chosen One; listen to Him!" (Luke 9:35). Appearing with Jesus at His transfiguration are two Old Testament prophets. Moses represents the Law and Elijah signifies the prophets. In other words, the Law and the Prophets testify to Jesus. On the mountain, Moses and Elijah speak with Jesus about "His departure, which He was about to accomplish at Jerusalem" (Luke 9:31). The Greek word translated as "departure" is *exodon* ("exodus"), thus recalling the Old Testament deliverance of Israel from Egypt, a sequence of events that began with the death of the Passover lamb (see Exodus 12).

What does the transfiguration tell us about the origin and use of the Scriptures? Some Christian denominations diminish the place of Scripture by arguing that it is historically conditioned or bound to an ancient culture and so is not applicable to us today. But in his second Epistle, the apostle Peter links the inspiration of Scripture to the incarnation of the Son of God (2 Peter 1:16–21). The apostles, who are the eye and ear witnesses (see 1 John 1:1–4) of the coming of our Lord, testify to His reality. The story of Jesus Christ is not mythology, but factual history in time and space. The apostles testify to the glory of God made manifest in the humanity of Jesus. The Scriptures are to be interpreted in light of their origin. Interpretation is not left to the imagination of the reader because the Scriptures were not the product of human impulses, but Spirit-sent from the Father through the Son.

WHERE DO WE HEAR GOD?

The Holy Scriptures and Christian preaching go hand in hand. Luther called the Church a "mouth house" rather than a "pen house" as a way of stressing the oral character of God's Word. God caused His Word to be put into writing, and thereby He gave it a fixed and permanent location in order that it might be proclaimed truthfully through all generations. The Bible is not just a book about God, and preaching is not just talk about God. In and through both the Scriptures and the sermon, God is speaking. The aim of His speaking is to bestow the forgiveness of sins, to bring life out of death.

The Divine Service moves sequentially from the reading of texts from the Old Testament (prophet), an Epistle (letter of an apostle), and the Gospel (evangelist) to a sermon preached by the pastor (see Ephesians 4:11). Peter confesses that Jesus has "the words of eternal life" (John 6:68), and this Bible passage is the text we sing in anticipation of the reading of the Holy Gospel in the Divine Service. The proclaimed Word of the sermon that follows almost immediately after the Gospel reading is based on and governed by the written Word of Holy Scripture. Preaching is the living voice of the Gospel as it conforms to Holy Scripture in proclaiming the forgiveness of sins for Christ's sake. When we hear such preaching that is faithful to His Word, we are hearing Jesus (see Luke 10:16). The Lutheran Confessions state:

> According to this Gospel authority, as a matter of necessity, by divine right, congregations must obey them, for Luke 10:16 says, "The one who hears you hears Me." But when they teach or establish anything against the Gospel, then the congregations are forbidden by God's command to obey them.[5]

and

> Ministers act in Christ's place and do not represent their own persons, according to Luke, "The one who hears you hears Me" (10:16). Ungodly teachers are to be deserted because they no longer act in Christ's place, but are antichrists. Christ says, "Beware of false prophets" (Matthew 7:15). Paul says, "If anyone is preaching to you a gospel contrary to the one you received, let him be accursed" (Galatians 1:9).[6]

SPIRITUAL EXERCISES

◈ Before worship, read the Scripture texts assigned in the lectionary for the Divine Service. How is God's Law operative in these texts to unmask your own sin? How is God's Gospel at work to forgive your sins and comfort you with Christ's promises?

◈ Review Luther's explanation to the Third Commandment in the Small Catechism as part of your preparation for the Divine Service. Luther does not focus on the Sabbath day per se, for the requirement of a specific day for worship has been fulfilled in Christ. Instead, Luther contends that we may not "despise preaching and His Word, but hold it sacred, and gladly hear and learn it."[7]

5   AC XXVIII 22–23; *Concordia*, p. 59.
6   Ap VII & VIII (IV) 47–48; *Concordia*, p. 151.
7   *Concordia*, p. 319.

◈   Pray Psalm 119:33–40 as you ask God to instruct you with His words and confirm in you the promises of His Gospel.

POINT TO REMEMBER _____

Truly, truly, I say to you, whoever hears My word and believes Him who sent Me has eternal life. He does not come into judgment, but has passed from death to life. *John 5:24*

The Words That Kill and Give Life

I learned to distinguish between the righteousness of the law and the righteousness of the gospel. I lacked nothing before this except that I made no distinction between the law and gospel. I regarded both as the same thing and held that there was no difference between Christ and Moses except the times in which they lived and their degrees of perfection. But when I discovered the proper distinction—namely, that the law is one thing and the gospel is another—I made myself free. *Martin Luther* [8]

God speaks in two completely different voices in the Scripture. His Law is the preaching of wrath against sin. It is that voice from Sinai's lofty heights that thunders with condemnation of the sinner and his sin. The Gospel stands in distinct contrast from the Law. While the Law makes demands and threatens punishment, the Gospel makes promises and bespeaks peace with God in the blood of Jesus Christ. The Bible is misused when the Law is not clearly distinguished from the Gospel. The Bible is misused when Law and Gospel are not used together to teach and meditate. If Jesus is transformed into something other than a Savior—perhaps a "new Moses," a spiritual coach, a teacher of moral precepts, or the pattern for the pious life—the Bible is misused and the Gospel is abandoned. Lutheran spirituality practices the highest art of all: rightly reading the Scriptures so that threat is distinguished from God's promises in Christ Jesus. C. F. W. Walther, a nineteenth-century pastor and one of the founders of The Lutheran Church—Missouri Synod, writes: "To rightly distinguish Law and Gospel is the most dif-

_____

8   AE 54:442–43.

ficult and highest Christian art—and for theologians in particular. It is taught only by the Holy Spirit in combination with experience."[9]

God's Law functions to show us our sin, that is, our unbelief, which is made manifest in our thoughts, words, and deeds. In contrast, the Gospel speaks the forgiveness of sins. The distinction between Law and Gospel is made difficult because the old Adam clings to what Luther called the *opinio legis*, that is, the inborn "opinion of the law" that human efforts must in some manner contribute to salvation. When human beings take God's Law in hand, it is natural that its use ends either in despair or self-righteousness. The Gospel does not declare man's righteousness but the righteousness of God. The Law is all about man and his sin. The Gospel is all about God and the redemption He has won for the world in the blood of Jesus. The Gospel declares pardon to the guilty, righteousness for the unrighteous, and life for those who are dead in sin.[10]

A LIFE-AND-DEATH DISTINCTION

In 2 Corinthians 3:7–11, the apostle Paul describes the office of the Law. He calls it "the ministry of death" (verse 7). In contrast, Paul describes the office of the Gospel as "the ministry of the Spirit" (verse 8). The ministry of death results in condemnation, for the Law convicts and executes sinners who trust in themselves and live in opposition to God. The ministry of the Spirit is called "the ministry of righteousness" (verse 9) because it serves the redeeming work of Christ Jesus, who justifies the ungodly, declaring them righteous through faith in His atoning sacrifice. The ministry of death has a fading glory. It finds its end in Jesus, who was put to death for our sin and raised to life for our justification. His Gospel, therefore, has a permanent glory because Christ's victory over sin, death, and the devil is eternal. Death will never put Jesus back in the grave. He lives to impart life in the forgiveness of sins to all who trust the promise of His Gospel.

In his Epistle to the Romans, Paul demonstrates what is at stake in the right distinction of the Law and the Gospel. According to Romans 3:19 and 23, the Law speaks to all people, for all have sinned.

---

9   *Law and Gospel: How to Read and Apply the Bible*, trans. Christian C. Tiews, gen. ed. Charles P. Schaum (St. Louis: Concordia, 2010), 49

10   For additional help with the distinction between Law and Gospel, review Article V in the Formula of Concord Solid Declaration (*Concordia*, pp. 552–57). Also see Walther, *Law and Gospel: How to Read and Apply the Bible*, or John T. Pless, *Handling the Word of Truth: Law and Gospel in the Church Today* (St. Louis: Concordia, 2004).

It condemns the Jews, for they were given the Law in written form in the Decalogue transmitted through Moses at Mount Sinai. The Gentiles are not able to plead exemption from the Law because God has written it in their hearts (Romans 2:15). All are held accountable by God's Law.

Paul writes that "by works of the law no human being will be justified in [God's] sight" (Romans 3:20). The Law lacks the power to save; it is impotent to give sinners righteousness before God. Instead, the Law gives us the knowledge of our sinfulness. The great Reformation hymn "Salvation unto Us Has Come" states succinctly:

> It was a false, misleading dream
> That God His Law had given
> That sinners could themselves redeem
> And by their works gain heaven.
> The Law is but a mirror bright
> To bring the inbred sin to light
> That lurks within our nature.[11]

The righteousness of God, on the other hand, is His redeeming work to save sinners accomplished by His Son. Jesus Christ has reconciled us to God by taking our sin upon Himself and dying in our place (see 2 Corinthians 5:18–21). Paul concludes his discussion of the Law in Romans 3 by declaring that God justifies sinners through the atoning death of His Son (verses 23–25). As he declared that under the Law all are condemned, now Paul declares that all are justified by God's grace as a gift through the redemption that is in Christ Jesus. This gift of salvation is received by faith alone.

Because justification is received, not achieved, the apostle writes that our boasting is excluded on the basis of faith (Romans 3:27). Faith is not a human work, but the work of God through His Word. It renders us passive in the sense that we have contributed nothing to our salvation. It is a gift. Thus all human boasting of merit or effort is excluded.

Justification "by faith apart from works of the law" (Romans 3:28) does not overthrow the Law so that we become lawless (Antinomianism) or so that we "continue in sin that grace may abound" (Romans 6:1). Rather, the Law finds its proper end or goal in Christ: "For Christ is the end of the law for righteousness to everyone who believes" (Romans 10:4). The condemnation of the Law is answered in Christ alone, for He is our righteousness. Living by faith in Him we are freed from condemnation (see Romans 8:1) even as the Law continues to

---

11 *LSB* 555:3.

put to death the old man who still lives within us, uncovering and convicting us of every impulse to walk by the flesh rather than by the Spirit. Thus justification by faith alone does not overthrow the Law but confirms the Law's verdict of our sinfulness. Since Christians are at one and the same time both saint and sinner (*simul iustus et peccator*), the Law cannot be dismissed, but it remains in place to put to death all that is not of Christ and to guide us away from self-chosen good works that tempt us to establish our own righteousness apart from faith in Jesus.

TO MIX IS TO MUDDLE

To mix the Law and the Gospel is to lose both. When the Gospel is blended with the Law, we are deceived into thinking that with the right amount of willpower, discipline, perseverance, and effort we can make ourselves right before God. Likewise, when the Law is seen as an additive to the Gospel, Christ Jesus becomes less of a Savior and more of an example. There is no good news in an offer of salvation that depends on emulating Christ. In fact, we would be lost from the start. Who of us has been born of a virgin and lived a life of complete perfection without sin? Sinners do not need a teacher or an example; sinners need a Savior. That is exactly what God has given us in His Son.

In reading the Scriptures and in speaking God's Word, we are to distinguish the Law from the Gospel. The Law comes by way of demand. It speaks to what we must do or leave undone. The Gospel is never about what I must do; rather, it is about what God as my Savior has done and what He continues to do for me. As you read the Bible and hear God's Word preached, pay attention to who it is that is carrying the action of the verbs of salvation. It is always the Lord. And that is good news!

In recent years, we have witnessed the popularity of books and programs that see the Christian life in terms of principles for sanctified living or the Bible as a "how-to" manual. The emphasis is on a life lived by conformity to biblical principles, which will cause God to shower blessings on those who "do the right thing." But this confusion of Law and Gospel is in direct contrast with the Scriptures' portrayal of the Christian life as a life lived by faith: "Therefore, as you received Christ Jesus the Lord, so walk in Him, rooted and built up in Him and established in the faith, just as you were taught, abounding in thanksgiving" (Colossians 2:6–7). Contrary to popular Christianity, God does not smile on us because of our obedience or good works, but solely on account of what Jesus has done for us.

In his letters to the Christians in Galatia and Ephesus, Paul speaks clearly of the life that is lived in Christ by faith (see Galatians 2:17–21; Ephesians 2:8–10). Good works have absolutely nothing to contribute to salvation. Good works are a fruit of faith. They are not offered to God as an attempt to satisfy Him, but they are directed to the need of the neighbor. God does not need our good works, but our neighbor does. We insult God when we attempt to drag our piety and works into heaven. God is honored most when we cling to His promises by faith, and, set free from every attempt to make ourselves righteous, when we focus on the good works that God has prepared beforehand, works defined by His commandments and directed toward the well-being of our neighbor.

THE GOSPEL PREDOMINATES

We observed in Romans 3:19–31 that all have sinned and fall short of the glory of God. Although all have sinned, sinners come in two varieties. There are secure sinners, like the Pharisee in Jesus' parable recorded in Luke 18:9–14. He was proud of his own piety and trusted in it. But there also are the broken sinners, like the tax collector in the same parable. He knew the verdict of the Law all too well, yet he "beat his breast, saying, 'God, be merciful to me, a sinner!' " (Luke 18:13).

Luther described the preaching of God's Law and Gospel as God's *alien* and *proper* work. Preaching the Law is alien work because it is actually foreign to God's nature. He takes no delight in crushing sinners and condemning them with His wrath. Yet that is just what His Law does. God does this alien work so that He can finally do His proper work, the work that God loves to do, namely, forgiving sinners who have been broken by their sin and who look to His mercy, not their own merit. Law and Gospel are both in the Bible, but the Gospel is the goal. It is God's ultimate Word of forgiveness and peace. You have not finished your study of any biblical text until you get to that Good News.

In Luke 15:11–32, the parable of the prodigal son, we have another example of the two types of sinners: those who recognize their sin and are broken by it (the prodigal son) and those who are secure in the knowledge that they have lived a life of obedience (the older son). The younger son sins in his rebellion, in his attempt to live life on his own terms apart from his father's house. The older son sins in his self-righteousness, his belief that his obedience merits blessings and benefits. The Gospel in the parable is found in the father who humiliates himself to embrace and reclaim the son whose life was broken by the Law and who extends the invitation to the banquet even to the ungrateful, selfish older brother.

Another example of these two types of sinners is found in the account of Jesus' crucifixion. He was crucified between two thieves, two obvious sinners. One went along with the crowd, abusing Christ verbally (Luke 23:39). The other thief, made all too aware of his sinfulness, confessed that he was being justly punished. Then he appealed to Jesus for salvation: "Jesus, remember me when You come into Your kingdom" (Luke 23:42). And Jesus answered with the Good News: "Today you will be with Me in Paradise" (Luke 23:43). Perhaps these were the last words this man heard, but they communicated to him the forgiveness that Jesus was even then earning for him.

Today we do not hear Jesus in any other way than through Scripture. Jesus said: "You search the Scriptures because you think that in them you have eternal life; and it is they that bear witness about Me" (John 5:39). To refuse to hear the Scriptures is to refuse to hear Jesus. The Jews had Moses (the Law) and claimed allegiance to the Old Testament—yet in their refusal to believe Jesus, they stand accused by their own Scriptures (see John 5:39–47).

SPIRITUAL EXERCISES

◈ Study and pray the following hymns that are models of proper distinction of Law and Gospel:

"Dear Christians, One and All" (*LSB* 556)
"Salvation unto Us Has Come" (*LSB* 555)
"These Are the Holy Ten Commands" (*LSB* 581)
"The Law of God Is Good and Wise" (*LSB* 579)
"The Gospel Shows the Father's Grace" (*LSB* 580)
"All Mankind Fell in Adam's Fall" (*LSB* 562)
"I Trust, O Lord, Your Holy Name" (*LSB* 734)

◈ How might your study of Law and Gospel sharpen your listening to preaching? As you listen to the sermon, intentionally listen for the distinction of Law and Gospel.

◈ Pray that God would deepen in you the ability to rightly distinguish Law and Gospel in the opportunities that He gives you to speak His Word to others in daily life.

POINT TO REMEMBER _____

For I am not ashamed of the gospel, for it is the power of God for salvation to everyone who believes, to the Jew first and also to the Greek. For in it the righteousness of God is revealed from faith for faith, as it is written, "The righteous shall live by faith." *Romans 1:16–17*

Word and Spirit

The Holy Spirit does not do one thing and the Word another in working out God's saving purpose in man; by the same action they perform one work and accomplish one effect, just as the mind and eyes see by one and not by different actions. It is only by virtue of the fact that God is in the Word that this Word has the power to accomplish anything spiritual. The Word is powerless if God is not present in it. Any Word which proceeds from God brings God with it. All this is very important. If the Spirit is separated from the Word of God, it is no longer the Word of God. And because God is always with His Word, the power of the Word is the power of God. *Robert Preus*[12]

Wherever God's Word is, there is His Spirit also. The Hebrew word for *breath* and *spirit* is the same. Without breathing there can be no speaking. Words are shaped and carried out of the mouth as we breathe. In Psalm 33:6, we see how the Lord's breath and His Word are held together: "By the word of the LORD the heavens were made, and by the breath of His mouth all their host." So when Jesus promises to send His Spirit, the Spirit of Truth, He ties the Spirit to His Word: "If anyone loves Me, he will keep My word, and My Father will love him, and We will come to him and make Our home with him" (John 14:23). It is the Spirit dispatched by Jesus who causes the disciples to remember all that Jesus said (see John 15:26). Word and Spirit are inseparable. The Word is never Spiritless and the Spirit is never Wordless. Where the one is, there is the other also.

Spirituality is one of the buzz words of our culture, and it comes in a variety of shapes and forms. More often than not, the word *spirituality* is used to refer to anything that is vaguely religious, such as the New Age Movement, Eastern religions, or even American civil religion with its

_____

12 *Inspiration of Scripture*, 184.

generic and inclusive descriptions of the deity. But not all talk of *spirituality* is of the Holy Spirit. Spirituality leaves us with the hidden God, a deity of our own imagination. We know the Holy Spirit only in Christ, who is revealed in the Scriptures. Mark Twain said, "In the beginning, God created man in His own image and ever since, man has returned the compliment." Faith relies not on imaginative efforts to reshape God in our own image, but in the true God, who has made Himself known in Jesus Christ.[13]

LET NOT MAN PUT ASUNDER _____

From the very beginning, Satan has been contradicting God's words, offering his own brand of "spirituality." When the serpent approaches Eve in the garden, he tells her that she "will not surely die" from eating the fruit of the forbidden tree. In fact, the fruit will have the opposite effect, according to the serpent—it will make her wise and "like God" (Genesis 3:4–5). The serpent's brand of spirituality is beyond Eve's comprehension, offering her the knowledge of good and evil. So Eve relies on what she can see with her eyes, rather than on the word that God had spoken ("You shall not eat . . ."). She considers sight to be more real than hearing, and she takes the fruit, eats, and shares it with Adam. Then the eyes of Adam and Eve are indeed opened—but they see themselves, not God. They see themselves as naked, and in their shame they try to hide themselves.

Eve's spirituality is a sensual spirituality because it relies on her own five senses rather than on what God had given her in His Word. She is no longer content to live under God's pronouncement that His creation is "very good" (see Genesis 1:31). The tempter seduces her into the false belief that being like God is superior to being a creature who lives trusting God's Word. For Eve, the Spirit is not to be found in the Word but in having her eyes opened by eating the fruit forbidden by God.

In contrast to the tragic account of our first parents in the garden, our Lord stands victorious in His battle with Satan in the wilderness

---

13 The historical-critical method of studying the Bible questions the reliability of the biblical Gospels. This yields a "Christ of faith" who is not the same as the "historical Jesus." For a brief but thoughtful response to this approach, see Craig Parton, *The Defense Never Rests: A Lawyer's Quest for the Gospel* (St. Louis: Concordia, 2003), 49–96. For those who want to explore the impact of postmodernism on the interpretation of the Bible, David F. Wells offers an excellent and reliable guide in *Above All Earthly Pow'rs: Christ in a Postmodern World* (Grand Rapids: Eerdmans, 2005).

(see Matthew 4:1–11). Instead of ignoring or taking God's Word out of context or not trusting God to be true to His words, Jesus relies on the written Word of God and uses it as weaponry against Satan.

A TRAGIC DIVORCE

Attempting to divide God's Word from His Spirit means that we, in fact, lose both. We see this in every attempt to pit God's Word against His Spirit. For example, there are those who would assert that while the Scriptures forbid the ordination of women to the pastoral office or condemn homosexual activity, the Holy Spirit has led the church today into a new truth that now makes these practices acceptable. Here the Spirit is not confessed as residing in His Word but as moving beyond it. This is what Luther and the Lutheran Confessions identified as Enthusiasm. Luther writes:

> In issues relating to the spoken, outward Word, we must firmly hold that God grants His Spirit or grace to no one except through or with the preceding outward Word [Galatians 3:2, 5]. This protects us from the enthusiasts (i.e., souls who boast that they have the Spirit without and before the Word). They judge Scripture or the spoken Word and explain and stretch it at their pleasure, as Münzer did. Many still do this today, wanting to be sharp judges between the Spirit and the letter, and yet they do not know what they are saying [2 Corinthians 3:6]. Actually, the papacy too is nothing but sheer enthusiasm. The pope boasts that all laws exist in the shrine of his heart. Whatever he decides and commands within his church is from the Spirit and is right, even though it is above and contrary to Scripture and the spoken Word.
>
> All this is the old devil and old serpent [Revelation 12:9], who also turned Adam and Eve into enthusiasts. He led them away from God's outward Word to spiritualizing and self-pride [Genesis 3:2–5]. And yet, he did this through other outward words. In the same way, our enthusiasts today condemn the outward Word.[14]

In Galatians 1:6–9, Paul strongly condemns the Galatians' version of Enthusiasm, what he calls "turning to a different gospel" (Galatians 1:6). Enthusiasm leads away from the real Jesus to a false christ, who is no Savior at all. This is the point of Paul's harsh condemnation of the Galatians.

---

14 SA III VIII 3–6; *Concordia*, p. 280.

What happens when Christians forsake the Holy Scriptures as the Spirit's Word? According to 2 Timothy 4:3–4, they become captivated by teachers of their own choosing, who satisfy their spiritual cravings by telling them what they want to hear. In short, they get a deity who is domesticated to their own desires and who affirms them in their personal notions of who God is and how He ought to act.

THE WORD WORKS

Because God's Word is filled with His Spirit, it is never static but always living and working God's own purposes. God's Word says what it does and does what it says. Alive with God's Spirit, His Word bestows what it promises. It does not merely describe who Christ is and what He does as our Savior; it delivers Him to us, creating faith, which receives Him. The knowledge that God's Word is potent enlivens in us patience to hear and speak His Word with confidence, knowing that it will accomplish His will.

The prophet Isaiah demonstrates the connectedness between Word and Spirit:

> For My thoughts are not your thoughts, neither are your ways My ways, declares the LORD. For as the heavens are higher than the earth, so are My ways higher than your ways and My thoughts than your thoughts. For as the rain and the snow come down from heaven and do not return there but water the earth, making it bring forth and sprout, giving seed to the sower and bread to the eater, so shall My word be that goes out from My mouth; it shall not return to Me empty, but it shall accomplish that which I purpose, and shall succeed in the thing for which I sent it. *Isaiah 55:8–11*

God's Word comes from the Lord's mouth, and it accomplishes the purpose for which He sends it. God's Spirit (His breath) is in His speaking. The prophet Jeremiah says that God is watching over His Word to perform it (1:11–12) and that God's Word is like a "hammer that breaks the rock in pieces" (23:29). Both of these passages reveal that God's Word is efficacious as it does what the Lord wills it to do.

The writer to the Hebrews tells us that God's Word is "living and active, sharper than any two-edged sword, piercing to the division of soul and of spirit, of joints and of marrow, and discerning the thoughts and intentions of the heart" (4:12). As we have observed, it is really the Scriptures that interpret our lives because we stand under their authority. We do not conform the Scriptures to our notions of truth and rationality, but we are conformed to the Scriptures as God's Law and Gospel work.

SPIRITUAL EXERCISES _____

◈ Meditate on Luther's explanation to the Second Petition of the Lord's Prayer in the Small Catechism. Notice especially the way the Spirit and the Word are linked together as we confess: God's kingdom comes "when our heavenly Father gives us His Holy Spirit, so that by His grace we believe His holy Word and lead a godly life here in time and there in eternity."[15]

◈ Study the hymn "O Morning Star, How Fair and Bright" (*LSB* 395). How does this hymn confess the unity of Word and Spirit and the gifts that Christ bestows on us therein?

◈ Pray for all preachers and hearers of the Word of the Lord, asking God to strengthen those who proclaim His Word in truth and that those who hear it might, through His Spirit, trust Him in life and in death.

POINT TO REMEMBER _____

It is the Spirit who gives life; the flesh is no help at all. The words that I have spoken to you are spirit and life. *John 6:63*

Inwardly Digesting the Word

Secondly, you should meditate, that is, not only in your heart, but also externally, by actually repeating and comparing oral speech and literal words of the book, reading and rereading them with diligent attention and reflection, so that you may see what the Holy Spirit means by them. And take care that you do not grow weary or think that you have done enough when you have read, heard, and spoken them once or twice, and that you then have complete understanding. . . . Thus you see in this same Psalm [Psalm 119] how David constantly boasts that he will talk, meditate, speak, sing, hear, read, by day and night and always, about nothing except God's Word and commandments. For

---

15 *Concordia*, p. 333.

God will not give you his Spirit without the external Word; so take your cue from that. *Martin Luther*[16]

The words of an ancient prayer ask God to bless our use of His Scriptures so that we may "read, mark, learn, and inwardly digest them that, by patience and comfort of Your holy Word, we may embrace and ever hold fast the blessed hope of everlasting life."[17] To meditate on God's Word is to let that Word reside in heart and mind. It is to be at home in the Scriptures and to let the Scriptures be at home in you, so that your mind is formed by their truth and your tongue is untied to declare the redeeming work of our Savior. Luther, in his usual graphic way, compares meditation to a cow chewing its cud. He does this in his commentary on Deuteronomy 14:1, where he states: "To chew the cud, however, is to take up the Word with delight and meditate with supreme diligence, so that (according to the proverb) one does not permit it to go into one ear and out the other, but holds it firmly in the heart, swallows it, and absorbs it into the intestines."[18]

The word *meditation* is often associated with mysticism and Eastern religions that attempt to clear the soul of earthly concerns so that one may enter into a purified communion with the divine. Others might think of quiet time spent in contemplation or reflection. Christian meditation is not an introspective dwelling on self nor is it an attempt to transcend time and space by way of some mystical technique. Rather, the Christian is like the Virgin Mary, who "treasured up all these things, pondering them in her heart" (Luke 2:19). Christian meditation is attentiveness to the Word of God read and heard.

CONTINUING IN JESUS' WORD

The author of Psalm 1 contrasts the righteous and the wicked, believers and unbelievers. Believers are compared to sturdy and fruitful trees with roots that are refreshed by streams of living water. They do not wither in the heat of a summer drought, but produce fruit in season. On the other hand, unbelievers are like husks blown away by the breeze.

According to Psalm 1:2, the blessed man delights "in the law [*Torah*] of the LORD." English translations often render *Torah* as *Law*, but it is essential to remember that the Torah contains both Law and Gospel. Thus verse 2 is really speaking of God's Word. In many ways Psalm

---

16 AE 34:286.
17 *Lutheran Service Book: Altar Book* (St. Louis: Concordia, 2006), 171.
18 AE 9:136.

119:33–48 is an extended commentary on Psalm 1:2. Note especially that the psalmist implores God to teach, guide, preserve, and confirm him in His Word. These sections of Psalm 119 also speak of meditation (verse 48) and delight in God's Word (verses 35 and 47). Meditation on God's Word is set in contrast with those who meditate, that is, set their hearts and eyes on, worthless things (verses 36–37).

If meditation is a worthy discipline for the Christian, how often should it be practiced and where? Psalm 1 says the blessed man's meditation on God's Word occupies his heart both day and night (verse 2). Also, the blessed man does not walk in the way of wickedness but stands in the company of God's people, who are righteous through faith in the Messiah. Thus rooted and grounded in God's Word, the blessed man bears the fruit of faith even as a well-watered tree is abundant with good fruit. The prophet Jeremiah says that such a believer "does not fear when heat comes" and "is not anxious in the year of drought" because his roots are in the stream of God's Word (Jeremiah 17:8; cf. Luke 6:43–45).

According to the psalmist, unbelievers will not abide in the Lord's presence. They stand under His judgment, and without faith they perish (Psalm 1:5–6). In John 15, Jesus speaks of Himself as the vine and believers as the branches. It is only through faith in Jesus that our lives are fruitful. His words live in us and keep us connected to Him by faith, and such faith bears fruit that remains.

CHEWING ON THE WORD

In Psalm 119:103, David extols the sweetness of God's Word, calling it "sweeter than honey to my mouth!" The prophet Ezekiel is commanded to take the scroll and eat it. When he does, it is as sweet as honey to his taste (see Ezekiel 3:1). In Deuteronomy 8:3, Moses records how God fed His people manna in the wilderness, declaring that "man does not live by bread alone, but man lives by every word that comes from the mouth of the LORD." Jesus quotes this verse against the tempter in Matthew 4:4.

Why does Scripture frequently refer to "feeding" on God's Word? More than a simple rhetorical device, the use of food imagery in context with study of God's Word emphasizes our dependence on this source of nutrition for our faith. Just as lack of food starves the body and depletes its energy stores, ultimately resulting in death, so lack of the bread of God's Word causes us to perish spiritually. Even as God opens His hands to satisfy us with daily bread for the body, He also gives us His words, that we might be satisfied with the gifts of forgiveness of sins, peace with Him, and the sure hope of eternal life. Therefore Jesus says, "Blessed . . . are those who hear the word of God and keep it!" (Luke 11:28).

We devour God's Word by "inwardly digesting" it as the ancient prayer of the Church says. We hear it over and over again like a cow chewing her cud, to paraphrase Luther. Faith holds fast to God's Word and digests every particle so we may use the gifts that God has put there to nourish us in faith and love.

STRENGTHENED FOR LIFE IN THE WORLD ____

To meditate on God's Word is to cherish it, to cling to it as our dearest treasure in life and death. Nourished by the Word, we are built up in faith and set free for a life of love toward the neighbor. During a con-versation with some of His followers, Jesus said: "If you abide in My Word, you are truly My disciples, and you will know the truth, and the truth will set you free" (John 8:31–32). Those who heard this statement pointed out to Jesus that they did not need to be set free; they were not slaves. Jesus replied that "everyone who commits sin is a slave to sin," but "if the Son sets you free, you will be free indeed" (John 8:34–35).

Apart from the Word, we are captive to sin. Freedom is not to be had apart from God's Word. And this freedom is not only a freedom *from* sin, death, and hell, but it is also a freedom *for* a life of faith in Christ and love for our neighbor. God's Word is the truth that sets us free.

In His High Priestly Prayer, Jesus revealed much about the connec-tion between His promises and His Word. Jesus has made God's name manifest to His disciples (John 17:6). With the Lord's name, He gives us His words, and in these words we know the truth that Jesus is the Son sent from the Father to redeem us by His blood and to sanctify us for a life with Him. In His High Priestly Prayer, Jesus intercedes for us in view of the fact that Christians will be hated and persecuted because they have and confess God's Word.

SPIRITUAL EXERCISES

◈ In an open letter, Luther suggested a simple way to meditate on God's Word. He advised his readers to take each commandment (or another text from the Scripture) "in their fourfold aspect, namely, as a school text, songbook, penitential book, and prayer book."[19] In other words, Luther advises that four questions be put to the text: What am I taught about God? For what should I give Him thanks? What sins are uncovered that I should confess? For what does this text teach me to pray? Each day pray one of the Ten Commandments and apply Luther's questions, using them as a schoolbook, songbook, penitential book, and prayer book.

◈ In his Genesis lectures, Luther wrote:

> Let him who wants to contemplate in the right way reflect on his Baptism; let him read his Bible, hear sermons, honor father and mother, and come to the aid of a brother in distress. But let him not shut himself up in a nook . . . and there entertain himself with his devotions and thus suppose that he is sitting in God's bosom and has fellowship with God without Christ, without the Word, without the sacraments.[20]

How does Luther's advice keep you both in the Word and the world?

◈ In 1521, Luther wrote a guide for Bible study entitled *A Brief Instruction on What to Look for and Expect in the Gospels*. In this tract, he said:

> When you open the book containing the gospels and read or hear how Christ comes here or there, or how someone is brought to him, you should therein perceive the sermon or the gospel through which he is coming to you, or you are being brought to him. For the preaching of the gospel is nothing else than Christ coming to us, or we being brought to him. When you see how he works, however, and how he helps everyone to whom he comes or who is brought to him, then rest assured that faith is accomplishing this in you and that he is offering your soul exactly the same sort of help and favor through the gospel. If you pause here and let him do you good, that is, if you believe that he benefits and helps you, then you really have it. Then Christ is yours, presented to you as a gift.[21]

Follow Luther's advice as you hear the Holy Gospel read in church.

POINT TO REMEMBER

Sanctify them in the truth; Your word is truth. *John 17:17*

---

19 AE 43:209.
20 AE 3:275.
21 AE 35:121.

Praying the Word

The richness of the Word of God ought to determine our prayer, not the poverty of our heart. *Dietrich Bonhoeffer* [22]

Prayer is the voice of faith, and faith comes by hearing God's Word (see Romans 10:17). God speaks His Word, which creates and sustains faith. The strong Word of the Gospel unlocks lips to call upon God in prayer and thanksgiving. God even gives us words to pray, as we see in the Psalms and the Lord's Prayer. His Word sets the agenda for our praying. Adolph Köberle, a Lutheran theologian of the last century, wisely counsels that prayer anchored in God's Word avoids disorder and confusion and a poverty of ideas, faith, and love. When we pray in concert with Scripture, we pray with confidence and clarity. [23]

If we pray relying on our words or our actions (past or future) to motivate God to act, we pray self-righteously and with pride. Our heart deceives us into believing that on our own merit we can approach God. Jesus reminds us that our hearts are full of evil (Matthew 15:19–20; cf. Jeremiah 17:9). However, Jesus and the Holy Spirit pray for us (see John 17; Romans 8:26). Certainty that our prayer is heard is not anchored in our hearts, untrustworthy as they are, but in God's Word, which both commands us to pray and promises that those who pray in Jesus' name will be heard. When we pray in Jesus' name, we are praying on the basis of who Jesus is (God's Son and our Savior) and all that He has promised us in His name (see John 16:23–24).

In his introduction to the Lord's Prayer in the Small Catechism, Luther reminds us that we can call on God "confidently with all assurance, as dear children ask their dear father." [24] And he concludes his discussion of the Lord's Prayer by explaining that the word *Amen* means that we can "be certain that these petitions are acceptable to our Father in heaven and are heard by Him. For He Himself has commanded us to pray this way and has promised that He will hear us." [25]

---

22 Dietrich Bonhoeffer, *Psalms: The Prayer Book of the Bible* (Minneapolis: Augsburg Fortress, 1970), 15.

23 See Adolph Köberle, *The Quest for Holiness* (Minneapolis: Augsburg, 1938), 176–77.

24 *Concordia*, p. 331.

25 *Concordia*, p. 338.

A COMMAND AND PROMISE _____

In John 16:12–16, Jesus says that all that the Father has is His and that the Spirit will glorify the Son by taking what belongs to Him and declaring it to the apostles. The Spirit speaks not on His own authority, but with the authority of the one who sends Him. Commenting on this section of John 16, Luther writes:

> Here Christ makes the Holy Spirit a Preacher. He does so to prevent one from gaping toward heaven in search of Him, as the flutter-ing spirits and enthusiasts do, and from divorcing Him from the oral Word or the ministry. One should know and learn that He will be in and with the Word, that it will guide us into all truth, in order that we may believe it, use it as a weapon, be preserved by it against all the lies and deception of the devil, and prevail in all trials and temptations. . . . The Holy Spirit wants this truth which He is to impress into our hearts to be so firmly fixed that reason and all one's own thoughts and feelings are relegated to the background. He wants us to adhere solely to the Word and to regard it as the only truth. And through this Word alone He governs the Christian Church to the end.[26]

The Spirit is at work in God's Word to declare all that Jesus has done for us in coming to be our Savior. Luther writes in the Smalcald Articles: "Therefore, we must constantly maintain this point: God does not want to deal with us in any other way than through the spoken Word and the Sacraments. Whatever is praised as from the Spirit—without the Word and the Sacraments—is the devil himself."[27] God's will is to be found by us and to speak to us in the Word. He carries out that will through the Holy Spirit's work in the very words of Scripture. The Spirit caused the holy authors to write the very words that He intended, yet in a way that followed the contours of the lives, experiences, and literary styles of the authors without introducing human error. As we believe that Jesus is God and man in one person, so we are reassured that the Bible is divine and human language: neither confused together nor changed, neither divided nor separated.

Chapters 13–17 of John's Gospel record Jesus' farewell discourse to His disciples on the night of His betrayal. In John 15:26–27, Jesus says that the Spirit of truth, who is sent from the Father, will bear witness to Jesus. He also reveals that the apostles will bear witness because they have been with Him from the beginning. After Jesus' resurrection and ascension, the apostles were able to bear witness to Jesus because they

---

26 AE 24:362.
27 SA III VIII 10; *Concordia*, p. 281.

had seen Him with their own eyes, heard Him with their own ears, and touched Him with their own hands (see 1 John 1:1–4; Acts 1:2–3). In Acts 1:21–26, we observe that the replacement for Judas had to be a man who was with Jesus from His Baptism to His ascension, and, like the other apostles, this man had to be a witness of His resurrection.

Another gift that Jesus gave His disciples that night was the invitation to "ask of the Father in My name" (John 16:23). But how is this invitation connected with the Scriptures? Because God has "exalted above all things [His] name and [His] word" (Psalm 138:2), all that is given us in Jesus' name is there for us in the Scriptures. To pray in Jesus' name is to pray on the basis of His Word. Thus in John 16:23–24, Jesus promises that prayers in His name will be answered and our joy will be made full.

SEEKING GOD'S FACE

In Jesus Christ, God's fatherly heart is revealed. We do not worship a nameless deity or an unknown God. God is never generic. The true God has revealed Himself to us in the Word made flesh, and it is to Him that the Scriptures testify. Because the Scriptures are the Word of the Lord, who does not lie or deceive, we rightly speak of their inerrancy and infallibility. In the Scriptures, God invites us to seek His face (Psalm 27:8), and it is from the Scriptures that He causes His face to shine upon us with favor (see Numbers 6:25).

The evening before Jesus' crucifixion, Philip asked, "Lord, show us the Father" (John 14:8). Jesus replied that "whoever has seen Me has seen the Father" (verse 9). Luther observes that Philip wanted to see God, but Jesus pulls him back down to earth so that he sees Jesus: "For this reason true theology and recognition of God are in the crucified Christ."[28] Outwardly, Jesus does not much look like God, but He is God in the flesh. Outwardly, the Scriptures do not look like what human imagination would envision God's Word to be. But as surely as Jesus is the Son of God, so, too, the Scriptures are God's Word. To see Jesus is to see the Father. To hear or read the Scriptures is to hear or read God's Word.

---

28 AE 31:53.

THE GIFT OF CERTAINTY

At the end of his explanation of each article of the Creed in his Small Catechism, Luther confesses: "This is most certainly true." God is at work in His Scriptures to dispel the fog of doubt and uncertainty so that we lay hold of His promises with faith. The certainty is not in us but in the steadfast works of God. If God does it, you can be certain that it is done. He inspired the Scriptures, using His eye and ear witnesses to proclaim to us the truth of Jesus' incarnation, death, and resurrection for us. The Scriptures are not "cleverly devised myths" (2 Peter 1:16) generated by human impulse. They are the Word of God. The clarity and efficacy of the Holy Scriptures give us the certainty of our salvation. That gives us boldness and confidence in believing and in praying.

After a reading from Holy Scripture in the Divine Service, the pastor usually says, "This is the Word of the Lord," to which the congregation responds: "Thanks be to God." This ancient response reminds us that the Scriptures are read and received not as the words of men but as the very Word of God. In 1 Thessalonians 2:13, Paul gives thanks that the Thessalonians received the apostolic words "not as the word of men but as what it really is, the word of God, which is at work in you believers." Thus the liturgical response is one way we can publicly acknowledge the authority of the Scriptures.

Some people argue that the Bible is a complex book, open to multiple interpretations, its words easily twisted, so that no one reading can be correct. And if we allow this argument to be carried to its end, we are left with uncertainty as to what God actually says. However, any perceived lack of clarity is not in the Scriptures, but in our own minds, which are blinded by sin (see 2 Peter 1:19–21). The fact that human beings can and do twist the Scriptures, and ignore or distort God's Word, does not mean that the Scriptures are at fault. It is often the case that people appeal to diversity of interpretations or perceived contradictions in Scripture as a way to avoid the claims that the Bible makes about God Himself. In other words, the real argument comes down to the First Commandment's divine assertion that we are to have no other gods.

34 LUTHERAN SPIRITUALITY

SPIRITUAL EXERCISES _____

◈ Luther writes: "Hence it is that the Psalter is the book of all saints; and everyone, in whatever situation he may be, finds in that situation psalms and words that fit his case, that suit him as if they were put there just for his sake, so that he could not put it better himself, or find or wish for anything better."[29] Begin and end each day with the praying of a psalm. In the morning, pray Psalm 3, and in the evening, pray Psalm 4.

◈ The Lord's Prayer is both God's words to us and our words to God. It is a template for all our praying. Prepare your personal list of intercessions and thanksgiving using the Lord's Prayer as a guide.

◈ The Lord's Prayer and the Book of Psalms mutually inform each other. Identify one psalm that best exemplifies each petition of the Lord's Prayer. How does this psalm deepen your praying of the Lord's Prayer?

POINT TO REMEMBER _____

O Lord, open my lips, and mouth will declare Your praise. *Psalm 51:15*

The Comfort of the Word

Firstly, you should know that the Holy Scriptures constitute a book which turns the wisdom of all other books into foolishness, because not one teaches about eternal life except this one alone. Therefore you should straightway despair of your reason and understanding. With them you will not attain eternal life, but, on the contrary, your presumptuousness will plunge you and others with you out of heaven (as happened to Lucifer) into the abyss of hell. But kneel down in your little room [Matthew 6:6] and pray to God with real humility and earnestness, that he through his dear Son may give you his Holy Spirit, who will enlighten you, lead you, and give you understanding.
Martin Luther[30]

Contrary to folk wisdom, the conscience is not a reliable guide. When the Law's accusing force scares it with the memory of sin, the first instincts of the conscience are to accuse and condemn, or else it seeks to suppress the knowledge of sin by excusing sinfulness with eager self-justifications. Sooner or later, the conscience is trapped like a snarling

---

29 AE 35:256.
30 AE 34:285.

beast. It either hardens against the Word, or the Spirit leads it to the soothing Gospel. God's Scriptures were written to bring consolation to consciences terrorized by sin. We exercise ourselves in Holy Scripture so that we might draw on God's comfort for our own distressed souls. Having thus been comforted, we are able to speak the Lord's words of consolation to others. So Luther writes:

> Therefore I admonish you, especially those of you who are to become instructors of consciences, as well as each of you individually, that you exercise yourselves by study, by reading, by meditation, and by prayer, so that in temptation you will be able to instruct consciences, both your own and others, console them, and take them from the Law to grace, from active righteousness to passive righteousness, in short, from Moses to Christ. In affliction and in the conflict of conscience it is the devil's habit to frighten us with the Law and to set against us the consciousness of sin, our wicked past, the wrath and judgment of God, hell and eternal death, so that thus he may drive us into despair, subject us to himself, and pluck us from Christ.[31]

It is all too common for us to fall to the pressure of society to be tolerant and inclusive—even in the face of situations that God's Word definitively addresses, such as abortion or same-sex marriage. But God's Word does not conform to scientific understandings of the beginnings of life or current gender development theory. God's Word is truth; it is not incorrect and it does not deceive. God's Word has been given to us to reveal the truth of our sinfulness and the truth of God's plan of salvation in Jesus.

WRITTEN FOR YOU

The apostle Paul explains that the books of the Old Testament were "written for our instruction, that through endurance and through the encouragement of the Scriptures we might have hope" (Romans 15:4). The Old Testament was written to give us hope in the Messiah, whose coming as Savior it promised. Paul writes of endurance and encouragement in Romans 15:4, and then he repeats these two words in verse 5 because they have to do with faith that clings to God when trial and temptation seem to contradict His promises. James 1:2–18 speaks of such testing and the blessing that God gives even amid life's trials and tests. Luther called these times of testing *tentatio*. As we noted earlier,

---

31 AE 26:10.

Luther describes *tentatio* as the third part of a triad that includes *oratio* (prayer) and *meditatio* (meditation). Luther says that this *tentatio*

> is the touchstone which teaches you not only to know and under-
> stand, but also to experience how right, how true, how sweet, how
> lovely, how mighty, how comforting God's Word is, wisdom beyond
> all wisdom. . . . For as soon as God's Word takes root and grows in
> you, the devil will harry you, and will make a real doctor of you, and
> by his assaults will teach you to seek and love God's Word.[32]

Thus the outcome of the use of Scripture is hope. And hope is faith that is focused toward the future. It does not disappoint, because Jesus has been raised from the dead. His future belongs to all who are His by faith (see Romans 5:1–5; 1 Peter 1:3–9).

Paul also states in Romans 15 that "Christ became a servant to the circumcised to show God's truthfulness, in order to confirm the prom-ises given to the patriarchs" (verse 8). By sending His Son, the promised Seed of the woman (Genesis 3:15) who came in the form of a servant (see Philippians 2:7; Matthew 20:28) to reconcile the world to Himself by the shedding of His blood on the cross, God fulfilled every promise in the Old Testament that He would send the Messiah. Following the statement that Christ had come for the descendants of Abraham, Paul offers a sampling of Old Testament texts (Romans 15:9–12). This dem-onstrates that the Gentiles are included in God's promised redemption. The Holy Spirit, who caused the Scriptures to be written in ancient times, is working through those same Scriptures today to give joy and peace in believing (Romans 15:13), and through that faith He causes us to abound in hope.

LIGHT IN THE DARKNESS

We find comfort in the Scriptures because they are clear. The clarity of the Scriptures is in Christ Jesus, who is the "light of the world" (John 8:12). He is the light that shines in the darkness and is not overcome by it (see John 1:4–5). By His Gospel, He has called us out of darkness into His marvelous light (see 1 Peter 2:9; 2 Corinthians 4:6). And in His light we see light (Psalm 36:9). The Scriptures shine clear and pure with the radiance of their Lord so that the psalmist testifies: "Your word is a lamp to my feet and a light to my path" (Psalm 119:105). The apostle Peter echoes this as he writes that we have the sureness of the prophetic word shining as a lamp in a dark place (see 2 Peter 1:19). The Scriptures

---

32 AE 34:286–87.

do not leave us with a hidden God (*Deus absconditus*) but God revealed in Christ, specifically in the Means of Grace (*Deus revelatus*).

The Lutheran Church holds to interpretation of doctrine by means of *sola scriptura*, that is, the Holy Scriptures alone are "the pure, clear fountain of Israel. They are the only true standard or norm by which all teachers and doctrines are to be judged."[33] Human reason, personal experience, and the tradition of the Church are subjected to the normative character of the prophetic and apostolic Scriptures. In one way or another, those who would set reason, experience, or tradition alongside Scripture argue that Scripture is either unclear or insufficient. Some will argue that Scripture must be taken as a "conversation partner" in contemporary debates on issues such as homosexuality. But when Scripture is reduced to a mere conversation partner, you can be sure that it will not be given the last word. Ultimately, when Scripture is deemed to be lacking either in clarity or sufficiency, struggling sinners are left without the comfort God wills to give us in Jesus.[34]

Mark Twain once quipped that what troubled him about the Bible was not those passages that were unclear or beyond his understanding but those clear passages that he understood all too well. Arguments about the clarity of Scripture often reveal that the darkness resides not in the Scriptures, but in its detractor. The Scriptures are all too clear about those who live in unbelief: "Whoever believes in the Son has eternal life; whoever does not obey the Son shall not see life, but the wrath of God remains on him" (John 3:36).

WORDS TO SPEAK

We study the Scriptures not to become better Bible trivia players but so that God's Word will dwell in us richly. We hear the reading and the preaching of Scripture that we might be strengthened in our faith in Jesus Christ. We read the Bible so that we might be comforted in the forgiveness of sins and enlivened in the hope of life eternal. Our ears and hearts are filled with the Word of God so that we might also speak it to both our fellow believers and to those who are still in the darkness of unbelief. (See Colossians 3:16–17.)

The apostle Paul tells us that God "comforts us in all our affliction, so that we may be able to comfort those who are in any affliction"

---

33 FC SD Summary 3; *Concordia*, p. 508.

34 For more on the application of the Reformation principle *sola scriptura*, see Wenz, "Justification and Holy Scripture," 12.

(2 Corinthians 1:4). As we read and study the Scriptures, we discover and commit to memory words that we can speak to those whose souls are seared with the bitter memory of sin, those whose consciences have been rubbed raw with the accusations of the Law. As we read earlier, God's will is to take Christians "from the Law to grace, from active righteous to passive righteousness, in short, from Moses to Christ."[35]

The apostle Peter says that we should always be ready "to make a defense to anyone who asks you for a reason for the hope that is in you" (1 Peter 3:15). When we are grounded in God's Word, when we read and study it and meditate upon it, we are prepared to give a reason for the hope we profess. Confessing the faith is not a matter of sharing opinions about what God's Word means to me—it is sharing the very words of God that I believe as truth! God has given us His Word, and we are to speak truthfully, rightly dividing the Law and the Gospel (see 2 Timothy 2:15).

SPIRITUAL EXERCISES _____

◈ Luther complied a list of Bible passages called "Sayings in Which Luther Found Comfort" (AE 43:171–77). Start a journal of biblical texts that you find especially comforting.

◈ Pray your way through Psalm 119, marking all the places that speak of God's Word as giving light, guidance, and comfort.

◈ Learn by heart the hymn "God's Word Is Our Great Heritage" (*LSB* 582) or "Lord, Keep Us Steadfast in Your Word" (*LSB* 655).

POINT TO REMEMBER _____

Heaven and earth will pass away, but My words will not pass away.
Matthew 24:35

---

35   AE 26:10.

Lutheran Teaching on the Word

The Lutheran Confessions are accepted because they are in agreement with the Holy Scriptures. Lutheran theology holds that the Scriptures are the normative standard that norms all others (*norma normans*) and that the Lutheran Confessions are the "norm that is normed" (*norma normata*) by the Bible. Lutherans accept the authority of the Lutheran Confessions because they hold the Scriptures to be authoritative. The *Book of Concord* always draws us back to the Scriptures, especially to Christ, the justifier of the ungodly, who is at the heart of the Bible.

THE WORD HAS DIVINE AUTHORITY

We believe, teach, and confess that the only rule and norm according to which all teachings, together with ‹all› teachers, should be evaluated and judged are the prophetic and apostolic Scriptures of the Old and New Testament alone. (FC Ep Summary 1; *Concordia*, p. 473)

Because we know that God does not lie. . . . God's Word cannot err. (LC IV 57; *Concordia*, p. 429)

THE WORD IS THE SOURCE OF DOCTRINE

[This confession] . . . shows, from the Holy Scripture and God's pure Word, what has been . . . taught in our churches. (AC Preface 1; *Concordia*, p. 27)

It will not do to frame articles of faith from the works or words of the holy Fathers. . . . [N]ot even an angel can do so (Galatians 1:8). (SA II II 15; *Concordia*, pp. 265–66)

First, ‹we receive and embrace with our whole heart› are the prophetic and apostolic Scriptures of the Old and New Testaments as the pure, clear fountain of Israel. They are the only true standard or norm by which all teachers and doctrines are to be judged. (FC SD Summary 3; *Concordia*, p. 508)

GOD'S WORD IS A MEANS OF GRACE

God's Word is the true "holy thing" above all holy things. Yes, it is the only one we Christians know and have. . . . God's Word is the treasure that sanctifies everything. (LC I 91; *Concordia*, p. 369)

So justification happens through the Word, just as Paul says in Romans 1:16, "[The Gospel] is the power of God for salvation to everyone who believes." . . . [I]f justification happens only through the Word, and the Word is understood only by faith, it follows that faith justifies. (Ap IV [II] 67; *Concordia*, p. 91)

We should not think of this call of God, which is made through the preaching of the Word, as a juggler's act. But we should know that God reveals His will by this call. . . . It is God's will that we should receive the Word, believe it, and obey it. (FC SD XI 29; *Concordia*, p. 606)

We, too, are simply to believe . . . our Creator and Redeemer's plain, firm, clear, solemn words . . . . He can do and accomplish everything He promises. (FC SD VII 47; *Concordia*, p. 570)

In issues relating to the spoken, outward Word, we must firmly hold that God grants His Spirit or grace to no one except through or with the preceding outward Word. (SA III VIII 3; *Concordia*, p. 280)

GOD'S WORD IS LAW AND GOSPEL

God's two chief works among people are these: to terrify; to justify and make alive those who have been terrified. Into these two works all Scripture has been distributed. . . . The one part is the *Law* . . . . The other part is the *Gospel*. (Ap XIIa [V] 53; *Concordia*, p. 164)

All Scripture ought to be distributed into these two principal topics: the Law and . . . the promises about Christ. (Ap IV [II] 5; *Concordia*, p. 83)

We unanimously believe, teach and confess . . . the distinction between the Law and the Gospel (2 Corinthians 3:6–9). (FC SD V 17, 26; *Concordia*, pp. 555, 557)

PRAYER
We Speak to God[1]

Since Christian spirituality depends on God's grace, it differs from all pagan forms of spirituality, which promote spiritual self-development and self-improvement. Christian spirituality is not based on our performance but on our reception from God. We are not producers of spiritual growth but receivers of spiritual life. We have nothing that we have not received from God (1 Corinthians 4:7), who has sent His Son and His Holy Spirit to give of Himself to us. In keeping with this, our praying has to do with our ongoing reception from the God who interacts with us in Word and deed in His Means of Grace. Our reception has to do with faith—our faith in Jesus and His Spirit-giving Word.

In His three years with them, Jesus taught His disciples, and us, about the close connection between faith in Him and prayer. Before He provided healing, Jesus commended the faith of those who asked Him for help. From this the disciples learned that faith was something like the empty hands of a beggar: the hands hold nothing to give but they receive everything from Jesus. Faith in Jesus led to prayer that received what He promised to give. So when we pray, we live by faith, we act in faith, we exercise our faith in Jesus. We, who are justified by faith in Jesus, have access to the grace of God the Father through Him. We use our faith and our access to God's grace to pray for ourselves and for others.

---

1 Adapted from *The Lutheran Spirituality Series: Prayer*, written by John W. Kleinig, edited by Robert C. Baker. Copyright © 2006 Concordia Publishing House.

As disciples of Jesus, we therefore are called to live by faith in a life of prayer. If we stop praying, then we fall asleep spiritually. We may still be spiritually alive, but we become unaware of God's gracious dealings with us. So the Holy Spirit seeks to keep us awake and watchful in prayer. In everything that happens to us, God is training us to become people of prayer, wakeful people who take Him at His Word and receive from Him His gifts. God is equipping His people, who are sure that He withholds nothing good from us and all His creatures.

Our Secret Vocation

Sons are entitled to speak in the family of the Father. Prayer is the permission which God accords His sons to join their voices in the discussion of His affairs. *Peter Brunner* [2]

Imagine that you received a written invitation from the president of the United States to join the administration as a department secretary in Washington DC. You would be a member of the president's cabinet, with access to the president and all the other people who govern the United States. You would have a say in the administration of this land and would help to decide how its resources are distributed. Think of all the good that you could do!

In the same way that we imagine how we would wield power in business or government, we Christians often think about prayer in terms of what we *should* do compared with what we *actually* do. We think about our obligation to pray as Christ has commanded us and our failure to fulfill His command to pray. The topic of prayer therefore touches the conscience of every disciple. It can arouse a sense of guilt that disheartens us or the determination for improvement that results in further failure. So a chapter on prayer can all too easily end up focused on our performance, a self-justification before God and others by measurement of progress in piety.

By the power of the Holy Spirit working through God's Word, we can rejoice in prayer as a great privilege rather than a burdensome obligation. We can come to understand the call to pray as part of our secret priestly vocation to reign with Christ here on earth as we together

2   *Worship in the Name of Jesus* (St. Louis: Concordia, 1968), 202.

with Christ pray for the people whom God has placed under our care in our family, social group, and congregation. In this chapter we will shift the focus away from ourselves and our efforts at spiritual self-improvement to a focus on God's grace and the privilege of involvement in the administration of His grace. The comparison of a Christian to a member of God's royal cabinet is therefore meant to highlight the honor and privilege of prayer. We are partners with Jesus in prayer, and He supports us in becoming people of prayer.

FRIENDS OF THE KING

In contemporary democracies, department secretaries are close to and assist the president. In the ancient world, the person who was closest to the king, his personal advisor, was given the title "Friend of the King." Not only did this individual sit in the royal council, he lived with the king as his secretary, his chief of staff, the man who had the king's ear.

In the Old Testament, God chose leaders and prophets such as Moses and Abraham to be members of His cabinet, His courtiers, His royal servants (see Exodus 33:11; Isaiah 41:8). As intercessors, they spoke for God's people and advised God on the decisions that He made. They had the privilege of working with God in the administration of His Word in wrath and grace, in judgment and salvation.

Through faith in Christ, we are even more privileged than Old Testament leaders and prophets. We are friends of Jesus, the Son of the King. We are His personal advisors; we have the ear of our King. Yet we have no power by ourselves. We depend on Jesus for our position and our vocation. He does not just call us to work with Him; He gives us His full backing.

GRAFTED IN

In John 15, Jesus develops a picture of Himself as a grapevine and us as His branches that pass on His love, just as a branch passes on its sap to produce bunches of grapes (see verses 1–8). Jesus also pictures His Father as the King of the world and Himself as His royal deputy (see verses 9–17). The agricultural metaphor teaches us that we are completely dependent on Jesus. We receive everything from Him; we achieve nothing spiritually if we are separated from Him.

The relationship between a friend of a king and the king is different from the relationship of a servant and a royal master. In a royal bureaucracy, servants did what they were told to do. They carried out the decrees of the king even if they did not seem to make sense. The friends of the king, however, were involved in the decision-making process and could see how the decision fit into the policy of the king. Thus they could speak for the king and act on his behalf. Friends of the king not only work for the king, they also work with him and share in his rule. In John 15:14, Jesus says, "You are My friends if you do what I command you."

The use of *friends* unpacks the practical implications of our total dependence on Jesus. As disciples of Jesus and through His Word, we know what Jesus is doing and why. He has taught us everything that He has learned from His heavenly Father (see John 15:11). He has briefed us fully on His Father's policy, His good and gracious will for us and His whole creation. We therefore know our Master's business. We do not merely work *for* Jesus by carrying out His commands; we work *with* Him by loving others as He has loved us. He honors us by involving us in His royal work.

In John 15:7 and 16 Jesus connects spiritual fruitfulness with prayer in His name to God the Father. When we pray, we draw on what Jesus brings to us from God the Father—His life and love—like branches that draw their nourishing, life-sustaining sap from the vine. We who receive the love of the Father from Jesus and our attachment to Him are meant to pass on that love to others. We do that best by praying for others, for when we pray for them according to God's Word, we love them with God's love. Just as Jesus laid down His life for us and put Himself at our disposal by dying for us, so we lay down our lives and put ourselves at the disposal of others by asking God the Father to give them what they need.

In part of His Sermon on the Mount, Jesus teaches His disciples how they are to deal with sin in God's royal family. They should not use the Law to condemn the sinner (Matthew 7:1–5), nor should they use the Gospel to excuse sin (Matthew 7:6). Instead, believers should use their access to God the Father to pray for the sinner (Matthew 7:7–12). Jesus urges us to lay our requests before God because we are sons of God the Father (verses 7–11). The Golden Rule of Matthew 7:12 is introduced by the word *so*, which indicates that we fulfill the Golden Rule by praying for the brother or sister who has sinned. By praying for God's mercy on them, we do what we as disciples of Jesus would like them to do for us if we were in their predicament. We therefore can claim God's grace for them and convey His good gifts to them by asking God to judge and forgive them just as He has judged and forgiven us through Christ.

REIGNING WITH CHRIST

In Revelation, John gives us a picture of our heavenly reign in connection with prayer. The four living creatures (Revelation 4:6–8) are the archangels who represent all the angels. The twenty-four elders (Revelation 4:10–11) represent the whole Church in heaven and earth. As they stand in a circle around Jesus and God the Father, they hold in their hands bowls of incense, which symbolize the prayers of all God's people (Revelation 5:8).

Jesus has purchased us with His own blood, says John in Revelation 5:9–10, in order to make us royal priests together with Him. That is our secret vocation, our heavenly calling here on earth (Hebrews 3:1). Since we have access to the presence of God the Father, the heavenly King, we reign with Christ by praying for the world and its citizens. We do so publicly in the Divine Service and privately in our personal prayers. We overcome evil and the powers of darkness in our environment as we use our access to God's grace to claim His help for those who need the gift of divine aid.

We are united with Jesus Christ our Lord in Baptism, and we now reign with Him here on earth. Each Christian is a member of God's royal priesthood. We are all called to serve as priests together with Jesus, our High Priest. As priests we have access to God the Father and His grace. We also reign as kings with Christ on earth and work with Him in the administration of God's grace, which we do by praying for our world. Yet unlike Jesus, we are responsible for only a small part of God's kingdom here on earth: the area that we know best, the place where He has put us. We exercise our priestly vocation, our area for prayer, as we are responsible for the spiritual welfare of the people around us. Our area of responsibility as a person of prayer, our department, is defined by our station in life, in our family, in our employment, in our circle of friends, and in our congregation.

THE PRIVILEGE OF PRAYER

As members of God's royal priesthood you have access to the presence of God the Father and His grace. Jesus has not made you merely a citizen of His Father's heavenly kingdom; He has made you part of

God's royal family and has appointed you to reign with Him by praying for others.

An essential aspect of the Lutheran teaching on vocation is God's call for us to pray for the people in our spiritual care in our family, society, and congregation. Thus Luther concludes the Table of Duties in the Small Catechism with the admonition from 1 Timothy 2:1: "I urge that supplications, prayers, intercessions, and thanksgivings be made for all people."[3] This means that we are not called to pray generally for everyone, but quite particularly for those with whom we interact in our station and daily routine. We should not only pray for their physical needs but also for their spiritual needs. We can use our status as friends of Jesus to intercede for two groups of people. On the one hand, when we discover that someone has sinned, we can ask God to have mercy on that person and protect him or her from the condemnation of Satan. On the other hand, we can note those who are not Christians, or who no longer attend church, and bring them to Christ in prayer for their conversion and salvation.

SPIRITUAL EXERCISES

Jesus calls us to live double lives here on earth. We are to live as citizens of this world in our daily work. We are also called to work with God as priests by praying for the people around us. That is our secret heavenly calling, our lifelong vocation (see Hebrews 3:1). Jesus uses everything that happens to us to equip us in this task and to help us become praying people as we grow more spiritually mature.

◈ List those people whom you are to serve as a priest. Pray for them by yourself or with your spouse.

◈ Begin each day by praying for the people whom you will meet and with whom you will work.

◈ End each day by thanking God for the people who crossed your path and by praying for them according to their needs.

POINT TO REMEMBER

If you then, who are evil, know how to give good gifts to your children, how much more will your Father who is in heaven give good things to those who ask Him! *Matthew 7:11*

---

3 *Concordia*, p. 348.

The Intercession of Jesus

There is no harder work than prayer. . . . But the Christian's prayer is easy, and it does not cause hard work. *Martin Luther* [4]

If we wish to be healthy, we need to eat well, exercise often, and adopt a balanced routine of work and leisure. Most of us fail to do this, so those who can afford to do so hire a lifestyle coach to help them to live well.

We Christians know that we are called to pray. Most of us would like to be people of prayer who pray regularly, ardently, and spontaneously. Yet we fail most dismally in this. No matter how hard we try, we do not seem to master the art of prayer. The devastating effect of original sin is evident in this problem with prayer because it reveals that we are "without trust in God." [5] We therefore find prayer to go against the grain. We do not like to ask God, or anyone, for help; rather, we prefer to manage by ourselves.

However, by the power of the Holy Spirit working through God's Word, we can come to regard our difficulties in prayer positively as opportunities to learn to pray with Jesus. He lets us fail when we pray by ourselves so that we will turn to Him for His help. Our success in prayer comes from our personal failure as we let Jesus take over from us. We can give thanks for the ongoing intercession of Jesus for the human family and see our reliance on the intercession of Jesus in worship and private prayer as God's perfect plan for our life of prayer.

New Christians often find it much easier than mature Christians to pray regularly and wholeheartedly. Mature Christians often go through periods of intense prayer followed by arid periods with little prayer. When we are successful in prayer, we feel good about our spiritual condition and use that as an index of spiritual progress. But that sense of achievement sets us up for eventual spiritual disillusionment when we run out of steam and become slack in our prayer life once again. On the other hand, when we fail in prayer, we feel guilty, and Satan uses our guilt to question our faith or to get us to give up trying to pray.

Problems with prayer are not new. An early Christian teacher named Agathon said:

> I think there is no labor greater than that of prayer to God. For every time a man wants to pray, his enemies, the demons, want to prevent him, for they know that it is only by turning him from prayer that

---

4   AE 21:142–43.
5   AC II 1; *Concordia*, p. 31.

they can hinder his journey. Whatever good work a man undertakes, if he perseveres in it, he will attain rest. But prayer is warfare to the last breath.[6]

Why are Satan and the demons determined to turn Christians from prayer? Because they want to win the spiritual war for souls. Satan is determined to sabotage our prayers because he knows that when we pray we receive divine help. So Satan's strategy is to stop us from praying, for whenever we pray, he suffers another defeat and his power is diminished. The more mature we are in the faith, the more we will come under attack because we are more of a threat to his interests. Satan knows far better than we do that prayer is a spiritual lifeline for us.

JESUS THE MAN OF PRAYER

Unlike us, Jesus is an expert in prayer. In fact, He is the only expert in prayer—its best practitioner. So Jesus takes over from us and fulfills God's call to us to be praying people. That is part of what He meant when He told John the Baptist at His Baptism, "Let it be so now, for thus it is fitting for us to fulfill all righteousness" (Matthew 3:15). In the first two commandments of the Decalogue, God gives us His name and tells us to use it in prayer. We, however, fail to keep that commandment, even though we benefit so much from observing it. Even as He fulfills the entirety of God's Law, Jesus keeps the Second Commandment of the Decalogue for us by praying for us. The life of prayer that God requires is given to us by our union with Christ in Baptism and our faith in Him as our High Priest. Jesus is our righteousness (1 Corinthians 1:30).

Although each of the Gospel accounts mentions this hidden side to the work of Jesus, St. Luke highlights it: "But [Jesus] would withdraw to desolate places and pray" (Luke 5:16). We learn that Jesus *often* withdrew to solitary places to spend time by Himself in prayer. Elsewhere we discover that He prayed in the evening after His work was done (Matthew 14:23), or all night (Luke 6:12), or early in the morning before a busy day (Mark 1:35). Jesus did not pray for Himself, but for the people who came to Him for help. In His ministry, He not only spoke the Father's word to them, but He also brought them and their needs to His heavenly Father. Luke implies in 5:17 that Jesus received the power to heal by staying in touch with His heavenly Father in prayer.

---

6   Benedicta Ward, trans., *The Sayings of the Desert Fathers* (London: Mowbray, 1980), 21f.

Jesus did not pray occasionally; His whole ministry, from His Baptism to His death on the cross, was an act of intercession for sinners on earth. Luke emphasizes this by telling us that Jesus prayed at all the important points in His earthly ministry.

- At His Baptism before the opening of heaven, the descent of the Spirit, and His Father's recognition of Him as His Son (3:21–22)
- Before forgiving and healing the paralyzed man (5:16–26)
- Before choosing the twelve disciples (6:12–16)
- Before Peter's confession of Him as Christ (9:18–27)
- Before His transfiguration on the mountain (9:28–36)
- Before the gift of His own prayer to His disciples (11:1–13)
- Before His betrayal, trial, and crucifixion (22:41–46)
- At His crucifixion (23:34) and as He died (23:46)

By saying that His ministry was an act of intercession, we mean that Jesus stood for us before God and represented us in His presence, just as at the temple the high priest bore the names of the twelve tribes of Israel on his breastplate and represented them before God in the daily service (Exodus 28:9–12, 21, 29). Luke's emphasis on the time Jesus spent in prayer teaches us three things. First, Jesus prays for us at every stage of our journey with Him—from the font to the moment of death. Second, the work of Jesus in word and deed flows out of His ministry of prayer for the people whom He serves. Third, our praying depends on His praying for us.

JESUS FOR US

God's solution to the problems that we have in our life of prayer is the incarnation of His Son and His life of prayer for us. Jesus did what we could not do for ourselves. Yet His work of prayer for us does not end at His death. Instead, it culminates in His ascension and exaltation as our High Priest in the presence of His heavenly Father. There Jesus continues to pray for all people on earth. He prays not only for our forgiveness but also for all our needs.

The most unique aspect of the Christian teaching and practice of prayer is its dependence on Jesus. He no longer intercedes for a few people at a time as He once did. As High Priest for the whole human family, Christ intercedes for all sinners in the presence of God the Father in heaven itself. Yet, amazingly, Jesus is also present with us here on earth in the Church. That is where He connects with us and involves us in His intercession.

The Book of Hebrews contrasts the ongoing work of Jesus in heaven with the work of the priest at the temple in Jerusalem. The priest interceded for all the Israelites each day as he stood in place of them before God in the Holy Place and burnt incense on their behalf. Because of this intercessory act, the people could approach God confidently and present their prayers to Him. Likewise, Jesus acts for us. The writer to the Hebrews states: "[Jesus] is able to save to the uttermost those who draw near to God through Him, since He always lives to make intercession for them" (7:25). The Greek verb translated as "draw near" is a technical liturgical term for approaching the Father in the Divine Service (see Hebrews 4:16; 10:1, 22; 11:6; 12:22). The Apology of the Augsburg Confession explains this verse in this way:

> He is our High Priest, who intercedes for us. So prayer relies upon God's mercy, when we believe that we are heard for Christ's sake. He is our High Priest, as He Himself says, "Whatever you ask in My name, this I will do, that the Father may be glorified in the Son. If you ask Me anything in My name, I will do it" (John 14:13–14). Without this High Priest we cannot approach the Father.[7]

In the Divine Service performed at the temple in Jerusalem, the people of Israel could approach God confidently with their offerings and prayers because the high priest had done two things for them. He had performed the rite of atonement with the blood of the sacrificed lamb to cleanse the people from their sins, and he had entered the Holy Place to intercede for them and to secure God's acceptance of them by burning incense before the Lord. Jesus is our great High Priest. He not only cleanses us with His blood so that we now have a good conscience, but He also now stands in for us before God the Father (Hebrews 9:24) and intercedes for us (Hebrews 7:25). He does not intercede for us in our absence, but He ushers us into His Father's presence where He puts in a word for us and presents our needs to the Father. Jesus covers us with His righteousness and prays us into the Father's presence. We therefore can approach God the Father boldly and confidently together with Jesus. As He intercedes for us, Jesus leads us into His Father's presence and gives us access to His grace (Hebrews 4:16). He also brings us full salvation from God the Father. We therefore can join with Jesus as He prays for us and our complete salvation.

---

7   Ap V (III) 212 [333]; *Concordia*, p. 133.

CARRIED ALONG

When my children were young, they often asked me to take a walk with them. When I did, they soon ran out of steam. Then came the part they enjoyed most. I would pick them up and piggyback them.

In the same way, we are not left to carry on by ourselves and find our own way in prayer. Jesus comes to us most fully in the Divine Service to help us by praying for us. That is why the pastor often introduces a prayer by greeting the congregation with the words, "The Lord be with you." He announces the presence of Jesus as our intercessor, our leader in prayer, and offers His assistance to us. In the Divine Service, Jesus comes to us and offers to carry us along in prayer. We, as it were, attach ourselves to Him and are piggybacked by Him into His Father's presence. We join in with Jesus when and as we are able, but He does it for us. He makes it easy for us in our weakness and helplessness.

So when we come to church, we do not need to worry about how to pray, or what to pray for, because Jesus prays for us. He includes us in His praying and moves us to join with Him as He prays. He offers Himself to us as our intercessor and gives His prayer to us as our prayer.

SPIRITUAL EXERCISES

◈ The common liturgical prayer "Lord, have mercy" was a beggar's cry for help in the ancient world. Use it as an admission of failure in prayer and as a plea to Jesus to pray for you and to help you in your praying.

◈ Pray the Lord's Prayer each day as the prayer of Jesus for you and your prayer together with Jesus and the whole communion of saints.

◈ Use an order of prayer (*LSB*, pp. 282–89, 294–98) to guide your time of prayer with Jesus.

POINT TO REMEMBER

Therefore, brothers, since we have confidence to enter the holy places by the blood of Jesus, by the new and living way that He opened for us through the curtain, that is, through His flesh, and since we have a great priest over the house of God, let us draw near with a true heart in full assurance of faith, with our hearts sprinkled clean from an evil conscience and our bodies washed with pure water. *Hebrews 10:19–22*

The Gift of Prayer

The Head of this Body prays together with the Body. *Hermann Sasse*

We live in a do-it-yourself society. Authors and speakers make a living selling programs for self-help and self-improvement. These range from methods of losing weight to methods of overcoming cancer. In each case, the assumption is that if we adopt the right technique, we will experience success. Even Christian bookstores feature pamphlets and books that claim to teach the method for successful prayer so you can improve your spiritual life! We believe in justification by grace through faith in Jesus our Lord. Yet all too often we fail to live by faith and grace. In our spirituality and our devotions, we, in practice, all too easily slip back into justification by works.

Much of the popular Christian literature and teaching on prayer reinforces the notion that improvement in prayer depends on us, on our knowledge, our faith, our discipline, our attitude, and our technique. Such books are popular because they are practical and helpful. But they also feed on our guilt and offer to allay it. They boost our spiritual self-confidence and overlook our spiritual impotence. They promise to empower us and to make us experts in prayer. Yet they disconnect prayer from Jesus and His atonement for us.

LORD, TEACH US TO PRAY

Although most people pray when they are in trouble, they find it difficult to pray regularly even when they wish to do so. That is why for millennia religious teachers, including the Jewish rabbis and John the Baptist, have taught their followers how to pray. So it was natural for the disciples of Jesus to ask Him to teach them how to pray.

Although Jesus assumed that His disciples would pray, He differed from the religious leaders in Israel by teaching little about the theory and practice of prayer. This was not because prayer was unimportant for Him; He was, after all, a man of prayer and an expert in it. The one thing that Jesus emphasized repeatedly and forcefully was the importance of faith in Him and His Word rather than self-confidence. He taught that God-pleasing prayer depended on Him rather than the person at prayer.

Luke records that "one of [Jesus'] disciples said to Him, 'Lord, teach us to pray, as John taught his disciples'" (Luke 11:1). This request shows that the disciples expected Jesus to teach them how to pray (the right method of prayer) and what to pray for (the content of prayer). Contrary to that expectation, Jesus answered the request by giving them His own prayer: the Lord's Prayer. He responds to their "prayer" for teaching on prayer by inviting His disciples to join with Him in His prayer to God the Father. In Luke 11:2, Jesus says, "When you pray . . . ," and He uses the plural form of "you" to address the disciples corporately.

The Lord's Prayer is the prayer that Jesus prays for His disciples and for the whole world. By giving us His own prayer, Jesus does three things:

- He puts His disciples on the same footing with God the Father as He has and helps them to impersonate Him.
- In the first two petitions, Jesus teaches His disciples to identify with Him as God's only Son and with His mission as the King of Israel.
- In the last three petitions, Jesus identifies Himself with the disciples and their needs.

We are so accustomed to praying the Lord's Prayer that we no longer are struck by it and our use of it. It is, first and foremost, the prayer of Jesus the Son to His heavenly Father, as unique to Him as that relationship. As such it is remarkable in three ways. First, since Jesus is the only Son of the Father, He alone may approach and address Him as Father. Yet Jesus shares His sonship with us (Romans 8:14–15; Galatians 4:4–6). By giving us His prayer He includes us in His relationship with the Father and allows us to act as if we were Him, dressed up as Him (Romans 13:14; Galatians 3:26–27). Second, by sharing His own status with us Jesus involves us in His mission, His vocation as the royal Son of God. We may therefore identify ourselves with Him and pray with Him for the coming of His Father's kingdom through Him and with us. Third, in the last three petitions Jesus identifies Himself with us and the whole human family by His use of "us" and "our." This is rather odd, for He does not need daily bread, forgiveness, and protection from temptation. Yet Jesus identifies Himself with us and our necessities, our sins, and our temptation. He sides with us and speaks up for us.

Most of us are too proud to ask people for anything unless they owe us a favor. We would rather do without than beg for ourselves. Yet we become quite shameless in seeking help for someone close to us, such as a sick child or a needy spouse. God therefore gets us to pray by confronting us with people who make demands on us that we cannot fulfill, people with needs that we cannot meet from our own resources.

Luther repeatedly taught that our neediness teaches us to pray. He writes:

> People must feel their distress, and such distress presses them and compels them to call and cry out. Then prayer will be made willingly, as it ought to be. People will need no teaching about how to prepare for it and to reach the proper devotion. . . . We all have enough things that we lack. The great problem is that we do not feel or recognize this.[8]

After giving the disciples His own prayer, Jesus answers their request for teaching on prayer with the parable of an unexpected visitor (Luke 11:5–8). Rather ironically, Jesus compares God the Father with a grumpy friend next door. Like the person in that parable, we often are confronted by needy friends who are seeking help. Like that person, we have nothing to set before them. But we do have access to God the Father, who has what we lack. We can borrow from Him by praying persistently for our friends. So Jesus teaches us to pray by sending needy people into our lives, people who expose our own poverty, people whom God alone can help.

RECEIVING FROM GOD

What is the point of praying? We do not need to inform God about our needs or the needs of others, because He knows them better than we do. We do not need to pester God, as if He were reluctant to give His gifts to us. We do not need to twist His arm, like a miserly parent, to get a treat from Him. God is, in fact, far more generous than we could ever imagine and far more willing to give us good things than we are ready to receive.

In Luke 11:9–10, Jesus teaches us the point of praying: "Ask, and it will be given to you; seek, and you will find; knock, and it will be opened to you. For everyone who asks receives, and the one who seeks finds, and to the one who knocks it will be opened." Here, as in Luke 11:1, Jesus uses the plural "you." In Matthew 6:7–8, Jesus says, "Do not heap up empty phrases . . . for your Father knows what you need before you ask Him." This reminds us that we do not need to use prayer to wear down God by pestering Him or to inform Him about what we need. The point of prayer is to receive from God. Jesus gives us His own prayer so that we can use it and our faith in Him to receive the good things that He has promised to give us. We cash in His promises in

---

8   LC III 26–27; *Concordia*, p. 411.

prayer. Jesus teaches us how to pray by promising that God will give us what we ask for when we pray His prayer for ourselves and for others.

Luther reminds us in the Small Catechism that we pray because God the Father "has commanded us to pray . . . and has promised that He will hear us."[9] Jesus' promise teaches us that we pray in order to receive from God the Father. Yet when we pray together with Jesus, we get much more than we ever ask for, in fact, we receive "far more abundantly than all that we ask or think" (Ephesians 3:20). Jesus explains this by comparing prayer to knocking at the door of His Father's house. When we knock at the door of our parents' house, they do not ask us what we want; they invite us in. Like our earthly parents, God the Father opens the door for us and lets us in when we come to ask Him for something. We therefore receive more than just something from God when we pray—we receive the Father Himself, His company, and life with Him. That is the unexpected bonus of prayer!

BEST OF ALL

So far we have had three surprises in the teaching of Jesus on prayer: instead of telling us how to pray, Jesus gives us His own prayer; we pray because of unexpected "visitors" whose needs we cannot meet; and Jesus has promised that we receive God and His gifts by approaching Him in prayer. But the final part of Jesus' teaching on prayer in Luke 11 contains the biggest surprise of all.

When Jesus mentions bad parents who give good gifts to their children (Luke 11:11), the expectation is that He will compare this to His Father's greater readiness to give good gifts to us His children, which He does in Matthew 7:9–11. Instead, Jesus says, "How much more will the heavenly Father give the Holy Spirit to those who ask Him!" (Luke 11:13). Superficially, this promise of the Spirit seems to have nothing whatsoever to do with the request for teaching on the practice of prayer. Yet at a deeper theological level, it has everything to do with the practice of prayer. Here, Jesus recognizes that the basic problem for us is our human weakness, our spiritual impotence, our inability to pray as we wish and as God requires. His solution to that problem is the provision of the Holy Spirit as our helper, as the one who prompts and empowers us to pray.

9   SC III; *Concordia*, p. 338.

Paul explains this promise more fully in Romans 8:26–27:

> Likewise the Spirit helps us in our weakness. For we do not know what to pray for as we ought, but the Spirit Himself intercedes for us with groanings too deep for words. And He who searches hearts knows what is the mind of the Spirit, because the Spirit intercedes for the saints according to the will of God.

So when we pray, we can follow the urging of the Holy Spirit, follow His prompting, even if it is evident only in sighing and groaning and deep distress. The Holy Spirit is the Spirit of prayer. The Holy Spirit is, as Zechariah 12:10 prophesies, the "Spirit of grace and pleas for mercy," the Spirit who gives us faith in the grace of our heavenly Father and who lays claim to that grace for us in prayer. The Holy Spirit assures us that we are sons of God quite practically by getting us to pray to God as our Father together with Jesus (Romans 8:14–17; Galatians 4:4–7). So the best help that Jesus gives to us for our practice of prayer is His Holy Spirit. By prayer we receive the Holy Spirit, who, in turn, makes us people of prayer.

SPIRITUAL EXERCISES

Naturally, we regard prayer as something that we do for God by engaging in conversation with Him. Jesus turns around this assumption and tells us that prayer is His gift to us, a gift that involves all three persons of the Holy Trinity. Jesus gives us His own prayer so that we can use it to enter His Father's house and to receive Him and His gifts for ourselves and for others. He also gives us His Spirit to help, guide, and prompt us as we pray.

◈ Pray to God the Father for the gift of the Holy Spirit and be ready to follow the Holy Spirit in discerning how to pray.

◈ List the unexpected "visitors" that God has sent to you and pray for them.

◈ Follow Paul's advice in Philippians 3:6 and thank God for some gift before you ask for something that you need. In this way, a sense of gratitude and of confidence in God's goodness will displace your anxiety and diffidence.

POINT TO REMEMBER

> Ask, and it will be given to you; seek, and you will find; knock, and it will be opened to you. *Luke 11:9*

Praying with Jesus

One who does not have the Word cannot pray. *Martin Luther* [10]

We learn to do something new by doing it with experts in that task. Boys and girls learn how to cook by helping their mother or father in the kitchen. Teenagers learn how to drive under the watchful eye of a parent or an older sibling. I taught my son how to garden by having him help me. I learned to sing by singing together with others.

Most people learn to pray by participating in family prayers, congregational prayer, and bedtime prayer. They learn to pray from their parents and other members of the family, as well as from their pastors and teachers. This usually involves joining in traditional prayers, such as the Lord's Prayer and table grace, and memorizing them through repeated use. We learn to pray by joining in with others. They hand on the gift of prayer to us by praying with us.

IN THE SHOES OF JESUS

The story is told of two British soldiers in the First World War who looked like twins even though they were unrelated. They came from the opposite ends of society. The one who came from a good family was married with a young son and had a share in his family's business. The other came from a broken family. The two became the best of friends. The young man with a good family spent much of his time telling his friend about his wife and family. He even told his friend that if he was killed his friend should take on his name and impersonate him. That is what happened. The man without any family and prospects in life swapped places with his friend who died.

The soldier who impersonated his friend took more than simply an identity. The name brought membership in a family with loving parents and siblings, a loving wife and son, part of the family business and the social status that went with it. All this became his at the death of his friend by his word and the gift of his name.

Jesus has done something far greater by His incarnation and His sacrificial death. He involves us in a great exchange. In His Baptism, Jesus takes on our sin and guilt, our death and damnation; in our Baptism, He gives us His place with God the Father and His status as the only Son of

---

10 AE 2:19.

the Father. He offers all that He is and has to us. From Jesus we receive a new self and a new life.

In John 16, Jesus is speaking to His disciples on the night before He died. He explains why He needs to return to His Father through His death, resurrection, and ascension. He speaks about two different ways of praying. There is the old way, in which the disciples ask Jesus to speak to God the Father for them. It looks like this:

God the Father

▲ asks on behalf of them

Jesus the Son

▲ ask

The disciples of Jesus

But after Jesus' death and resurrection, the disciples will be able to pray in a new way because they will have direct access to the Father. They will pray in the name of Jesus, in His shoes, as it were. They will pray together with Him like this:

God the Father

▲ ask in the name of Jesus

The disciples

In John 16:23–29, Jesus speaks about the old way of praying in which His disciples did not have access to God the Father and His grace. Therefore they asked Jesus to put their requests to His Father. But by His death and His return to the Father, Jesus provided a new way of praying that was symbolized by the splitting of the curtain of the temple at His death (Matthew 27:51). Jesus describes this new way of praying as asking the Father in His name (John 14:13; 15:16; 16:23, 24, 26). After His ascension, Jesus' disciples could use His name to approach the Father directly in prayer together with Jesus. As St. Paul says in Ephesians 2:18: "For through [Jesus] we both have access in one Spirit to the Father." The most remarkable thing about this new way of praying is that it overcomes our anxiety about our performance and acceptability. God hears our prayers as if they came from the mouth of Jesus. He is just as pleased with us and our prayers as with Jesus and His prayers. The Father listens to us as we are in Jesus, dressed up in Him and all His qualities.

Luther explains:

What greater honor could be paid us than this, that our faith in Christ entitles us to be called His brethren and coheirs, that our prayer is to be like His, that there is really no difference except that our prayers must originate in Him and be spoken in His name. . . . Aside from this, He makes us equal to Himself in all things; His and our prayer must be one, just as His body is ours and His members are ours.[11]

Luther also explores what is meant by praying in the name of Jesus:

"Christ prayed for me, and for this reason my prayers are acceptable through His." Accordingly, we must weave our praying into His. . . . Through Him we come to God. In Him we must incorporate and envelop all our prayers and all that we do. As St. Paul declares (Rom. 13:14), we must put on Christ; and everything must be done in Him (1 Cor. 10:31) if it is to be pleasing to God. But all this is said to Christians for the purpose of giving them the boldness and the confidence to rely on this Man and to pray with complete assurance; for we hear that in this way He unites us with Himself, really puts us on a par with Him, and merges our praying into His and His into ours.[12]

In keeping with this teaching we normally address our prayers to God the Father. We may, of course, also pray to Jesus and to the Holy Spirit. But that is not typical. We conclude our prayers to God the Father by saying that we pray "through Jesus Christ" or "in the name of Jesus." We thereby acknowledge that we pray together with Jesus, who intercedes for us and leads us in our prayers. We use the name of Jesus and our faith in Him to approach the Father with a good conscience, without fear of condemnation or rejection by Him. This teaching makes us bold in prayer for two reasons. First, we need not be anxious about whether God is pleased with us and whether He will give us a favorable hearing (see 1 John 3:21–22; 4:13–15). Second, we need not worry about what to pray for, and how, because Jesus covers us with His righteousness and perfects our prayers. Our performance does not matter; everything depends on Jesus and our faith in Him.

PROMPTING

We do not pray by ourselves, but we pray together with Jesus, who prays for us. Jesus does not just give us His own prayer, but He gives us His Spirit-filled Word to prompt, move, and guide us in our praying. God's Word differs from human speech because it is "spirit and life" (John 6:63). Since His words are inspired by the Holy Spirit, they bring the Holy Spirit to us and fill us with the Holy Spirit. In the Smalcald

11 AE 24:407.
12 AE 24:407.

Articles, Luther therefore asserts: "God grants His Spirit or grace to no one except through or with the preceding outward Word."[13] Jesus helps us to pray together with Him by giving us His Word and His Holy Spirit with His Word. So when we use His Word to pray, we pray by the Spirit.

In John 15, Jesus compares Himself to the stalk of a vine and us to branches that are attached to Him. He shares His Holy Spirit with us so that we can bear much fruit. Jesus also teaches that prayer is the key to spiritual fruitfulness. He does not refer to just any kind of prayer, but to prayer that comes from union with Him. There is one important condition for fruitful prayer. Our praying must echo the words of Jesus that remain in us (John 15:7). His words teach us to pray and prompt us as we pray. We therefore pray, as Luther so often tells us, in obedience to God's Word, in obedience to His commands and promises, because through His Word we remain in Jesus and He remains in us. When His words remain in us, they move and empower us with His Holy Spirit. The more the words of Jesus dwell in us, the more they transform our wishes and desires so that they are in tune with the will of God and with the intercession of Jesus (1 John 5:14). The Father will give us whatever we wish because we will desire what He wants to give us. This has far-reaching implications for the practice of prayer. In our Lutheran tradition, we usually begin our devotions with the reading of God's Word and meditation on it so that His Word can prompt us as we pray. We pray in accordance with His commands and promises, because they harmonize with the intercession of Jesus and synchronize us with the intercession of the Holy Spirit in us.

WORKING WITH JESUS

Although God commands us to pray and promises to hear us when we pray to Him in the name of Jesus, prayer is not a Means of Grace. But when we pray as believers, we exercise our faith in God's Word and so use His Means of Grace. In prayer, by faith, we receive what God offers to us by His Spirit-giving Word, and God does His work in and through us.

In John's Gospel, Jesus performed seven miracles as signs of what He does through the ministry of Word and Sacrament in the Church:

1. The transformation of water into wine (2:1–11)

2. The healing of the official's dying son (4:46–54)

13 SA III VIII 3; *Concordia*, p. 280.

3. The healing of an invalid (5:1–15)

4. The feeding of the five thousand (6:1–15)

5. Walking on the lake at night (6:16–21)

6. The gift of sight to a man born blind (9:1–7)

7. The resuscitation of Lazarus (11:1–44)

In John 14:12–14, Jesus says, "Whoever believes in Me will also do the works that I do; and greater works than these will he do . . . . Whatever you ask in My name, this I will do, that the Father may be glorified in the Son." Here Jesus says that we work together with Him by praying to the Father in His name. The "greater things" performed by the disciples are the "miracles" that are worked by baptizing, preaching, and celebrating the Lord's Supper. Jesus emphasizes the importance of faith in doing His work because, by ourselves, we have no power to do God's work. We are completely dependent on Christ and His Word. He does His work in and through us as we use our faith in Him to ask the Father for everything.

SPIRITUAL EXERCISES

The praying of a Christian is different from the praying of an unbeliever. We do not make conversation with a god who is silent and separated from us. Instead, we join in the conversation of Jesus the Son with God the Father by the power of the Holy Spirit. We pray together with Jesus and follow Him.

◈ Begin your time of prayer by calling on Jesus and asking Him to teach you to pray.

◈ Use a promise that Jesus has made, such as Matthew 11:28, as a guide when you pray.

◈ Begin your time of prayer with a Bible reading and base your prayers on that reading.

POINT TO REMEMBER

If you abide in Me, and My words abide in you, ask whatever you wish, and it will be done for you. *John 15:7*

Complaining

God also requires that you weep and ask for such needs and wants, not because He does not know about them [Matthew 6:8], but so that you may kindle your heart to stronger and greater desires and make wide and open your cloak to receive much [Psalm 10:17]. *Martin Luther*[14]

Most leaders keep themselves aloof from those whom they lead. They do not welcome criticism. Imagine a boss who not only welcomed complaints but also did his best to discover what had gone wrong, so that he could fix the problems. Imagine, too, that this boss made it easy for his employees to lodge their complaints by appointing one of his senior staff to act as an advocate, an ombudsman who spoke up for employees in his presence.

We do not need to be taught how to complain. When something goes wrong, or when we feel that we have been wronged, complaining comes naturally. And that is good. It allows us to let off steam, and when we do not cover up the hurt or bottle up our anger we can be in a better position to deal with what has happened. But often when we complain, we do so because we want someone to vindicate us. We want someone to affirm that we are in the right and that our "enemy," the person who has injured us, is in the wrong. Such affirmation helps us to ignore our own complicity in the matter. It proves our innocence and allows us to occupy the moral high ground against our enemies. The advantage of an ombudsman is that those adversely affected actually have someone to address discreetly the problems without resorting to the law and causing further alienation.

When we complain, we seldom do so directly to anyone who could fix the situation. Instead, we sound off to those around us and take out our frustrations on them. We may, of course, complain to God because He is our Judge. Yet many Christians feel it is wrong to be angry and even worse to be angry with God. Therefore they believe they must put on a happy face with God.

DARING TO COMPLAIN

The Bible is full of God's promises to hear the prayers of His people. For example, Psalm 34:17 states: "When the righteous cry for help, the LORD hears and delivers them out of all their troubles." Popular piety

---

14 LC III 27; *Concordia*, p. 411.

holds that if you are a good Christian, you will prosper. Yet our own experience contradicts that expectation. Quite often things go wrong for us. God does not appear to keep His promises. He does not provide for what we need. He may not heal us when we are sick. He does not deliver us from evil nor defend us when we experience injustice. When God fails to answer our prayers, we feel that either He is not what He claims to be (just, gracious, compassionate, generous) or He is so angry with us that He has abandoned us.

In Luke 18, Jesus uses the parable of the persistent widow to teach His disciples that they should keep on praying even when God seems silent and unresponsive. The widow has experienced injustice in a court of law, but she does not give up. She appeals directly to the judge outside the court, because she knows that he is not a stickler for legality and conventional morality but rather is interested in his reputation.[15] Jesus urges His followers to pray regularly, day and night (Luke 18:7). Unlike that judge, God is truly just. Like that judge, God exercises grace and vindicates us apart from the Law. Christians therefore copy this widow by trusting that God will deliver them from their adversary, the devil, and vindicate them. In fact, Jesus commands Christians to bring their complaints to God daily. These complaints are evidence of their faith because they assume that, even though God may appear to be indifferent, unresponsive, and unhelpful, actually He is just, gracious, and merciful. They appeal to God's grace in the face of His apparent wrath.

We are reluctant to complain to God because we fear that we will wear out His goodwill and exhaust His compassion. Yet He wants us to dump on Him. That is why He has provided the laments in the Book of Psalms. By giving us these psalms that cover almost every situation, He not only tells us that it is right, and even good, to complain to Him when we are wronged, but He also shows us how to complain in a way that pleases Him. The laments have four main components:

- Complaint to God about what has gone wrong, the enemies that have wronged us, and God's failure to provide help.
- Pleas for help from God
- Confession of faith in God's goodness
- Promise of praise for God's help

There are far more laments in the Psalter than psalms of thanksgiving and praise. The most surprising part in many of these laments is the

---

15 This comes out more clearly in the Greek than in our English translation, for the judge does not fear that the widow "will wear him down" but that she "will give him a black eye" if he does not consider her complaint.

complaint, which typically goes in three directions. First, the psalmist describes his trouble in imagery that is vivid and general enough to suit any circumstance from sickness to social disgrace. This focus on trouble shifts to a description of the injuries sustained and a graphic description of the enemies themselves in all their demonic malevolence. Last, the complaint is often directed against God Himself for His dereliction of duty. It is not as if God has caused the evil that has come upon the psalmist. Rather, the psalmist complains that, despite all His promises, God either has abandoned him or has decided to do nothing to help him. These complaints use anger as a stimulus for prayer. In them God's people pour out the bitterness of their hearts to God and argue angrily with Him. They refuse to accept disaster as the proper condition for God's people and protest vehemently against it. By their vivid portrayal of trouble, they appeal to God's compassion. They appeal to God's justice in the face of injustice, to God's grace in the face of His wrath. Despite their troubles, they assume that God is still involved with them and committed to them. They take God at His word and refuse to shut up until He intervenes and deals with their troubles.

One particular psalm fits almost any kind of trouble and any experience of injustice. King David, who wrote Psalm 13, feels angry with God for rejecting him. "How long will You hide Your face from me?" David questions (Psalm 13:1). He is upset because God seems inattentive and indifferent to him. Yet even as David complains that God has done nothing to fix his problems, he does not blame God for causing his trouble. He simply repeats the cry, "How long?" (four times in the first two verses). In verse 3, David asks for three things:

1. God's attention
2. An answer to his prayer
3. Deliverance from the threat of death

And David gives three reasons for making these requests—the prospect of death apart from God's deliverance (verse 3), the triumph of his enemies over him (verse 4), and God's commitment to him (verse 5). David's promise of praise in Psalm 13:5–6 is not an attempt to manipulate God; rather, he is expressing his confidence in God's grace.

OUR OMBUDSMAN

In Psalm 22, an afflicted man (David) complains that God has forsaken him so completely that he has been handed over to death and the powers of darkness. Jesus claimed this psalm for Himself as He hung on the cross. On the cross, Jesus identifies Himself with our human lot and suffers for us. Thus He prays two laments. First, he prays, "My God, My God, why have You forsaken Me?" (Psalm 22:1; cf. Matthew 27:46). Our Savior prayed these words for us and all people who have ever felt abandoned by God. Jesus willingly suffered God's wrath for us and descended into hell for us, so that we could pray this lament and all the psalms of lament together with Him. With nearly His final breath, Jesus prayed, "Into Your hands I commit My spirit" (Psalm 31:5). Thus He committed Himself to God the Father for His vindication.

The risen Lord Jesus is our advocate before the Father, our heavenly ombudsman. He sides with us in our suffering and intercedes with God for us. Not only does He pray for our justification, but He also pleads with God to "graciously give us all things" that He has promised to provide for us (Romans 8:32).

Because Jesus is our ombudsman, we can confidently say with the apostle Paul: "If God is for us, who can be against us?" (Romans 8:31). In fact, the verses surrounding this statement (Romans 8:31–34) can be considered in the light of Paul's instruction on the intercession of the Spirit in Romans 8:26–27 and his claim that in all things God works for good to those who love Him (Romans 8:28). By His intercession, Jesus pleads for our justification before God but also for our reception of all good gifts from Him. Because Jesus acts as our ombudsman and intercedes for us, we can be sure that He backs us when we bring our troubles to God. We can be sure that no matter how much our experience seems to contradict God's promises of blessing, He will bring good out of all the bad things that happen to us. Since Jesus intercedes for us, we can be bold in lamenting and complaining to God because we know that He would have to spurn His own Son if He rejected us and our complaints.

DUMPING

When things go wrong, we feel anger and hurt, especially as we consider God's apparent failure to look after us. We either bottle up our anger (which then produces self-pity, bitterness, resentment, and hatred against those who have hurt us) or we lash out verbally or physically against others. By itself, anger is not sinful because God Himself is angry at sin, abuse, and injustice. As with guilt, anger is a gift of God, the proper healthy reaction to evil. But Satan uses our anger negatively to destroy our confidence in God's goodness and to turn us into hard-hearted cynics.

How can we be angry without sinning? The apostle Paul tells the Ephesians that they can "be angry and . . . not sin," but this happens when they "do not let the sun go down on your anger" (Ephesians 4:26) and when they "let all bitterness and wrath and anger and clamor and slander be put away from you" (verse 31). First, Paul is telling us that we must not let our anger get out of hand. He is not saying that we can rid ourselves of anger; instead, we need someone to remove it. And this happens when we hand over our anger with its fruits—bitterness, rage, quarrelling, slander, and malice—to Jesus in prayer and unload it on Him. He alone can take it away from us and heal the hurt that has produced it. But Jesus cannot remove it unless we acknowledge, release, and hand it over to Him. So God uses our anger to teach us to complain to Him and to pray for help from Him.

SPIRITUAL EXERCISES

◈ List your "enemies" who have abused you. Tell God how you feel about them. Ask Him to undo the damage they have done.

◈ Use Psalm 13, or another psalm of lament, to complain to God about your trouble and those who have wronged you.

◈ Pray "Lord of Our Life" (*LSB* 659) or Psalm 74 as your lament for the Church, which is under attack by Satan.

POINT TO REMEMBER

Humble yourselves, therefore, under the mighty hand of God so that at the proper time He may exalt you, casting all your anxieties on Him, because He cares for you. *1 Peter 5:6–7*

Praying Together

Prayer is the greatest prerogative of Christians, which God conferred on them as He placed them, justified by faith, into their filial relationship. *Peter Brunner* [16]

---

16 *Worship in the Name of Jesus*, 202.

Some years ago a minister's conference in the city where I live conducted a survey of the local agencies involved in public life. It set out to discover what these agencies wanted the churches to do in the community. The survey listed options such as childcare, food aid, shelters for women, housing for the homeless, and so on. When the churches assessed their responses, they found that most respondents had added something that they had not even considered. They asked the churches to pray for them. Luther agrees with the survey respondents. He maintains that "the true office and function" of Christians is their work of praying for others who have not yet come to faith.[17] Only believers can do this, for they alone have access to the grace of God the Father.

One way in which we as the Body of Christ carry out this function is in the Divine Service when we join together in the Prayer of the Church. In this vital part of our worship, the congregation prays for itself and for the world and all people in need, no matter who they are. Luther says about congregational prayer:

> Such prayer is a precious thing and a powerful defense against the devil and his assaults. For in it, all Christendom combines its forces with one accord; and the harder it prays, the more effective it is and the sooner it is heard. . . . Thus it is certain that whatever still stands and endures, whether it is in the spiritual or in the secular realm, is being preserved through prayer.[18]

The Church serves the world best by praying for it and its rulers in the Prayer of the Church.

COMMON PRAYER

People in all religions pray to their gods. The normal practice in paganism is individual prayer. Yet we Christians never pray alone even when we pray privately; we pray together with Jesus and the whole Church. Thus Luther says, "Never think that you are kneeling or standing alone, rather think that the whole of Christendom, all devout Christians, are standing there beside you and you are standing among them in a common, united petition which God cannot disdain."[19]

In Matthew 5:44, Jesus commands us to "pray for those who persecute you." The worship of early Christians differed from the rituals performed by their neighbors in their practice of common prayer. The

---

17 AE 24:87.
18 AE 21:140.
19 AE 43:198.

critics of the Church were astonished that in addition to their families and community, Christians prayed for people who were unrelated to them, for foreigners, and even for their enemies. This was, and still is, a countercultural feature of Christian piety. In the Divine Service, all Christians pray for the world, and they offer these prayers with Jesus and the whole Church.

After the people who believed were baptized on the day of Pentecost, they devoted themselves to four communal activities in the Divine Service:

1. The teaching of God's Word by the apostles
2. The presentation of common offerings
3. The celebration of the Lord's Supper
4. The saying of congregational prayers

This practice of common prayer, which had its origins in Jewish worship at the temple and in the synagogue, began with the mother church in Jerusalem. Acts 2:41–43 shows that, from the beginning, all baptized believers were involved in this common prayer. The people of Jerusalem were filled with awe at the solidarity in prayer exhibited by the first Christians. They were amazed that by joining in common prayer, Christians put aside their own concerns and focused on the needs of others.

Paul instructs the young pastor Timothy in how to repair the church in Ephesus. He says that the most important task of the congregation, the thing that it needs to do "first of all" (1 Timothy 2:1) in response to hearing the Gospel, is to engage in communal prayer. Not only will such prayer be "pleasing in the sight of God our Savior" (verse 3), but Paul connects prayer directly to the fact that God "desires all people to be saved and to come to the knowledge of the truth" (verse 4). Prayer is the basis for the work of evangelism in the community, for sharing the Good News flows from intercessory prayer for those who have not yet "come to the knowledge of the truth." Corporate prayer is how the Body of Christ best serves the world in the Divine Service.

Paul goes on to connect the prayers of Timothy's congregation in Ephesus with the work of Jesus among them. He writes that the "man Christ Jesus, who gave Himself as a ransom for all" (1 Timothy 2:5–6), is the "one mediator between God and men" (verse 5). Since God wants all people to be saved, Jesus intercedes for all people and prays for their salvation. Thus the congregation joins with Jesus in His ministry of intercession for the world. Paul says that the Church should pray for two groups of people. First, it should pray generally for "all people" without exception, because God "desires all people to be saved" (1 Timothy 2:4; cf. verse 1). Second, the Church should pray specifically for "kings and all who are in high positions" (verse 2). Whether they are good or bad rulers, governmental leaders need our prayers because they have the God-given vocation of ruling His world. They cannot do so without God's help and the prayers of the Church. Paul's reference to kings needs to be translated into modern terms that fit our democratic system of government with its dispersal of powers rather than the Roman system with its concentration of power in a single person. We need to pray for those who work in all levels of government, from the local to the international sphere. Those in the government either can use their authority to advance the spread of the Gospel by promoting justice, peace, and good order, or they can abuse their power to hinder the work of the Church by unleashing the powers of darkness.

Paul tells Timothy's congregation in Ephesus to offer four different kinds of prayer for the human family:

1. *Supplications* or *petitions* for people in their need. In these prayers, the people of Ephesus were to pray as if the needs of others were their needs.

2. *Prayers* for prosperity. In these prayers, the people of Ephesus were to pray as if their access to God the Father and His grace was given to them for the benefit of others.

3. *Intercessions* for those who have done wrong. In these prayers, the people of Ephesus were to pray for God's pardon as if the sins of others were their sins.

4. *Thanksgivings* for those who have prospered. In these prayers, the people of Ephesus were to pray as if the blessings others had received from God had been given to them.

When we pray for others, we identify ourselves with them just as Jesus does. First, we stand in for them as we petition God concerning their needs. If they are in trouble, we do not distance ourselves, but we act as if their needs were ours. We plead with God to help others in their need, whether they are sick, depressed, unemployed, divorced, or whatever. Second, even if others are not in trouble, we pray to God for their prosperity. We act as if their lives were ours. We ask God to give them His good gifts, such as health, success at work and at home, and any other gift available to them in the order of creation. Third, we intercede on behalf of others before God when they have sinned. If they have done something evil, we do not damn them, but we act as if their sins were ours. We ask God to have mercy and to provide the opportunity to repent. Fourth, we stand in for others by our thanksgivings for the blessings they have received from God. If they prosper and things go well, we do not envy them and begrudge them their happiness. Instead, we act as if their blessings were ours. We use our access to God to thank Him on their behalf for His generosity, because they are not yet in the position to do so for themselves.

AGREEMENT WITH JESUS

In Matthew 18, Jesus taught us what a congregation should do if a member is lost (verses 10–14) and how a congregation should deal with one member who sins against another (verses 15–18). Then Jesus says, "If two of you agree on earth about anything they ask, it will be done for them by My Father in heaven" (verse 19). The Greek word in this verse that is translated as "agree" means that we are to speak with one voice, a common voice. Jesus does not stress only the importance of common congregational prayer, but He emphasizes agreement in a common confession of faith and verbal assent to the content of liturgical prayers. If we disagree with what is prayed for, we dissociate ourselves from the congregation and disagree with Christ, who leads us in prayer. Through our agreement with one another and with Jesus in our common prayers, the Father does His work among us and through us. We most commonly voice our agreement and assent with the use of the Hebrew acclamation "Amen." By its use we pray together with one voice, the voice of Jesus.

USING OUR FAITH FOR OTHERS

The healing of the paralyzed man in Mark 2:1–12 is a unique story in the Gospels. Usually Jesus healed people who used their faith in Him to request something of Him. But this man could not bring himself to Jesus because he was paralyzed. So his friends used their legs and their faith in Jesus to bring the man to Jesus. This is the only recorded case where Jesus healed someone because of the faith of his friends rather than his own faith.

The account of this healing illustrates what we do when we pray for unbelievers. We use our faith in Jesus to bring others to Him. Unbelievers are like this paralyzed man because they cannot approach God with a good conscience, since they do not yet have faith and have not yet received forgiveness. They may desire help from God, but they lack the ability to come to Him. Faith gives us legs to walk in the way of the Lord. As believers, we use our faith in Jesus and our access to the Father's grace for the benefit of others by praying for them. We do this corporately in the Prayer of the Church. We bring unbelievers with us to church and place them before Jesus by interceding for them.

SPIRITUAL EXERCISES

When we pray for others, we use our faith in Jesus and our access to God's grace for them. We bring them to Jesus and gain His help for them.

◈ Pray for the people close to you who do not attend church. Pray for them also each Sunday, either in the Prayer of the Church or at Holy Communion.

◈ Read the words of Jesus in Matthew 5:43–48 and show your love for your enemies by praying for them.

◈ Recall the people whom you envy and thank God for the blessings they enjoy.

POINT TO REMEMBER

Again I say to you, if two of you agree on earth about anything they ask, it will done for them by My Father in heaven. *Matthew 18:19*

Lutheran Teaching on Prayer

The first Lutherans took great pains to distinguish prayer as a God-pleasing good work of a justified person from prayer as a good work that earned God's approval. They emphasized three things. First, Christian prayer depends on God's commands and promises rather than the performance of the person, for by His Word God gives access to His grace. The power of prayer therefore comes from God's Spirit-filled Word. Second, prayer is an act of faith by which a believer receives a good conscience before God and all His promised gifts. Third, Christ encourages and helps His disciples to pray by giving them the Lord's Prayer. God therefore "expects us and He Himself arranges the words and form of prayer for us. He places them on our lips for how and what we should pray."[20]

PUTTING HIS WORDS IN OUR MOUTHS

Our Father who art in heaven. *What does this mean?* Answer: By these words God would tenderly encourage us to believe that He is our true Father and that we are His true children, so that we may ask Him confidently with all assurance, as dear children ask their dear father. (SC III; *Concordia*, p. 331)

Amen. *What does this mean?* Answer: I should be certain that these petitions are acceptable to our Father in heaven and are heard by Him. For He Himself has commanded us to pray this way and has promised that He will hear us. Amen, Amen; that is, "Yes, yes, it shall be so." (SC III; *Concordia*, p. 338)

We have now heard what we must do and believe, in what things the best and happiest life consists. Now follows the third part, how we ought to pray. For we are in a situation where no person can perfectly keep the Ten Commandments, even though he has begun to believe. The devil with all his power, together with the world and our own flesh, resists our efforts. Therefore, nothing is more necessary than that we should continually turn towards God's ear, call upon Him, and pray to Him. We must pray that He would give, preserve, and increase faith in us and the fulfillment of the Ten Commandments [2 Thessalonians 1:3]. We pray that He would remove everything that is in our way and that opposes us in these matters. So that we might know what and how to pray, our Lord Christ has Himself taught us both the way and the words [Luke 11:1–4], as we shall see.

But before we explain the Lord's Prayer part by part, it is most necessary first to encourage and stir people to prayer, as Christ and the apostles also have done [Matthew 6:5–15]. And the first thing to know is that it is our duty to pray because of God's commandment. For that's what we heard in the Second Commandment, "You shall not take the name of the LORD your God in vain" [Exodus 20:7]. We are required to praise that holy name and call upon it in every need, or to pray. To call upon God's name is nothing other than to pray [e.g., 1 Kings 18:24]. Prayer is just as strictly and seriously commanded as all other commandments: to have no other God, not to kill, not to steal, and so on. Let no one think that it makes no difference whether he prays or not. Common people think this, who grope in such delusion and ask, "Why should I pray? Who knows

---

20 LC III 22; *Concordia*, p. 410.

whether God heeds or will hear my prayer? If I do not pray, someone else will." And so they fall into the habit of never praying. They build a false argument, as though we taught that there is no duty or need for prayer, because we reject false and hypocritical prayers [Matthew 6:5]. (LC III 1–6; *Concordia*, pp. 408–9)

But praying, as the Second Commandment teaches, is to call upon God in every need. He requires this of us and has not left it to our choice. But it is our duty and obligation to pray, if we would be Christians, just as it is our duty and obligation to obey our parents and the government. For by calling upon God's name and praying, His name is honored and used well. This you must note above all things, so that you may silence and reject thoughts that would keep and deter us from prayer. It would be useless for a son to say to his father, "What good does my obedience do me? I will go and do what I can. It makes no difference." But there stands the commandment, "You shall and must obey." So here prayer is not left to my will to do it or leave it undone, but it shall and must be offered at the risk of God's wrath and displeasure.

‹This point is to be understood and noted before everything else. Then by this point we may silence and cast away the thoughts that would keep and deter us from praying, as though it does not matter if we do not pray, or as though prayer was commanded for those who are holier and in better favor with God than we are. Indeed, the human heart is by nature so hopeless that it always flees from God and imagines that He does not wish or desire our prayer, because we are sinners and have earned nothing but wrath [Romans 4:15]. Against such thoughts (I say), we should remember this commandment and turn to God, so that we may not stir up His anger more by such disobedience. For by this commandment God lets us plainly understand that He will not cast us away from Him or chase us away [Romans 11:1]. This is true even though we are sinners. But instead He draws us to Himself [John 6:44], so that we might humble ourselves before Him [1 Peter 5:6], bewail this misery and plight of ours, and pray for grace and help [Psalm 69:13]. Therefore, we read in the Scriptures that He is also angry with those who were punished for their sin, because they did not return to Him and by their prayers turn away His wrath and seek His grace [Isaiah 55:7].›

Now, from the fact that prayer is so solemnly commanded, you are to conclude and think that no one should in any way despise his prayer. Instead, he should count on prayer. He should always turn to an illustration from the other commandments. A child should in no way despise his obedience to father and mother, but should always think, "This work is a work of obedience. What I do I do for no other reason than that I may walk in the obedience and commandment of God. On this obedience I can settle and stand firm, and I can value it as a great thing, not because of my worthiness, but because of the commandment." So here also, we should think about the words we pray and the things we pray for as things demanded by God and done in obedience to Him. We should think, "On my account this prayer would amount to nothing. But it shall succeed, because God has commanded it." Therefore, everybody—no matter what he has to say in prayer—should always come before God in obedience to this commandment. (LC III 8–13; *Concordia*, pp. 409–10)

For we let thoughts like these lead us astray and stop us: "I am not holy or worthy enough. If I were as godly and holy as St. Peter or St. Paul, then I would pray." But put such thoughts far away. For the same commandment that applied to St. Paul applies also to me. The Second Commandment is given as much on my account as on his account, so that Paul can boast about no better or holier commandment.

You should say, "My prayer is as precious, holy, and pleasing to God as that of St. Paul or of the most holy saints. This is the reason: I will gladly grant that Paul is personally more holy, but that's not because of the commandment. God does not consider prayer because of the person, but because of His Word and obedience to it. For I rest my prayer on the same commandment on which all the saints rest their prayer. Furthermore, I pray for the same thing that they all pray for and always have prayed. Besides, I have just as great a need of what I pray for as those great saints; no, even a greater one than they."

Let this be the first and most important point, that all our prayers must be based and rest upon obedience to God, regardless of who we are, whether we are sinners or saints, worthy or unworthy. We must know that God will not have our prayer treated as a joke. But He will be angry and punish all who do not pray, just as surely as He punishes all other disobedience. Furthermore, He will not allow our prayers to be in vain or lost. For if He did not intend to answer your prayer, He would not ask you to pray and add such a severe commandment to it.

In the second place, we should be more encouraged and moved to pray because God has also added a promise and declared that it shall surely be done for us as we pray. He says in Psalm 50:15, "Call upon Me in the day of trouble; I will deliver you." And Christ says in the Gospel of St. Matthew, "Ask, and it will be given to you; . . . for everyone who asks receives" (7:7–8). Such promises certainly ought to encourage and kindle our hearts to pray with pleasure and delight. For He testifies with His own Word that our prayer is heartily pleasing to Him. Furthermore, it shall certainly be heard and granted, in order that we may not despise it or think lightly of it and pray based on chance.

You can raise this point with Him and say, "Here I come, dear Father, and pray, not because of my own purpose or because of my own worthiness. But I pray because of Your commandment and promise, which cannot fail or deceive me." Whoever, therefore, does not believe this promise must note again that he outrages God like a person who thoroughly dishonors Him and accuses Him of falsehood.

Besides this, we should be moved and drawn to prayer. For in addition to this commandment and promise, God expects us and He Himself arranges the words and form of prayer for us. He places them on our lips for how and what we should pray [Psalm 51:15], so that we may see how heartily He pities us in our distress [Psalm 4:1], and we may never doubt that such prayer is pleasing to Him and shall certainly be answered. This ‹the Lord's Prayer› is a great advantage indeed over all other prayers that we might compose ourselves. For in our own prayers the conscience would ever be in doubt and say, "I have prayed, but who knows if it pleases Him or whether I have hit upon the right proportions and form?" Therefore, there is no nobler prayer to be found upon earth than the Lord's Prayer. We pray it daily [Matthew 6:11], because it has this excellent testimony, that God loves to hear it. We ought not to surrender this for all the riches of the world.

The Lord's Prayer has also been prescribed so that we should see and consider the distress that ought to drive and compel us to pray without ceasing [1 Thessalonians 5:17]. For whoever would pray must have something to present, state, and name, which he desires. If he does not, it cannot be called a prayer.

We have rightly rejected the prayers of monks and priests, who howl and growl day and night like fiends. But none of them think of praying for a hair's breadth of anything. If we would assemble all the churches, together with all churchmen, they would be bound to confess that they have never from the heart prayed for even a drop of wine. For none of them has ever intended to pray from obedience to God and faith in His promise. No one has thought about any need. But when they had done their best they thought no further than this: To do a good work, by which they might repay God. They were unwilling to take anything from Him, but wished only to give Him something.

But where there is to be a true prayer, there must be seriousness. People must feel their distress, and such distress presses them and compels them to call and cry out. Then prayer will be made willingly, as it ought to be. People will need no teaching about how to prepare for it and to reach the proper devotion. But the distress that ought to concern us most (both for ourselves and everyone), you will find abundantly set forth in the Lord's Prayer. Therefore, this prayer also serves as a reminder, so that we meditate on it and lay it to heart and do not fail to pray. For we all have enough things that we lack. The great problem is that we do not feel or recognize this. Therefore, God also requires that you weep and ask for such needs and wants, not because He does not know about them [Matthew 6:8], but so that you may kindle your heart to stronger and greater desires and make wide and open your cloak to receive much [Psalm 10:17].

Every one of us should form the daily habit from his youth of praying for all his needs. He should pray whenever he notices anything affecting his interests or that of other people among whom he may live. He should pray for preachers, the government, neighbors, household servants, and always (as we have said) to hold up to God His commandment and promise, knowing that He will not have them disregarded. This I say because I would like to see these things brought home again to the people so that they might learn to pray truly and not go about coldly and indifferently. They become daily more unfit for prayer because of indifference. That is just what the devil desires, and for which he works with all his powers. He is well aware what damage and harm it does him when prayer is done properly.

We need to know this: all our shelter and protection rest in prayer alone. For we are far too weak to deal with the devil and all his power and followers who set themselves against us. They might easily crush us under their feet. Therefore, we must consider and take up those weapons with which Christians must be armed in order to stand against the devil [2 Corinthians 10:4; Ephesians 6:11]. For what do you imagine has done such great things up till now? What has stopped or quelled the counsels, purposes, murder, and riot of our enemies, by which the devil thought he would crush us, together with the Gospel? It was the prayer of a few godly people standing in the middle like an iron wall for our side. Otherwise they would have witnessed a far different tragedy. They would have seen how the devil would have destroyed all Germany in its own blood. But now our enemies may confidently ridicule prayer and make a mockery of it. However, we shall still be a match both for them and the devil by prayer alone, if we only persevere diligently and do not become slack. For whenever a godly Christian prays, "Dear Father, let Your will be done" [see Matthew 6:10], God speaks from on high and says, "Yes, dear child, it shall be so, in spite of the devil and all the world." (LC III 15–32; *Concordia*, pp. 410–12)

CONFESSION
God Gives Us Truth[1]

In the memorable words of the sixth chief part of Luther's Small Catechism, "where there is the forgiveness of sins there is also life and salvation."[2] Lutheran spirituality has as its heart the forgiveness of sins. In contrast to competing forms of spirituality that might be characterized by moral improvement, celebration of the divine presence, or growth toward holiness, Lutheran spirituality is always a return to the baseline of the forgiveness of sins. The Absolution, spoken in liturgy and sermon and given with the body and blood of Jesus in the Lord's Supper, moves us back into the world where we live in our various callings. It is precisely in those callings that the continued reality of our sinfulness is made manifest. We fail to fear, love, and trust in God above all things, and thus we do not love our neighbors as ourselves. We are continually driven back to Jesus, to confess our sins and receive what only His blood can impart: forgiveness of sins, which carries with it both pardon and the power for the new life.

Forgiveness of sins is only for sinners. Those who do not see themselves as sinners will find this topic irrelevant at best and offensive at worst. But if you know yourself to be a real sinner who lives only by the promise of the Absolution, continue reading. This is not a chapter about how one might feel about his or her sins. It does not provide you with a few easy techniques to master those bad habits that make your life and the lives of those around you a misery. This is an exploration of truth. It

---

1   Adapted from *The Lutheran Spirituality Series: Confession*, written by John T. Pless, edited by Robert C. Baker. Copyright © 2006 Concordia Publishing House.
2   SC VI; *Concordia*, p. 343.

is a study of the truth of your sin in the eyes of God. In this chapter, we hear the truth that comes out of God's mouth in the word of the Law that convicts and kills you. Agreement with that truth is called confession. But our study cannot end there, for there is an ultimate word of truth about sinners that comes from the mouth of God. It is called Absolution. The word of the Gospel in all of its various forms—spoken, sacramental, written, or remembered—is nothing less than an Absolution. It is God's own verdict that the sinner will not die but live by trust in the promise.

This chapter will probe Confession and Absolution in the multiple ways that they are given us, such as the Lord's Prayer; the Divine Service; words of repentance and forgiveness spoken between brothers and sisters in Christ Jesus; and that often overlooked and underused gift of our heritage, individual Confession and Absolution before one's pastor. The goal of this chapter is to deepen in you the knowledge of Absolution as the comfort and consolation that Christ alone provides when the devil terrorizes you, tempting you to believe his lie that there is no forgiveness of your sins.[3]

The Truth of Sin

If sin were only disobedience, that is, the deviation from a norm, the damage could be repaired forthwith by obedience, and the problem of destiny would be solved by "composure." In reality, however, sin, in the strict sense, is "enmity against God," that is, active opposition to the will of God, which, to an equal degree, is active against sin. God replies to sin with a judgment that can terminate only in our death. *Werner Elert*[4]

---

3   For more information on this topic, see the following: Oswald Bayer, *Living by Faith: Justification and Sanctification*, trans. Geoffrey W. Bromiley (Grand Rapids: Eerdmans, 2003); Gerhard Forde, *On Being a Theologian of the Cross* (Grand Rapids: Eerdmans, 1997); Henry Hamann, *On Being a Christian* (Milwaukee: Northwestern, 1998); Herman Preus, *A Theology to Live By* (St. Louis: Concordia, 2005); and Harold Senkbeil, *Dying to Live: The Power of Forgiveness* (St. Louis: Concordia, 1994). Each of these authors in his own way has explored confession and forgiveness of sin and their insights are often reflected in this chapter.

4   *The Structure of Lutheranism* (St. Louis: Concordia, 1962), 27.

> Man is by nature unable to want God to be God. Indeed, he himself
> wants to be God, and does not want God to be God. *Martin Luther*[5]

Lutheran theology is nothing if it is not realistic! Like the Scriptures, Lutheran theology does not start with notions about human freedom and the potential (great or small) that human beings have. Theologies that start with assumptions about human freedom end up in bondage. Lutheran theology begins with man's bondage in sin and ends up with the glorious liberty of the Gospel.

The bondage to sin is not a slight defect that can be corrected by appropriate self-discipline. Neither is it a sickness that can be cured by the appropriation of the medication of regular doses of God's grace. Sin is alienation from the Creator and carries with it God's verdict of guilt and a divinely imposed death sentence. To be a sinner is to be held captive in death and condemnation. We need to see more clearly the biblical teaching of the depth of human sin as the evil and inborn failure to fear, love, and trust in God above all things. We have inherited this failure from Adam, and we daily express it in thought, word, and deed.

The distance between God and humanity is not the gap between the infinite and the finite. It is the gap between a holy God who is the judge and man who is the guilty defendant. When we name sin for what it is, we can better recognize and address contemporary denials of sin that would undermine the atonement of Christ. God has provided the answer to sin in the forgiveness obtained by Christ's sacrificial death and bestowed in the Gospel.

Paul describes life apart from faith in Christ Jesus as being dead in trespasses and sins (Ephesians 2:1). Just as a corpse cannot will itself to be alive, so those who are spiritually dead must be made alive by a power that is outside of the self. Sin places us in a prison from which we cannot escape. But Paul proclaims that "God, being rich in mercy, because of the great love with which He loved us, even when we were dead in our trespasses, made us alive together with Christ" (Ephesians 2:4). We are made alive and liberated by the promise of the Gospel, which creates faith.[6]

---

5   AE 31:10.
6   See AC II; *Concordia*, pp. 31–32.

SELF-DECEPTION IS THE ENEMY
OF THE TRUTH

Denial is the polar opposite of confession. According to 1 John 1:8 and 10, when we say that we do not sin, "we deceive ourselves, and the truth is not in us . . . we make [God] a liar, and His word is not in us." To deny that we are sinners demonstrates that we are sinners, for the essence of sin is unbelief, which calls God a liar. Through the prophet Jeremiah, God calls the human heart "deceitful" and "desperately sick" (Jeremiah 17:9). That is, the human heart cannot be trusted, for it is the center of that inborn mistrust of God called sin. As the heart is a veritable cesspool of anger, adultery, pride, and murder (see Mark 7:21–23), its directives are not to be trusted. God has given us something far more sure and certain than the fickle heart. He has given us His Word, which is truth (John 17:17).

In Psalm 32:3–5, the psalmist speaks of sin as a disease that causes anguish in body and soul as he poetically describes a wasting away of the bones. The heavy hand of God's wrath is unrelenting over and against the one who attempts to deny his sin. "Sin has its own hidden law of gravitation," says Adolph Köberle.[7] It pulls the sinner ever deeper into either denial or despair. When sin is not acknowledged, the sinner is hardened in his or her denial or is plunged into despair that will not trust in Christ's forgiveness.

The confessional prayer in Setting One of the Divine Service confesses that "we are by nature sinful and unclean," that is, we are afflicted with original sin. We also confess that we have committed actual sin when we have sinned against God in "thought, word, and deed." We acknowledge that we have sinned by commission and omission, that is, "by what we have done and by what we have left undone."[8] This confessional prayer is anchored in the Ten Commandments, especially the First Commandment. We recognize that we have not loved God with "our whole heart; we have not loved our neighbors as ourselves."[9] As we confess that we are poor, miserable sinners,[10] we are not making a statement about how we *feel*, but we are stating our need for divine mercy.[11]

---

7   *The Quest for Holiness* (Minneapolis: Augsburg, 1938), 216.

8   *LSB*, p. 151.

9   *LSB*, p. 151.

10   See the confessional prayer in Setting Three of the Divine Service: *LSB*, p. 184.

11   On this point, see the excellent essay by C. S. Lewis, "Miserable Offenders," in *God in the Dock: Essays on Theology and Ethics* (Grand Rapids: Eerdmans, 1970), where

Some argue that Confession and Absolution should be omitted from the Divine Service because this practice immediately "tells people how bad they are" instead of starting the service with something more upbeat and affirming. But the knowledge that we are sinners is exactly the correct starting point for the liturgy. The Divine Service is a service that God renders to sinners. Through the Divine Service, God proclaims to sinners a Word of promise that raises the dead and feeds them with the meal of His New Testament, Christ's body and blood. Without the Law, there is no need for the Gospel. When the Divine Service is turned into something other than God's vehicle for the delivery of His forgiveness, then we are left with our human celebration, affirmation, motivation, and so forth. All of that is finally in the category of the Law. Feeling affirmed is a poor substitute for being forgiven by Christ!

The Divine Service uses 1 John 1:8–9 to prepare us for the confession of our sins. The apostle reminds us that "if we confess our sins, [God] is faithful and just to forgive us our sins and to cleanse us from all unrighteousness" (verse 9). Without the confidence that God is the Lord who is merciful and promises to forgive the sins of all who repent, we would never come to confess our sins. It is this promise of God's merciful pardon for sinners that gives us the courage to confess our sins.

THE CLARITY OF CONFESSION _____

In the confession of sins—whether in the liturgy, before our pastor, to a Christian brother or sister, or in our prayers—we do not make excuses for our sins or whimper and whine over their bitter consequences in our lives. Instead, we confess them, that is, we acknowledge that God's judgment on our sin is altogether true and right. He is, indeed, justified in His judgment (see Psalm 51:4–5). We name sin for what it is, recognizing that it merits God's temporal and eternal punishment. When we confess our sins, we are not telling God something that He does not already know. Before Him there are no secrets. He sees into the deepest recesses of the human soul. Confession is not for God's sake but for our own sake, that we might know our sin for what it is.

But we are easily seduced into self-deception, and we evade the truth about ourselves. Thus one of the helpful features of individual

---

Lewis points out that the English word *miserable* is derived from the Latin word for one in need of mercy. This need for mercy is also reflected in the order for Individual Confession and Absolution, where the confessional prayer states: "I have lived as if God did not matter and as if I mattered most" (*LSB*, p. 292).

confession before our pastor is that we actually name our sins.[12] Naming our sins guards against what Herman Bezzel described as a "general repentance" that he called "the death of repentance."[13] A "general repentance" acknowledges sin as a generic reality but fails to come to terms with the concrete reality of one's own sin. Luther's advice that each person should examine his or her life in light of their place or station in life (i.e., mother, child, employee, etc.) and the Ten Commandments is brought into the order of Individual Confession and Absolution.[14] Thus we see our sin precisely at those points where God has called us to live in faith and love, but we have not fulfilled His Law.

While it is not possible or necessary to enumerate each and every sinful thought, word, or deed (see Psalm 19:12), naming our sins individually is a guard against attempting to hold any sin outside of Christ's forgiveness. As we name our sins, we acknowledge the truth of the Law's diagnosis, and this process is for our benefit, not to enable God to see things more clearly. God already sees us as we are. And He has already accomplished the very forgiveness that is announced to us.

Another tool to aid us in making confession of our sins is to review the Lord's Prayer. Repentance and faith, Confession and Absolution are implicit and often explicit in each petition (especially as Luther explains them in his Small Catechism). For example, we pray "hallowed be Thy name" as those who have profaned God's name. In praying "Thy kingdom come," we are praying that we might believe the Absolution. When we pray "Thy will be done on earth as it is in heaven," we are imploring God to deal with not only the evil plans and purposes of the world and the devil but also with our own sinful nature. The Fourth Petition is a prayer against the unbelief that will not receive God's provisions with thanksgiving. The Fifth Petition can be prayed only by sinners, for it is a prayer for the forgiveness of sins. In the Sixth Petition, we pray against the temptations from the devil, the world, and our sinful nature that constantly assault us. In the Seventh Petition, we cry out for the final deliverance from sin. Finally, we speak the "Amen" as the great word of faith—trust that God will indeed keep His promises.

---

12 See *LSB*, pp. 292–93.
13 Quoted in Köberle, *Quest for Holiness*, 214.
14 See *LSB*, p. 292.

GOD'S RIGHTEOUSNESS IS OUR FORGIVENESS

In his first Epistle, the apostle John does not stop with the confession of sin but moves quickly to the promise of the Gospel: that God will forgive the sins of those who confess (see 1 John 1:8–9). This forgiveness is no sentimental attitude of God toward sinners but the work of God, who in His faithfulness and justice actually speaks words that deliver what they promise: pardon and cleansing for Jesus' sake. Jesus achieved full atonement for our sins "not with gold or silver, but with His holy, precious blood and with His innocent suffering and death."[15] This atonement is the basis for Absolution. Without Jesus' vicarious death for sinners, there would be no Absolution of sinners.

Paul writes that we sinners are "justified by [God's] grace as a gift, through the redemption that is in Christ Jesus, whom God put forward as a propitiation by His blood, to be received by faith" (Romans 3:24–25). Absolution is the application of Christ's atonement to the sinner. It is spoken not on account of any righteousness on our part but by virtue of Christ's redeeming righteousness. It is a word that forgives sins because Christ was made sin for us on the cross, dying in our place so that we might be clothed with His righteousness. Without that atonement, there would be no Absolution. "For all who rely on works of the law are under a curse . . . . Christ redeemed us from the curse of the law," Paul writes (Galatians 3:10, 13). Christ was cursed for us so that in Him we might hear not God's curse, but His blessing. That blessing is Absolution. Absolution is justification by faith alone in action as God Himself is at work to raise to life those who have been killed by His Law (see Romans 3:26).

Luther provides helpful clarification concerning the relationship between atonement and Absolution:

> We treat of the forgiveness of sins in two ways. First, how it is achieved and won. Second, how it is distributed and given to us. Christ has achieved it on the cross, it is true. But he has not distributed or given it on the cross. He has not won it in the supper or sacrament. There he has distributed and given it through the Word, as also in the gospel, where it is preached. He has won it once for all on the cross. But the distribution takes place continuously, before and after, from the beginning to the end of the world.[16]

---

15 SC II; *Concordia*, p. 329.
16 AE 40:213–14.

SPIRITUAL EXERCISES _____

◈ North American culture seems to have lost the ability to speak about sin. Sin's target is God, and we wish to think of ourselves as autonomous, accountable only to self. As you read or listen to the news, note how other categories are substituted for sin. Why are these categories inadequate? What are the implications for Christian witness as we speak God's Law and Gospel to unbelievers?

◈ Meditate on the hymn "From Depths of Woe I Cry to Thee" (*LSB* 607) along with Psalm 90. Pray Psalm 90. If you have time, you may also wish to read Luther's commentary on this psalm.[17] Luther says of this psalm:

> In a magnificent manner, therefore, he [Moses] performs the ministry of the Law; he depicts death in the most repulsive colors and in this way demonstrates that God's wrath is the cause of our death. Yes, he shows that even before we die physically, we have been put to death and are overwhelmed with dreadful miseries.[18]

◈ Keep a journal of biblical passages that extol and magnify the greatness of the gift of the Gospel in light of the depth of our sin.

POINT TO REMEMBER _____

If You, O LORD, should mark iniquities, O Lord, who could stand? But with You there is forgiveness, that You may be feared. *Psalm 130:3–4*

The Truth of the Law

He who masters the art of exact distinction between the Law and the Gospel should be called a real theologian. These two must be kept apart. The function of the Law is to frighten men and drive them to despair, especially the coarse and secure sinners, until they realize their inability to meet the demands of the Law or to obtain grace. They will never obtain mercy, but must despair. Dr. Staupitz told me once: "I lied to God more than a thousand times, promising that I would become pious. I never kept the promise. Therefore I shall no longer form that resolve; for I see very well that I am unable to keep my promise, and I never again want to tell a lie." I myself had

_____

17 See AE 13:75–141.
18 AE 13:77.

the same experience. In the papacy I was zealously given to piety. But how long did it last? Only until I read Mass. After an hour I was worse than before. In the end one becomes weary and feels impelled to say: "I will lay piety, Moses, and the Law aside and cling to another Person, who says (Matt. 11:28): 'Come to Me, all who labor and are heavy-laden, and I will give you rest.' " Cherish these words: "Come to Me." *Martin Luther* [19]

As soon as reason and the Law are joined, faith immediately loses its virginity. *Martin Luther* [20]

Postmodernism is about "truth decay," or so we are told. But the truth of God's Law will not go away even if it is not recognized or it is denied. The Law keeps on irrevocably doing its work, putting sinners to death: "Therefore, just as sin came into the world through one man, and death through sin, and so death spread to all men because all sinned" (Romans 5:12). As we have seen, you may call the God of truth a liar by insisting that you are without sin, but such an accusation only confirms the Law's verdict. Law and Gospel are at work in Confession and Absolution as the Law brings us to acknowledge our sin and the Gospel gifts the broken sinner with the forgiveness of sins. The unflinching and irrevocable truth of the Law is that all have sinned and are under God's condemnation. We all have failed to fear, love, and trust in God above all things. Only where this truth is made plain will sinners be able to hear God's ultimate truth: the good news that, in Jesus Christ, God is not out to drive sinners into hell, but He wills to make them alive through Christ's death on the cross.

In 2 Samuel 11, the holy writer lays out the shocking sins of David, the man God had chosen as king of His people. For chapter after chapter, we have seen David trust in God, praise God, follow God's commands. Yet here we see that every human being is afflicted with sin. David sins in thought, word, and deed. David's sin had its genesis in his sinful heart as he looked in lust on his neighbor's wife (2 Samuel 11:2). He sends word to Bathsheba, inviting her to the palace (11:3–4), and he has sexual intercourse with her (11:4–5). The adulterous desires of David's heart lead to words that scheme to secure another man's wife for himself and eventuate in the deed of adultery.

---

19 AE 23:271.
20 AE 26:113.

COVER-UP OR CONFESSION? _____

When Bathsheba finds herself pregnant because of their sin, David believes that he can handle this situation with a bit of ingenuity. He brings Uriah back from the front lines for "rest and recreation" in Jerusalem. This furlough from the battle will allow people to assume that, since Uriah was home, he must be the father of Bathsheba's child. In the same way, we try to cover up our sins, whether we point the finger at someone else, resort to murder in the form of abortion to cover an affair, or simply refuse to acknowledge that our actions are sinful. In all these ways, we seek to justify ourselves rather than trust in God's justification given by faith alone.[21] And this will always lead to further problems. For David, his attempts to cover-up backfired when Uriah refused to go to his home. Uriah's conscience would not let him enjoy hearth and home while his fellow soldiers were afield and did not have the creature comforts or the opportunity to be with their wives. So David hatches yet another plot to silence Uriah before he could potentially accuse the king of sin. David devises a battle strategy that will lead to Uriah's death (see 2 Samuel 11:14–21).

Unconfessed sin is not static. It has an entangling dynamic all its own. Thus David gets himself ever deeper into sin because he does not want to suffer the humiliation entailed in repentance. Instead, David pursues a course of action that leads from adultery to murder. His sin becomes self-multiplying. One sin leads to yet another if the fatal chain reaction is not broken by repentance and forgiveness.

At the core in this sequence of events is David's lack of fear, love, and trust in God above all things. Perhaps he fears the loss of reputation and position, but David has no fear of God. David loves his own pleasure and security more than God. He trusts in his own ability to secure his future by well-laid schemes. When David is informed of Uriah's death, David treats his sin lightly as he gives Joab the hollow comfort that Uriah's death is not worth worrying over (see 2 Samuel 11:25). Soldiers die in war. Uriah was a soldier. Uriah died. Such a dismissive attitude toward our own sin tempts us also. We may use cultural or environmental constraints to rationalize our sinful actions. Or we may claim that we have the personal choice to determine for ourselves what is right or wrong rather than following an archaic culture-bound set of rules like the Ten Commandments. Either path displeases God, as we see with God's reaction to David's snowballing tally of sins.

---

21 For a helpful exposition of this point, see Bayer, *Living by Faith*, 1–26.

THE LAW MAKES A DIRECT HIT _____

Adam and Eve learned that you may run from the Creator but you cannot hide. Before God (*coram Deo*) no secrets can be hid. With its laser-like precision, the Law does not miss its intended target: the sinner secure in his or her sin. With inerrant accuracy, the prophet Nathan came to David and pronounced the Law. The parable of the wealthy rancher who steals his poor neighbor's pet lamb is a picture of David's own wretchedness (see 2 Samuel 12:1–4). Nathan's words were like the knife in the hand of a skilled surgeon. It cut deeply into David's flesh so that the cancer of his heart could no longer be ignored. When David says that "the man who has done this deserves to die" (2 Samuel 12:5), he is speaking the terrible truth about himself.

A head-on confrontation might have backfired for Nathan. Instead, Nathan tells a parable in such a way that the Law is let loose with full force. Nathan allows the word of preaching to reveal David's sin. David is brought to see himself in Nathan's parable, which is a mirror of David's own existence. The parable breaks through his security systems and catches him off guard.

Luther comments on the use of the Law:

> Therefore the proper and absolute use of the Law is to terrify with lightning (as on Mt. Sinai), thunder, and the blare of the trumpet, with a thunderbolt to burn and crush that brute which is called the presumption of righteousness. Hence God says through Jeremiah (23:29): "My Word is a hammer which breaks the rock in pieces." For as long as the presumption of righteousness remains in a man, there remain immense pride, self-trust, smugness, hate of God, contempt of grace and mercy, ignorance of the promises and of Christ. The proclamation of free grace and the forgiveness of sins does not enter his heart and understanding, because that huge rock and solid wall, namely, the presumption of righteousness by which the heart itself is surrounded, prevents this from happening.

> Therefore this presumption of righteousness is a huge and a horrible monster. To break and crush it, God needs a large and powerful hammer, that is, the Law, which is the hammer of death, the thunder of hell, and the lightning of divine wrath. To what purpose? To attack the presumption of righteousness, which is a rebellious, stubborn, and stiff-necked beast. . . . Then the Law is being employed in its proper use and for its proper purpose. Then the heart is crushed to the point

of despair. This use and function of the Law is felt by terrified and desperate consciences.[22]

Thus Nathan's preaching of the Law convicts David of his sin. He sees himself as the man whom he has just asserted deserves to die. He pronounces God's sentence on himself: guilty! And this is not an emotional reaction to wrongdoing. Rather, God renders a judgment, a forensic declaration, of guilt that is not dependent on the guilty individual's feelings of remorse. And after the judgment of guilt must come the penalty.

A WORD THAT ANSWERS THE LAW

The Law renders David helpless. He cannot undo his adultery or bring back from the grave the murdered Uriah. David can only confess, that is, he can only agree with God's verdict that he is the man God's Law declares him to be: the lustful adulterer and the plotting murderer whose hands are stained with Uriah's blood. For a man who could compose beautiful poetry, David says simply, "I have sinned against the LORD" (2 Samuel 12:13). In Psalm 51, which was written in reaction to Nathan's visit, David more eloquently though still directly says, "Against You, You only, have I sinned and done what is evil in Your sight" (verse 4). This psalm clearly points out that all sin is ultimately against the First Commandment. As the Lord hides Himself behind the mask of our neighbor, all sin is truly aimed at Him.

Once the Law has done its work, Nathan does not hesitate to speak the Absolution. He declares to David that God "has put away your sin; you shall not die" (2 Samuel 12:13). Nathan offers words from God that declare two things. First, Nathan's Absolution announces that the Lord has taken away David's sin. In the Scriptures sin has a location. It will either rest squarely on your own shoulders or it will be carried by the Lamb of God who takes away the sin of the world. In Absolution, Christ lifts the load from our backs and carries it in His own body. Second, the Absolution proclaims to David that he will not die under the condemnation of his sin. He has confessed his sin, and now he will live to confess the mercies and favor of the God who saved him. The Absolution is both pardon and the promise of the resurrection. It is words that judge David forgiven and promise him life instead of the death that his sin deserves. In the Third Article of the Apostles' Creed,

---

22 AE 26:310.

we also see the forgiveness of sins tied to the resurrection of the body and life everlasting.[23]

SPIRITUAL EXERCISES

◈ Use Luther's explanation of the Ten Commandments in the Small Catechism (*Concordia*, pp. 316–27) as a tool for self-examination under God's Law.

◈ Meditate on Luther's catechetical hymn on the Ten Commandments "These Are the Holy Ten Commands" (*LSB* 581). How might this hymn, used in tandem with the explanations of the Commandments in the Small Catechism, help you prepare for confession?

◈ Give thanks for the Gospel by praying "Salvation unto Us Has Come" (*LSB* 555).

POINT TO REMEMBER

Now we know that whatever the law says it speaks to those who are under the law, so that every mouth may be stopped, and the whole world may be held accountable to God. For by works of the law no human being will be justified in His sight, since through the law comes knowledge of sin. *Romans 3:19–20*

The Truth of Repentance

But repentance consists of acknowledging everything that is mine is sin. You will never acknowledge this by using reason. But Christ commands that repentance be preached in his name: "So that you are justified in your sentence and blameless when you pass judgment." This is repentance, and at the same time you have the forgiveness of sins, because you acknowledge your sins and you are a true Jew and confess according to the Word of God that everything is sin. This is not according to reason, which says: "If I perform external righteousness, then it is not sin." *Martin Luther*[24]

---

23 See *Concordia*, p. 330.
24 Irving L. Sandberg, trans., *The 1529 Holy Week Sermons of Dr. Martin Luther* (St. Louis: Concordia, 1999), 165–66.

"When our Lord and Master Jesus Christ said, 'Repent' [Matt. 4:17], he willed the entire life of believers to be one of repentance."[25] So wrote Luther in the very first of his *Ninety-five Theses*. Repentance is not an occasional guest in the Christian life, an episode of sorrow after a season of sin. The Christian is constantly living in repentance and faith, dying daily to sin and being made alive to walk by faith in the newness of life that is found only in Christ Jesus. Repentance is more than feeling sorrow for your sins, though as Paul puts it, "godly grief produces a repentance" (2 Corinthians 7:10). To repent is to be rendered defenseless before God, stripped of every self-justifying excuse that the old Adam can muster. To repent is to die to your sin. It is to see your sin as God sees it. Repentance embraces the whole Christian life, calling believers to see the connection between Baptism and repentance and to themselves repent and trust the Gospel.

In Psalm 51:2, David prays that God would cleanse him from his sin. In verse 1 and earlier in verse 2, David uses the synonyms *transgressions* and *iniquity*. Were these simply a poet's effort not to repeat himself? Far from it. *Transgressions* are the trespasses, the times of stepping over, of the boundaries that God has established. *Iniquity* is the bitter unrighteousness of a spoiled creation that now gives evidence of death and decay. Each of these synonyms brings out a dimension of sin: First, in unbelief it will not honor the Creator's boundaries (transgressions). Second, though sin appears to the eye and heart as beautiful and sweet, it is actually ugly and diseased.

GOD DOES THE TURNING

David's prayer as recorded in Psalm 51 reveals David's recognition that his salvation is completely the work of the triune God. Verses 1–12 recount David's confession of his sin, while verses 13–19 are a meditation on the blessing of the Absolution spoken by the prophet Nathan. Throughout the psalm, David implores God to carry the action of the verbs. David might wallow in self-pity, but only God can have mercy on him and blot out his transgressions (Psalm 51:1). Only God can wash David in such a way as to cleanse him from the filth of sin (verses 2 and 7). Only God can create in David a new heart (verse 10) and restore to him the joy of salvation (verse 12).

David identifies God's "delight in truth in the inward being" and asks God to "teach me wisdom in the secret heart" (Psalm 51:6). It is

---

25 AE 31:25.

this same honesty concerning our human condition before God that the apostle exhorts in 1 John 1:8–10. God delights in the *Amen* of faith embedded in the heart and confessed with the lips. Without the *Amen* of faith, the confession of sins is impossible. Wisdom in the Scriptures is to see life from God's perspective. The wisdom that the Spirit teaches us is the wisdom of Christ crucified for the sins of the world. This is the wisdom of God (see 1 Corinthians 1:18–25).

Nathan preaches God's Law to David, and David experiences God's judgment as a breaking of bones (see Psalm 51:8). Such crippling renders David unable to pursue his foolish attempts at evading his sin and the God from whom no secrets are hid. But even at the point of imploring God to rid him of his sins, to wash them away that their presence might not pollute his life (Psalm 51:7), David already knows that God stands ready to hear his confession and to forgive. He pleads for God's good word of Absolution: "Let me hear joy and gladness; let the bones that You have broken rejoice" (Psalm 51:8).

Luther states in his Small Catechism that "confession has two parts: the one is that we confess our sins; the other is that we receive Absolution, or forgiveness, from the confessor, as from God Himself, and in no way doubt, but firmly believe that our sins are forgiven before God in heaven."[26]

THE JOY OF REPENTANCE

Repentance is a turning *from* sin and a turning *to* the mercy of God in Jesus Christ. Crushed by the Law, we are restored by the Gospel. The Apology of the Augsburg Confession reminds us that the Law can kill, but it cannot vivify:

> So, in the preaching of repentance, it is not enough to preach the Law, or the Word that convicts of sin. The Law works wrath and only accuses. The Law terrifies consciences, because consciences never are at rest unless they hear God's voice clearly promising the forgiveness of sins. So the Gospel must be added, that for Christ's sake sins are forgiven and that we obtain the forgiveness of sins by faith in Christ.[27]

There is joy in repentance because of the Gospel alone.

Where do we hear the joy and gladness that David speaks of in Psalm 51:8? We hear this joy and gladness in the preaching of the forgiveness of sins as God declares to us the Good News that He has taken

26 SC V; *Concordia*, p. 341.
27 Ap V (III) 136 [257]; *Concordia*, p. 120.

away our sin and restored us to life with Him through the blood of Christ. Christ suffered death *for* our sins on the cross, and in Baptism we die *to* our sins as we are united with Christ (see Romans 6:1–11). The baptismal life is the life of repentance and faith, of death and resurrection. Thus God restores the joy of salvation (Psalm 51:12) by bringing us to Himself in repentance and faith. Jesus concludes the parables of the lost sheep and the lost coin by telling us that heaven and the angels rejoice "over one sinner who repents" (Luke 15:7, 10). Repentance does not end with the gloom of sin but in the promise of the glory of the resurrection. Absolution gives us the joy of the resurrection, for it brings us out of the death of sin into life with Christ.[28] The apostle Paul states: "So you also must consider yourselves dead to sin and alive to God in Christ Jesus" (Romans 6:11).

UNLOCKED LIPS

Jesus says that it is not what goes into a man that makes him unclean but rather that which comes out of him (see Matthew 15:11). We know what came out of David's mouth when he opened his own lips: the schemes to protect himself by arranging for Uriah's death, as well as the evasive and self-defensive speech that Uriah's death is just another casualty of war (see 2 Samuel 11:25). The only language that comes naturally to the sinner is that of the lie. Only when the Law silences the tongue made unclean by sin can lips be unloosed to speak the truth about self and about God. When God opens lips, then the truth is spoken—both the painful truth of our sin and the merciful truth that God seeks the life, not the death, of the sinner.

David concludes his penitential psalm by remembering that God will not despise "a broken and contrite heart" (Psalm 51:17). Such a heart is one that has been broken by sin and crushed by the Law, but that now looks to Christ alone for forgiveness. The broken heart is the heart that is severed from the object of its craving and split off from the idols for which it formerly lived.

---

28 Köberle writes: "The forgiveness of sins carries with it the power of the resurrection" (*Quest for Holiness*, 90).

SPIRITUAL EXERCISES

◈ Pray each of the penitential psalms: 51, 6, 32, 38, 102, 130, and 143. As you pray, keep a journal to record your reflections on each individual psalm. In your journal, answer these three questions: (1) How is the Law at work in the psalm? (2) How does the psalm proclaim the Gospel? (3) Which petition of the Lord's Prayer is best reflected in each psalm?

◈ Commit to memory the words of Psalm 30:4–5. Use these verses as your personal prayer in thanksgiving for holy Absolution.

◈ Pray "To Thee, Omniscient Lord of All" (*LSB* 613), noting the similarities of this hymn with Psalm 51.

POINT TO REMEMBER

Repent, for the kingdom of heaven is at hand. *Matthew 3:2*

The Truth of Jesus, the Friend of Sinners

The earthly righteousness ceases and does not stand the test. But there must be One who is eternally over death and devil. For this reason Paul will not tolerate that Christians be perplexed in the conscience. It is the greatest skill: a Christian must be protected so that no one nails a law to her or his conscience and heart. You must have this skill if you want to believe in Christ. This is over all laws. If a hundred thousand sins fell on you today, you would still have to say, I know of none because Christ, who is subject to neither sin nor death, is risen from the dead. *Martin Luther*[29]

A paralyzed man is brought to Jesus. Behind the physical paralysis there is a deeper bondage than confinement to the bed. Where is God in all of this? Luther often commented that a person has God as he or she imagines Him to be. What does this paralyzed man imagine about God? Does he conclude that God is angry with him? Is this disease the heavy hand of God punishing him for some transgression? Is God oblivious to his plight, so far removed from him in majesty and might as to be unconcerned with his misery?

---

29 Sandberg, *1529 Holy Week Sermons*, 141.

We are not told anything about the inner thoughts of this nameless man. But we do see Jesus speaking words of Absolution that forgive this man's sin and set him on his feet (see Mark 2:5). Jesus speaks as only God can speak. The Jews of Jesus' day expected God's vindication at some unknown point in the future, on the Last Day, but instead Jesus forgives sins right here on earth. Absolution disrupts the old order of sin and death. It is a word of powerful pardon that sets the captive free and causes the lame to walk (see Isaiah 35:4–6). Jesus has redeemed us by His precious blood, and in the life and ministry of Jesus we have countless vivid examples of how God is justifying the ungodly. Thus we can give thanks for the gift of salvation won for us by the Lamb of God, a gift we have access to right here and right now.

WHO IS JESUS?

According to Jesus' words and actions in Mark 2:1–12, especially verse 5, we know that Jesus is the Lord who forgives sin. Here Jesus reveals the fatherly heart of God (as Luther liked to put it), addressing the paralyzed man as His son and pronouncing a word of pardon that will accomplish what He promises. However, the scribes in the crowd hear these same words and determine that they are blasphemy rather than blessing. The scribes believed that since God alone can forgive sins, Jesus was claiming equality with God in this enactment of divine pardon.

In the very next section of Mark 2, Jesus calls Levi the tax collector to be one of His disciples. This serves as a dramatic commentary on Jesus' action in the Absolution of the paralytic as both events show Jesus to be the friend of sinners. On more than one occasion, Jesus receives notorious outcasts into His fellowship, demonstrating that He came to call not the "righteous" but sinners. And in these interactions, we have an example of what Luther referred to as the theology of the cross in opposition to a theology of glory. The theology of glory operates according to the *opinion legis*, the "opinion of the law," as it teaches that God rewards the righteous but punishes the unrighteous. Jesus turns this upside down as He goes to the cross to save those who should be condemned. Adolph Köberle has described Jesus' approach to tax collectors and sinners as the embodiment of the forensic justification described by Paul in his Epistle to the Romans.[30] How is this so? Tax collectors and sinners are obviously ungodly, but Paul writes in Romans 4:1–5 that God justifies the ungodly not by works but through faith

---

30 See *Quest for Holiness*, 57.

alone (see also Romans 5:6–11). As Luther liked to put it, Christ dwells only with sinners!

This event and the other times during His ministry that Jesus associated with sinners points ahead to Calvary. As Jesus hung on the cross, the thieves crucified with Him had differing reactions. The thief on the left joins with the crowd in mocking the suffering Christ. But the dying thief on Jesus' right side, who has no time for the amendment of his evil life, chastises his unrepentant companion in crime. He points out that "we are receiving the due reward of our deeds" (Luke 23:41) while Jesus is suffering unjustly. Then the thief turns to Jesus with a plea for mercy, a request to be remembered in His kingdom. And Jesus responds, "Truly, I say to you, today you will be with Me in Paradise" (Luke 23:43). Jesus' words open heaven to this dying thug.

The mission of the Church is to preach the Law and the Gospel, repentance and faith to all people, not only to those whom we would judge to be likely candidates for salvation. The mission of the Church is directed toward real, flesh and blood sinners. It is not a program of church growth or cultural accommodation, but it is the proclamation of the Gospel of the crucified and risen Lord. Mission involves the speaking of the Law to uncover and dethrone sin, the unbelief that delivers death, but ultimately the mission of the Church is to proclaim to sinners that God has reconciled them to Himself in Christ and that He forgives them their sin.

THE AUTHORITY OF THE ABSOLUTION

Returning to the account of the healing of the paralyzed man, Jesus speaks unexpected words. He says to the paralytic: "Son, your sins are forgiven" (Mark 2:5). With these words, Jesus shows Himself to be the Savior. His greeting is the vehicle for mercy. The kingdom of Christ is in the sentence "your sins are forgiven"; in these words there is no demand, no Law, and no works. Jesus' words give the paralyzed man nothing that he must do to attain health. The Lord comes not to provide him with a regimen for physical therapy or a plan of spiritual renewal that he is to work at to help him cope with his misfortune. Calling him "son," Jesus shows Himself to be present for this man as His Helper and Savior. Jesus has come not to mock him in his infirmity or to crush him with condemnation, but rather He has come as his Lord with words of peace and Absolution: "Son, your sins are forgiven you."

According to Mark 2:10, Jesus speaks the Absolution to show the authority that the Father has given to the Son of Man. It is the authority to forgive sins because the Son of Man is the one who has carried those sins to the cross and answered for them as our Brother. The sainted Gerhard Forde liked to explain that in the Absolution the verdict of the Last Day slips out ahead of time. In other words, when we hear the Absolution now in time, we are hearing what all believers in Christ will hear on that final day when He returns to judge the living and the dead.

Sometimes visitors to a Lutheran church service are offended when the pastor says: "As a called and ordained servant of Christ, and by His authority, I therefore forgive you all your sins in the name of the Father and of the Son and of the Holy Spirit."[31] But this pronouncement is part and parcel of the Gospel. God has committed to His servants the ministry of reconciliation (see 2 Corinthians 5:18–21). As Christ's ambassadors, His ministers do not speak their own words, but the words of the one who sent them. Of those whom He sends, Jesus says: "The one who hears you hears Me" (Luke 10:16). Jesus commissioned His apostles not merely to talk about the forgiveness of sins, but actually to forgive sins here and now (see John 20:23).

A PHYSICIAN FOR THE SICK

Forgiveness of sins is offensive on several levels. It is an offense against the rules of justice that insist each one should get what he deserves. It is also offensive because it is declared only to sinners. Forgiveness of sins assumes that the recipient of the Absolution is indeed a sinner. The self-righteous have no need for the righteousness of Christ, the righteousness of faith bestowed in the Absolution. But for those who know their sin, the forgiveness of sins is good news.

Thus Absolution differs radically from attitudes of tolerance or acceptance that often substitute for forgiveness in our culture. Absolution recognizes sin as so much more than an errant attitude, a misspoken word, or a hurtful deed. Sin is not merely something that is socially inappropriate. Sin is unbelief enacted in countless ways. Tolerance would put up with the failures of others. Acceptance would ignore the condition that is delivering death. Neither toleration nor acceptance will deliver the sinner from the ultimate outcome of his or her sin. Both leave the sinner in sin and under the illusion of health while in reality the sinner is fatally sick. One does not need the cross for tolerance and

31   *LSB*, p. 151.

acceptance. But Absolution necessitates the cross, for without the shedding of blood, there is no forgiveness of sins.

The Swedish theologian Gustaf Wingren once preached a sermon on the healing of the paralyzed man in which he noted that there are really two miracles. One is the divine healing granted through the forgiveness of sins. The other, Wingren said, is that the man picked up his bed and went home. He did not retreat to a monastery or go off on a religious tour to give his testimony! The forgiveness of sins is not only an amnesty but also a powerful pardon that enables us to live in the newness of life in those places where the Lord has put us. Forgiveness of sins does not draw the healed paralytic away from his home and family, but sends him back there to live in faith and love.

SPIRITUAL EXERCISES

◈ Review Luther's Explanation to the Second Article of the Apostles' Creed in the Small Catechism (*Concordia*, p. 329). If you have not already done so, learn it by heart.

◈ Review the Divine Service, marking every place where worshipers confess the person and work of Christ for sinners (e.g., the Agnus Dei confesses Christ as the Lamb of God, etc.).

◈ Learn Galatians 2:20 by heart.

◈ Meditate on this comment from Luther's 1531 lectures on Galatians as you think about how the Lord would use you to comfort penitent sinners:

> I wish that you students of Sacred Scripture would equip yourselves with such parables, in order to retain the distinction between Law and Gospel better, namely, that trying to be justified by the Law is like counting money out of an empty purse, eating and drinking from an empty dish and cup, looking for strength and riches where there is nothing but weakness and poverty, laying a burden upon someone who is already oppressed to the point of collapse, trying to spend a hundred gold pieces and not having even a pittance, taking clothing away from a naked man, imposing even greater weakness and poverty upon someone who is sick and needy, etc.[32]

POINT TO REMEMBER

Now the tax collectors and sinners were all drawing near to hear [Jesus]. And the Pharisees and the scribes grumbled, saying, "This man receives sinners and eats with them." *Luke 15:1–2*

---

32 AE 26:406–7.

The Truth
of the Absolution

The other part of Confession is the Absolution, which the priest speaks in God's place, and which therefore is nothing other than God's Word with which He comforts and strengthens our hearts against the sinful conscience. *Martin Luther*[33]

Dear God, what consolation can a weak conscience receive from a preacher, if it does not believe that these very words are the consolation of God, his Word, his way of thinking. Therefore, we simply conclude that God works through his Word or not at all. *Martin Luther*[34]

Jesus is risen from the dead, but the disciples remain confused and frightened. As they hide in the upper room, it is more than a lock that keeps them in seclusion on Easter evening, for they are held in bondage by fear and uncertainty. Then Jesus appears, and He says, "Peace be with you" (John 20:19). He shows them the marks of the nails and spear still present in His resurrected body. But this is more than just an appearance. Jesus speaks His benediction of peace a second time and adds: "As the Father has sent Me, even so I am sending you" (John 20:21). Thus our Savior institutes the Office of the Holy Ministry. He makes His disciples His apostles ("sent ones"), and their work is now to speak Jesus' words, forgiving the sins of the penitent and retaining the sins of the impenitent (see John 20:23). Here the Office of the Keys is set in motion, so that you might have the fruits of Jesus' death, the peace that was made in His sacrificial death. That peace is nothing less than the forgiveness of your sins.

As our understanding of the gift of Absolution deepens, we see it as justification by faith alone in action. And as our appreciation for the practice of private Confession and Absolution grows, we learn to trust Jesus' absolving words in Scripture, liturgy, sermon, and Sacrament.

Without the atoning work of Jesus on the cross and His resurrection from the dead, we would be left desolate in sin, destined for death, and without hope. But God "made Him to be sin who knew no sin, so that in [Jesus] we might become the righteousness of God" (2 Corinthians 5:21). By dying in our place, Jesus atoned for our sins, and by

---

33 Jon D. Vieker, trans., "An Open Letter to Those in Frankfurt on the Main," *Concordia Journal* 16, no. 4 (October 1990): 345.

34 WA Tr 3:671.21–24.

His rising from the grave, we are justified. Absolution would be empty without the atoning work of Christ. In Absolution Jesus sprinkles you with His blood (see Colossians 1:19–20) and applies His words of forgiveness specifically to you, a fact signified by the pastor making the sign of the cross over you as he speaks the words of Absolution. The words of Robert Preus are helpful and to the point:

> There is nothing fictional or untrue about this verdict. My justification is as true and valid as Christ's cursed death on the cross. . . . His verdict is effective: it accomplishes what it says. When he pronounces me righteous in Christ, then it is so, all accusations, inner doubts and empirical evidence to the contrary notwithstanding. Nor is God's verdict a mere possibility—to which I add my faith. And it will not be undone, just as Christ's incarnation, suffering and death cannot be undone.[35]

IN THE STEAD AND BY THE COMMAND OF CHRIST

As the risen Christ has left Scripture and the Sacraments as trustworthy and true means of His presence and forgiveness, so Christ has provided men to stand in His place to preach the Word and to administer the Sacraments. Scripture presents the exalted Christ as one robed in white (Matthew 17:2; 28:3; Mark 9:3; Luke 9:29). Likewise, the angels appear clothed in white (Mark 16:5; John 20:12; Revelation 19:14). More important for us, the full righteousness that Christians receive after death appears as a white robe washed clean in the blood of the Lamb (Revelation 2:17; 3:4–5, 18; 4:4; 6:11; 7:9, 13–14). Through the Church, God calls stewards of the mysteries (1 Corinthians 4:1) who serve the Church in Christ's place. It is little wonder, then, that the ancient Church adopted the use of white garments for pastors to signify their office.

Pastors forgive sins not by their own authority but by the command and in the stead of Christ, which historically has been called the "power of the order."[36] Since ancient times, ministers have worn vestments during the worship service, and it is suggested that pastors also wear vestments when hearing private confession. Such a practice reinforces

---

35 Robert Preus, *Doctrine Is Life: Essays on Justification and the Lutheran Confessions* (St. Louis: Concordia, 2006), 25.

36 See *LSB*, p. 151. For the Lutheran Confessions' exposition concerning the pastor as the representative of Christ, see Ap VII & VIII (IV) 28 (*Concordia*, p. 148). For more on the "power of the order," see Ap XXVIII (XIV) 13 (*Concordia*, p. 250).

100 LUTHERAN SPIRITUALITY

that the personal identity of the pastor is not important. The vestments, which cover the man, serve as a uniform to remind both pastor and people of what he is present to do: speak Jesus' words of forgiveness.

We confess before God that we are guilty of all sins, but in private confession before the pastor we confess only those sins that we know or feel in our hearts. Pastors are not detectives or judges, but shepherds and physicians of the soul. The pastor will not pry out of curiosity, but he may ask questions to better diagnose the sin so that the Absolution may be spoken.

In Article XXV, the Augsburg Confession argues for the retention of private confession for the sake of the Absolution and the consolation that it brings to the wounded conscience.[37] Absolution is prized as God's "voice from heaven" to be received through faith alone.

In Luther's "Brief Exhortation to Confession," which was appended to his Large Catechism, the reformer identifies abuses in Roman Catholic teaching regarding private confession. He specifically mentions that private confession was made mandatory so that people were using it under coercion and out of fear. Further, people were required to enumerate all their sins (an impossible task!), which tortured the already stricken conscience, and they were not taught the consoling benefits of the Absolution. Instead, the people were left to rely on their own works for satisfaction. In his "Brief Exhortation," Luther puts forth his plan to restore private confession in the Reformation churches. He envisions private confession standing alongside other forms of confession in Evangelical churches: the confession made in the Lord's Prayer and the confession made to the neighbor against whom we have sinned (see James 5:16). Luther points out that it would be an abuse of Christian freedom to dispense with private confession. It should be retained and used in the Church evangelically so that sinners might know the comfort of the Gospel.[38]

There are, no doubt, many reasons why private confession has been neglected in present-day Lutheran church life. Already at the time of the Reformation, Luther identified those who mistakenly neglected private confession in the name of Christian freedom. He did not want the Church to reject Confession and Absolution but to reclaim it for the comfort of penitent sinners. In the seventeenth century, the powerful Pietism movement stressed the subjectivity of personal religious experience instead of the objective character of God's Gospel. Pietism

---

37 See *Concordia*, p. 50.
38 See "A Brief Exhortation to Confession," in *Concordia*, pp. 649–53.

was detrimental to the practice of private confession. Great Lutheran churchmen such as C. F. W. Walther, Wilhelm Loehe, and Theodore Kliefoth battled against Pietism, urging Lutherans not to abandon private confession.[39] There are other reasons that private confession has declined in contemporary Lutheran churches. For example, pastors have not always spent sufficient time teaching about it or in finding ways to make it available. There is also the confusion of private confession with counseling.

When we neglect the gift of private Confession and Absolution, the vacuum is often filled with secular substitutes. While counseling and psychological therapies can be useful in making life functional, they do not provide Absolution. That is the great treasure in private confession. When Luther included the question "Do you believe that my forgiveness is God's forgiveness?" in his confessional rite in the Small Catechism, he sought to emphasize that it is Christ who forgives sin through the instrumentality of the pastor.[40] The pastor does not represent himself; the pastor represents Christ. As the confessors stated: "Ministers act in Christ's place and do not represent their own persons, according to Luke, 'The one who hears you hears Me' (10:16)."[41]

FORGIVEN!

One of the great blessings of private or individual confession is that the penitent hears the Gospel in a way that is unmistakably personal. When the pastor acting in the stead and by the command of the Lord says, "I forgive you all your sins," he is not just talking about forgiveness, nor is he proclaiming forgiveness in a general sort of way that may or may not be applicable to you. In his words lies the powerful consolation that Jesus is Lord *for you*. It is *your* sins that are forgiven, for the One who is the Truth incarnate does not lie or deceive.

In the Lutheran ordination rite, the pastor pledges that he will never divulge the sin that is confessed to him. Because the pastor is not a servant of the state (God's left-hand rule) but of the Church (God's right-hand rule), even the state may not invade the sacred trust of the confession. The pastor is hearing the confession of sins that the penitent renders to God, not to man. And the pastor has no authority to render

---

39 For a helpful summary of the place of private Confession and Absolution in Lutheran history, see Fred L. Precht, ed., *Lutheran Worship: History and Practice* (St. Louis: Concordia, 1993), 322–86.
40 See *Concordia*, p. 342.
41 Ap VII & VIII (IV) 47; *Concordia*, p. 151.

unto Caesar what belongs to God (see Matthew 22:17–22). The ear of the pastor is the tomb where those sins are buried. What does God do with the sins that are confessed to Him? The psalmist writes: "As far as the east is from the west, so far does He remove our transgressions from us" (Psalm 103:12). And through the prophet Isaiah, God tells us that He "will not remember your sins" (Isaiah 43:25). Pastors, as God's representatives on earth, are trained to forget the sins confessed to them.

When we confess our sins, they lie buried in Christ's empty tomb. Christians are not to live as grave robbers who exhume the rot of sin that God has crucified and buried with Christ. When the devil comes to tempt us with the lie that our sins are not forgiven and that we are under God's wrath and condemnation, we go to the words of Absolution. They are the words of One who is greater than our conscience. In Isaiah 6:1–7, Isaiah was driven to despair in the presence of God on account of his sin. "Then one of the seraphim flew to me, having in his hand a burning coal that he had taken with tongs from the altar. And he touched my mouth and said: 'Behold, this has touched your lips; your guilt is taken away, and your sin atoned for'" (Isaiah 6:6–7). The prophet was comforted by words of Absolution that touched his lips and removed his sin. Lutheran pastors will teach their people how to cling to the words of Absolution when the devil accuses tender consciences with memories of past sins and invites unstable hearts to doubt the truth of Christ's forgiveness.

RETAINED!

There is only one way to receive Absolution, and that is by repentance and faith. Those who harden themselves against God's Law and insist that they have no need for the forgiveness of sins are left with their sins. Pastors have the responsibility of retaining the sins of the unrepentant, that is, of announcing to them that they are stuck with their sins and the terrible judgment that unbelief brings. This word of unrelenting Law must be preached to sinners who are secure and comfortable in living with their sins, in living apart from the mercy and grace of God in Christ Jesus. Through such preaching, pastors pray that such people might recognize their sin for what it is, repent, and hear the word of forgiveness.

Foundational to the Office of the Keys are the words of Jesus in Matthew 16:19: "I will give you the keys of the kingdom of heaven, and whatever you bind on earth shall be bound in heaven, and whatever you loose on earth shall be loosed in heaven." The Word of forgiveness in Jesus' name spoken on earth releases the sinner from his or her sin. On the other hand, the word of Law spoken to the unrepentant sinner ties or binds the sinner to his or her sins.

The goal of evangelical church discipline is not retribution. Instead, it is a profound act of love for a brother or sister whose unbelief has hardened them to the point of impenitence. As Paul says, "If anyone is caught in any transgression, you who are spiritual should restore him in a spirit of gentleness" (Galatians 6:1). And Jesus has outlined the process of church discipline in Matthew 18:15–20. Excommunication is under-taken as a last resort after speaking privately and in a small group with the impenitent. Such an action is accompanied by the prayer that the Holy Spirit might still work repentance and faith.

SPIRITUAL EXERCISES

◈ Review the order for Individual Confession and Absolution in *Lutheran Service Book* or another Lutheran hymnal (see *LSB*, pp. 292–93). Consider making use of this gift with your pastor.

◈ Learn by heart the words of the Absolution in the Divine Service. Then when the devil tempts you to doubt that these words were spoken to you by your pastor as Christ's servant, you may recall them and use them to quench his devilish accusation.

◈ Study the Divine Service and identify the places where an Absolution is spoken, in addition to the formula of Absolution in the confession of sins.

◈ Meditate on these words from Luther's lectures on Hebrews:

> For since it [the conscience] cannot change a sin committed in the past and in any way avoid the future wrath, it cannot escape being distressed and troubled, no matter where it turns. Nor is it freed from these difficulties except through the blood of Christ; and if it looks at Him through faith, it believes and realizes that its sins have been washed away and taken away in Him. Thus through faith it is at the same time purified and made calm, so that out of joy over the remission of sins it no longer dreads punishments.[42]

POINT TO REMEMBER

> As far as the east is from the west, so far does He remove our trans-gressions from us. *Psalm 103:12*

---

42 AE 29:209.

The Truth of Freedom in the Forgiveness of Sins

> Our faith in Christ does not free us from works but from false opinions concerning works, that is, from the foolish presumption that justification is acquired by works. Faith redeems, corrects, and preserves our consciences so that we know that righteousness does not consist in works, although works neither can nor ought to be wanting; just as we cannot be without food and drink and all the works of this mortal body, yet our righteousness is not in them, but in faith; and yet those works of the body are not to be despised or neglected on that account. *Martin Luther* [43]

Christians are both forgiven and forgiving people. The gift of God's pardon received through faith in Christ Jesus is transmitted in love to those who sin against us. Where there is no forgiveness of sins, there is only bondage to sin. Christ Jesus has set us free from the prison house of sin and the domain of death by a word that liberates us from the tyranny of those powers that would destroy and damn us. In Christ Jesus, there is no condemnation (see Romans 8:1). God daily and richly forgives our sins and calls us to live by the forgiveness of sins in our various vocations. We can learn to cling to Absolution as the charter of evangelical freedom, a weapon for the fight against the devil, and a salve for the conscience inflamed by terror over past sins.

Our lives are hidden with Christ in God. This hiding occurs in Baptism. In Baptism, we are tucked away in Jesus' death. In Him, our future is secure because He has been raised from the dead, never to die again. We do not rely on what we see, for we still see the marks of sin in our thinking and doing. We still see the signs of death and decay in our bodies and in the world. The truth is, however, that we have been wrapped up in the righteousness of Christ and in Him we are forgiven sinners who await the consummation of our Baptism in the resurrection from the dead. The freedom that we now have by faith will be made manifest in the final liberation that will be given us on the Last Day.

---

43 AE 31:372–73.

FREEDOM FROM AND FREEDOM FOR _____

One day Jesus told His Jewish followers: "If you abide in My word, you are truly My disciples, and you will know the truth and the truth will set you free" (John 8:31–32). At the time Jesus spoke these words, the Jewish people were under Roman domination, and previously the Israelites had been in captivity under Pharaoh and even taken into exile by various nations, such as the Assyrians and Babylonians. But Jesus was not talking about a political freedom. He was speaking of the freedom we have in Absolution, which declares and delivers to us the truth that Jesus' death for sin is *for you*. In truth, you are set free from your sins by Jesus' blood and righteousness.

Christian freedom is liberty, not license. By the blood of Christ, we are set free from the guilt of sin, the condemnation of the Law, and the sting of God's wrath. Paul tells his readers that they are to "put to death therefore what is earthly in you," and then he catalogues the sinful attitudes and activities from which Baptism frees us: sexual immorality, impurity, passion, evil desires, covetousness, anger, wrath, malice, slander, and obscene talk (Colossians 3:5–8). In short, we are freed from all the practices of the old self, all the habits of hell that threaten us with bondage. Instead, in Baptism we "have put on the new self, which is being renewed in knowledge after the image of its creator" (Colossians 3:10).

This passage from Colossians parallels Romans 6:1–11, where Paul makes the argument that God's free grace in Christ Jesus is not an excuse to continue in sin. Rather, in Baptism we die to sin and so are raised to walk in the newness of life. Christ died for our sins on the cross. We die to our sins in Baptism. Confession and Absolution is a concrete form of our dying and rising.

The freedom of Absolution entails vocation or calling. We are called by the Gospel to live in Christ by faith and for the neighbor by love. The life of the forgiven sinner takes on the shape of being a "little Christ" to our neighbor, to borrow Luther's imagery. Living by faith in Christ, we are now free to give ourselves in love to our neighbor as we exhibit compassion, kindness, humility, meekness, patience, love, harmony, and so forth (see Colossians 3:12–17).

To slip back into the vices of our old life is to surrender the freedom we have in Christ and revert to bondage. The freedom we have in Christ is the freedom to serve freely and love our neighbor, not in order to gain something for ourselves, but because we already have all things in Christ (see Galatians 5:1).

In Colossians 3:15, Paul speaks of the rule of God's peace in the life of the believer. Recall the previous discussion of the peace of God as it relates to the forgiveness of sins. Luther once commented that the Pax Domini ("The peace of the Lord be with you always") in the Divine Service is "a public absolution of the sins of the communicants, the true voice of the gospel announcing remission of sins, and therefore the one and most worthy preparation for the Lord's Table, if faith holds to these words as coming from the mouth of Christ himself."[44] This peace of God permeates the Divine Service, giving us confidence in the work of Christ for us as:

- in the Kyrie, we pray to the Lord in peace.
- in the Hymn of Praise ("Glory to God in the Highest"), we acclaim the Father as the Giver of heaven's peace on earth in Christ.
- after the sermon, the pastor blesses the congregation with "the peace of God which passes all understanding."
- in the Agnus Dei, we implore the Lamb of God to grant us peace.
- in the post-Communion canticle (Nunc Dimittis), we sing of going in peace because God's Word has been fulfilled.
- in the second post-Communion collect, we give thanks for God's pardon and peace given us in the Sacrament.
- in the Benediction, the Lord gives us His peace.

LIVING IN THE ABSOLUTION _____

Luther's explanation to the Fifth Petition of the Lord's Prayer in his Small Catechism reminds us that we daily implore our Father for the forgiveness of our sins because "we daily sin much and indeed deserve nothing but punishment."[45] The Christian life is a constant struggle with the devil, the world, and our own proud flesh. It is a dangerous illusion to believe that we can live without the forgiveness of sins. The forgiveness of sins is never past tense; it is always a present-tense reality as we constantly crawl back to our Baptism in repentance and faith. It is a spiritual danger signal of the first order if a Christian begins to think of himself or herself as something other than a forgiven sinner. For we are always, on this side of the resurrection of the dead, *simul iustus et peccator*, at one and the same time both righteous and sinful.

---

44   AE 53:28–29.
45   SC III; *Concordia*, p. 336.

In Romans 7:7–25, the apostle Paul demonstrates our constant need for Absolution. He demonstrates that the Christian life is a constant struggle, beset with contradictions. The good that we desire to do, we fail to do. The evil that we abhor, we end up doing. Where will we find deliverance? Only in Christ Jesus, whose death gives us the victory. Forgiveness of sins is not just the starting point of the Christian life, but it is the foundation to which we must constantly return! In Luther's treatment of the ongoing significance of Baptism for the Christian life, he declares that the Christian life is a continual return to Baptism: "Repentance, therefore, is nothing other than a return and approach to Baptism."[46]

As we have already observed, the liturgy of the Divine Service is packed with the forgiveness of sins. God delights in extending His pardon to us in more than one way. Paul tells us that we are to let the word of Christ dwell in us richly as we teach and admonish one another, "singing psalms and hymns and spiritual songs" (Colossians 3:16). Luther's great hymn "Dear Christians, One and All, Rejoice" (*LSB* 556) tells the whole story of the Law and the Gospel in its ten stanzas. The hymn tells of our life under Law bound by sin and death. Then Luther confesses the wondrous gift of Christ's incarnation and atonement. Finally, the hymn speaks of the work of the Holy Spirit in the Gospel as He comforts us with the forgiveness of sin.[47]

VOCATION

When God calls us to faith by the Gospel, He does not call us out of the world but to a life of love that is lived within His creation. Yet it is precisely in our worldly callings that we sin. Our sin drives us back to the Divine Service and to Absolution. When we examine ourselves in preparation for Confession, Luther wisely counsels us in the Small Catechism: "Consider your calling according to the Ten Commandments, whether you are a father, mother, son, daughter . . . ."[48] Where our place in life (vocation) intersects with God's Law, there we see our sin. Vocation keeps us from ever outgrowing the Lord's Prayer—and Luther's evening prayer, for that matter, where we ask God to "forgive me all my sins, where I have done wrong, and graciously keep me this night."[49]

---

46 LC IV 79; *Concordia*, p. 430.
47 For a helpful exposition of this hymn, see Bayer, *Living by Faith*, 52–57.
48 SC V; *Concordia*, p. 341.
49 SC Evening Prayer; *Concordia*, p. 344.

God daily and richly forgives us our sin. He has also put the words of forgiveness on our lips. Paul directs the Colossian Christians to forgive "as the Lord has forgiven you" (Colossians 3:13). This is not telling the person who apologizes to you, "Oh, don't worry about it." Rather, a confession of sin should be followed with an Absolution: "For Jesus' sake I forgive you your sin." Christian people should practice Confession and Absolution, not merely apology, in their life together. The outcome of the words of Christ's forgiveness is praise both with lips and life as we "do everything in the name of the Lord Jesus, giving thanks to God the Father through Him" (Colossians 3:17). Forgiveness of sins frees us from fretting about ourselves, for we live under the righteousness of Christ Jesus as justified sinners. That means we can go in peace.

SPIRITUAL EXERCISES

◈ *The Hammer of God* by Bo Giertz is a great novel that illustrates the freedom of the forgiveness of sins that we have in Christ. Read this novel for your own edification.

◈ Pray the Fifth Petition of the Lord's Prayer along with the explanation in the Small Catechism (*Concordia*, p. 336), naming a person whom you are struggling to forgive.

◈ Use Compline—Prayer at the Close of the Day (*LSB*, pp. 253–59) as your evening devotion with your family. Note the way this service leads us to confess our sins and speak God's forgiveness to each other.

◈ When we confess our sins, we are returning to our Baptism. Pray the following baptismal hymns. Note how the hymn teaches us to rejoice in the present-tense reality of Baptism.

"The Gifts Christ Freely Gives" (*LSB* 602)
"All Christians Who Have Been Baptized" (*LSB* 596)
"Baptized into Your Name Most Holy" (*LSB* 590)
"God's Own Child, I Gladly Say It" (*LSB* 594)
"Once in the Blest Baptismal Waters" (*LSB* 598)
"O Gracious Lord, with Love Draw Near" (*LSB* 599)
"Baptismal Waters Cover Me" (*LSB* 616)

POINT TO REMEMBER

For freedom Christ has set us free; stand firm therefore, and do not submit again to a yoke of slavery. *Galatians 5:1*

Lutheran Teaching of Confession

Luther and the authors of the Lutheran Confessions did not want to abandon the practice of private Confession and Absolution. Rather they wanted to filter this practice through the sieve of justification by faith alone so that private Confession and Absolution would (a) be purified from abuses, (b) be set evangelically in the context of the doctrine of repentance, and (c) serve pastorally to comfort broken sinners with the certainty of Jesus' forgiveness.

REPENTANCE

Now, strictly speaking, repentance consists of two parts. One part is contrition, that is, terrors striking the conscience through the knowledge of sin. The other part is faith, which is born of the Gospel [Romans 10:17] or the Absolution and believes that for Christ's sake, sins are forgiven. It comforts the conscience and delivers it from terror. Then good works are bound to follow, which are the fruit of repentance [Galatians 5:22–23]. (AC XII 3–6; *Concordia*, p. 38)

To deliver godly consciences from these mazes of the learned persons, we have attributed these two parts to repentance: contrition and faith. If anyone desires to add a third—fruit worthy of repentance, that is, a change of the entire life and character for the better—we will not oppose it. We separate from contrition those useless and endless discussions regarding grief from loving God and from fearing punishment. We say that contrition is the true terror of the conscience, which feels that God is angry with sin and grieves that it has sinned. This contrition takes place when sins are condemned by God's Word. The sum of the preaching of the Gospel is this: to convict of sin; to offer for Christ's sake the forgiveness of sins and righteousness, the Holy Spirit, and eternal life; and that as reborn people we should do good works. So Christ includes the sum of the Gospel when He says, "Repentance and forgiveness of sins should be proclaimed in His name to all nations" (Luke 24:47). (Ap XIIa [V] 28–30; *Concordia*, p. 161)

Furthermore, the Power of the Keys administers and presents the Gospel through Absolution, which is the true voice of the Gospel. We also include Absolution when we speak of faith, because "faith comes from hearing," as Paul says in Romans 10:17. When the Gospel is heard and the Absolution is heard, the conscience is encouraged and receives comfort. Because God truly brings a person to life through the Word, the Keys truly forgive sins before God. According to Luke

10:16, "The one who hears you hears Me." Therefore, the voice of the one absolving must be believed no differently than we would believe a voice from heaven. Absolution can properly be called a Sacrament of repentance, as even the more learned scholastic theologians say. . . . So faith is conceived and strengthened through Absolution, through the hearing of the Gospel, through the use of the Sacraments, so that it may not give in to the terrors of sin and death while it struggles. This method of repentance is plain and clear. It increases the worth of the Power of the Keys and of the Sacraments. It illumines Christ's benefit and teaches us to make use of Christ as Mediator and the Atoning Sacrifice. (Ap XIIa [V] 39–43; *Concordia*, pp. 162–63)

But to this office of the Law, the New Testament immediately adds the consoling promise of grace through the Gospel. This must be believed. As Christ declares, "Repent and believe the gospel" (Mark 1:15). That is, become different, act differently, and believe My promise. John the Baptist (preceding Christ) is called a preacher of repentance, but this is for the forgiveness of sins. That is, John was to accuse all and convict them of being sinners. This is so that they can know what they are before God and acknowledge that they are lost. So they can be prepared for the Lord [Mark 1:3] to receive grace and to expect and accept from Him the forgiveness of sins. This is what Christ Himself says, "Repentance and forgiveness of sins should be proclaimed in [My] name to all nations" (Luke 24:47).

Whenever the Law alone exercises its office, without the Gospel being added, there is nothing but death and hell, and one must despair, as Saul and Judas did [1 Samuel 31; Matthew 27:5]. St. Paul says, through sin the Law kills. [See Romans 7:10.] On the other hand, the Gospel brings consolation and forgiveness. It does so not just in one way, but through the Word and the Sacraments and the like, as we will discuss later. As Psalm 130:7 says against the dreadful captivity of sin, "with the Lord is . . . plentiful redemption." (SA III III 4–8; *Concordia*, pp. 272–73)

ABUSES OF CONFESSION/ABSOLUTION

As we all know from experience, there had been no rule so burdensome as the one that forced everyone to go to Confession on pain of committing the most serious of mortal sins. That law also placed on consciences the heavy burden and torture of having to list all kinds of sin, so that no one was ever able to confess perfectly enough. The worst was that no one taught or even knew what Confession might be or what help and comfort it could give. Instead, it was turned into sheer terror and a hellish torture that one had to go through even if one detested Confession more than anything. These three oppressive things have now been lifted, and we have been granted the right to go to Confession freely, under no pressure of coercion or fear; also, we are released from the torture of needing to list all sins in detail; besides this we have the advantage of knowing how to make a beneficial use of Confession for the comfort and strengthening of our consciences. (Brief Exhortation to Confession 1–4; *Concordia*, p. 649)

So notice, then, that Confession, as I have often said, consists of two parts. The first is my own work and action, when I lament my sins and desire comfort and refreshment for my soul. The other part is a work that God does when He declares me free of my sin through His Word placed in the mouth of a man. It is this splendid, noble, thing that makes Confession so lovely, so comforting. It used to be that we emphasized it only as our work; all that we were then concerned about was whether our act of confession was pure and perfect in every detail. We paid no attention to the second and most necessary part of Confession, nor did we proclaim it. We acted just as if Confession were nothing but a good work by which payment was to be made to God, so that if the confession was inadequate and not exactly correct in every detail, then the Absolution would not be valid and the sin unforgiven. By this the people were driven to the point where everyone had to despair of making so pure a Confession (an obvious impossibility) and where no one could feel at ease in his conscience or have confidence in his Absolution. So they not only rendered the precious Confession useless to us but also made it a bitter burden [Matthew 23:4] causing noticeable spiritual harm and ruin. (Brief Exhortation to Confession 15–17; *Concordia*, p. 651)

THE EVANGELICAL USE OF CONFESSION/ABSOLUTION

Our churches teach that private Absolution should be retained in the churches, although listing all sins is not necessary for Confession. For, according to the Psalm, it is impossible. "Who can discern his errors?" (Psalm 19:12). (AC XI; *Concordia*, pp. 35, 37)

The people are very carefully taught about faith in the Absolution. Before, there was profound silence about faith. Our people are taught that they should highly prize the Absolution as being God's voice and pronounced by God's command. The Power of the Keys [Matthew 16:19] is set forth in its beauty. They are reminded what great consolation it brings to anxious consciences and that God requires faith to believe such Absolution as a voice sounding from heaven [e.g., John 12:28–30]. They are taught that such faith in Christ truly obtains and receives the forgiveness of sins. Before, satisfactions were praised without restraint, but little was said about faith, Christ's merit, and the righteousness of faith. Therefore, on this point, our churches are by no means to be blamed. (AC XXV 2–5; *Concordia*, p. 50)

Absolution, or the Power of the Keys, is an aid against sin and a consolation for a bad conscience; it is ordained by Christ in the Gospel [Matthew 16:19]. Therefore, Confession and Absolution should by no means be abolished in the Church. (SA III VIII 1; *Concordia*, p. 280)

In issues relating to the spoken, outward Word, we must firmly hold that God grants His Spirit or grace to no one except through or with the preceding outward Word [Galatians 3:2, 5]. This protects us from the enthusiasts (i.e., souls who boast that they have the Spirit without and before the Word). . . . Actually, the papacy too is nothing but sheer enthusiasm. The pope boasts that all rights exist in the shrine of his heart. Whatever he decides and commands within his church is from the Spirit and is right, even though it is above and contrary to Scripture and the spoken Word.

All this is the old devil and old serpent [Revelation 12:9] . . . . We have treated this well enough elsewhere. (SA III VIII 3–6; *Concordia*, p. 280)

‹*What is Confession?* Answer:› Confession has two parts: the one is that we confess our sins; the other is that we receive Absolution, or forgiveness, from the confessor, as from God Himself, and in no way doubt, but firmly believe that our sins are forgiven before God in heaven by this.

What sins should we confess? ‹Answer:› Before God we should plead guilty of all sins, even of those that we do not know, as we do in the Lord's Prayer. But before the confessor we should confess only those sins that we know and feel in our hearts.

Which are these? ‹Answer:› Here consider your calling according to the Ten Commandments, whether you are a father, mother, son, daughter, master, mistress, a manservant or maidservant. Consider whether you have been disobedient, unfaithful, or slothful. Consider whether you have grieved anyone by words or deeds, whether you have stolen, neglected, wasted, or done other harm. (SC V; *Concordia*, p. 341)

When I urge you to go to Confession, I am doing nothing else than urging you to be a Christian. If I have brought you to the point of being a Christian, I have thereby also brought you to Confession. (Brief Exhortation to Confession 32; *Concordia*, p. 653)

CROSS
We Suffer with Jesus[1]

artin Luther once identified three things that make a good theologian: prayer for the Holy Spirit to provide understanding of God's unique biblical Word; meditation on this Word; and, as the "touchstone," enduring afflictions because of both meditating on God's Word and putting the Word into practice. This chapter will explore what Scripture has to say about afflictions in the life of the Christian, that is, the cross we will endure in various shapes and sizes, not *even though* but *because* we are Christians.

Luther noticed a discrepancy in his day: On the one hand, Scripture is filled with passages about the constant suffering of the saints in the world as they follow their crucified Lord in their concrete daily vocations in church, home, work, and state. On the other hand, the teaching and practice of many seemed to be about avoiding suffering at all costs, or at least taking control of how and when to "suffer." Some people in the Middle Ages paid significant sums of money to avoid suffering in purgatory or to avoid the more demanding forms of penance in the Roman Church of the day. Others subjected themselves to a rigorous discipline of prayer, fasting, chastity, and poverty that in theory rejected the world and material gain, yet in practice resulted in greater social standing and earthly power. This paradox stands apart from any vocational discipleship in the biblical sense. In each and every case, Luther found self-chosen, controlled forms of "suffering" that were anxiously

---

1   Adapted from *The Lutheran Spirituality Series: Cross*, written by Holger Sonntag, edited by Robert C. Baker. Copyright © 2006 Concordia Publishing House.

sought as spiritual paths. In contrast, many of the ancient martyrs did not choose their path and were not glorified in life. Any path that seeks personal glory in a kind of "sainthood" in this life seeks to get around the real sainthood or martyrdom sent by God in His way and at His time. Distrusting God, that is, breaking the First Commandment, is the root of this "deformation," this large-scale medieval deviation from God's Word.

Clearly, a reformation, a return to Scripture also in this area of spirituality, had become necessary. By the time the Diet of Augsburg occurred in 1530, those who subscribed to this confession humbly stated that in their churches people were well instructed from God's Word concerning the cross in the life and vocation of the Christian.

Despite good instruction, however, some early Lutherans moved to the other extreme. Instead of worrying about how they might control Christian suffering, people began to reject altogether the need for suffering. In the last decade of his earthly life, Luther battled the notion that, since Christians are redeemed by Christ alone, they need not worry about sin in any serious way. Those holding this view were called "Antinomians" because they believed that God's Law, the Ten Commandments, no longer had a place among believers. The Antinomians taught that Christians had no need for their sins to be pointed out to them or to be encouraged to struggle daily against this sin in them; the proclamation of the Gospel was all that was needed.

Time and again Antinomianism rears its head in the Church. This is understandable because Christianity in many successful assemblies today has turned into a self-help club with an all but exclusive focus on the use of the Law as some inner guide. However, such a misuse of the Law provides the false impression that genuine faith could coexist with an unwillingness to fight sin. Thus Baptism's cross of lifelong struggle against sin is rejected.

As we shall read below, hearing and believing the Gospel and receiving the Sacraments in faith does not jibe with remaining in unrepentant sin. God's saving gifts are not static; they are living gifts that cannot be separated from Christ and His Spirit, the "Lord and Giver of Life." Freedom from sin is the freedom from God's just condemnation for sin on account of Christ. But it is not a license to sin. Rather, we are to use our freedom to show love and to "serve one another" (Galatians 5:13). Part of free self-denial, bearing our cross, is also to deny our sinful natures the opportunity to rule over us.

At times we will struggle with great temptations to sin. We are tempted to give in and say: "I can't handle that! Why not give in just this one time? I can always repent later!" This is not a Christian approach. We do not plan to sin in order to take advantage of God's forgiveness. Every sin that is not covered in the blood of Christ is a sin that can lead to death. Planning to sin brings one a step nearer to committing the unforgivable sin.[2] A cold heart is close to spiritual death.

Christians whose hearts have been warmed to life in the Gospel nevertheless do sin, yet they are not proud of it. A warm heart is saddened by its sins against God and neighbor. Thanks be to God, however, that He abounds in grace. Paul reminds us in 1 Corinthians 10:13 that "God is faithful, and He will not let you be tempted beyond your ability, but with the temptation He will also provide the way of escape, that you may be able to endure it." We can commend ourselves to God, look to His Gospel for strength to fight sin, and He will provide an escape. God has set a limit for every temptation.

Do popular forms of Christianity embrace these biblical ideas about struggling and suffering today? Or is "hip" Christianity promoted as a way to avoid the bad stuff and to achieve worldly success and self-improvement? Popular titles such as *Your Best Life Now* by Joel Osteen suggest the latter. Being religious is widely seen as a path to freedom from pain and failure. Suffering is often considered an invigorating challenge on the road to reaching one's full potential. Spiritual disciplines are observed to achieve personal fulfillment, even salvation, often at the expense of our God-given vocations and their trials.

We cannot serve two masters (Luke 16:13). Popular Christianity is at odds with biblical Christianity at key points. Lutherans faithful to God's Word hold out a biblical vision of Christianity and spirituality, one that is shaped by the cross of Christ and that daily flows from Baptism. We now enter this unique and life-giving world of biblical Christianity.

---

2 See Theses X and XXIV in C. F. W. Walther, *Law and Gospel: How to Read and Apply the Bible* (St. Louis: Concordia, 2010).

Cross Meets Man: Baptism

Who can blot out the Cross, which th' instrument
Of God, dewed on me in the Sacrament?
John Donne

The Christian life is based on the historical fact of God at work for us. Christians are reborn through the Word-filled waters of Baptism. We are marked with Christ's cross forever. Paul says this clearly in Romans 6:4: "We were buried therefore with Him by baptism into death, in order that, just as Christ was raised from the dead by the glory of the Father, we too might walk in newness of life." This verse explicitly draws the connection between the suffering, death, and resurrection of Christ on the one hand and His command to teach and baptize (Matthew 28:19–20) on the other. We arrive at Calvary and the empty tomb through Baptism, where God drowns our old Adam, our sinful flesh, in the water of life so the new man in Christ may arise (see Romans 5:12–21; 2 Corinthians 5:17; Colossians 2:11–14).

By God's design, our lives as Christians are connected to the cross from the start. Through Baptism, Christ's suffering and death on the cross gives us new life. As one of God's means of salvation that convey the forgiveness, life, and salvation won by Christ on the cross, Baptism is more than just a rite of initiation performed either when a child is born to church members or when an adult is brought into the Church. Baptism also provides an ongoing pattern for Christian living under the cross as we daily struggle against sin. Baptism also teaches us how to lead our eternal life in time as we serve God and our neighbor in our vocations in church, home, work, and state—as pastors and parishioners; as husbands and wives; as parents and children; as employers and employees; as rulers and citizens.

BAPTISM AND THE CROSS

Our crucifixion and burial with Christ through Baptism happens in a twofold manner: first by faith in the promise of the Gospel presented in Baptism—this is an instantaneous gift of the Holy Spirit—and then by love, that is, by struggling against sin by the power of the Holy Spirit (see Romans 6:6; Galatians 2:20). This struggle is an ongoing process that will not be completed in this life on earth. Christ, now living in us through faith, is also shaping our thoughts, words, and deeds. He is both saving gift and guiding example.

In Romans 6:1, Paul raises the rhetorical question of whether Christians should continue to sin. "By no means!" is his forceful answer (Romans 6:2). In the following verses of the chapter, the apostle goes on to explain the function of Baptism. This Means of Grace unites us with Christ in both His death and His resurrection (verses 3–4). Continuing to sin is out of the question for members of Christ's Body, "for one who has died has been set free from sin" (verse 7). Of course, each of us sins daily, so Paul means that the baptized believer should not continue in unrepentant sin. He says in verse 12: "Let not sin therefore reign in your mortal body, to make you obey its passions."

Our ongoing crucifixion in the post-Baptismal life takes place in our daily vocations as we strive to serve God and neighbor according to God's holy will, the Ten Commandments. Our "members" are to become in life what we are already by faith: God's instruments (see Romans 6:13) and God's slaves of righteousness (see Romans 6:16). This is what it means to live by the Spirit and not according to sinful flesh. The fact that we are no longer "under law but under grace" (Romans 6:14) means that we have passed from condemnation to pardon through faith in the Gospel. Obviously, however, this is no justification for willful sin. We continue to sin (which is why we need to strive against it), but sin is no longer the dominating force in our life; the Holy Spirit is (see Colossians 3:5–17).

The Ten Commandments clearly give us a picture of our new life in Christ. Luther expresses the abiding truth of the Commandments for the Christian in his Small Catechism. The Ten Commandments must not be replaced by a vaguely defined notion of "love" or "what would Jesus do." Love is the summary of the Ten Commandments, not its substitute. In His perfectly obedient life, Christ fulfilled the Ten Commandments for us so we would be liberated from the curse of the Law. Christ's fulfillment of the Law means we now strive with the Holy Spirit's help to follow His example. This includes Jesus' cross-bearing. Being baptized into His suffering and death means that our suffering bears witness to the atonement that Christ made with God for us. We love because He first loved us (1 John 4:19). Faith does not replace love; faith makes true love happen. The life we will enjoy in the new heaven and the new earth will be the full expression of the Ten Commandments; there we will be in life and body what we are now by divine imputation: perfectly righteous.

So if Christ has already accomplished our salvation, why is the life of the baptized a spiritual battle, with all the hardships of military service? In other words, why is it an ongoing "cross" of the Christian? The answer is both simple and complex: sin is forgiven, but our sinful nature is not removed by Baptism. As the apostle Paul writes: "For I have the desire to do what is right, but not the ability to carry it out. For I do not do the good I want, but the evil I do not want is what I keep on doing" (Romans 7:18–19). The old Adam (original sin) remains a potent force in us, always bringing forth actual sins and seeking to gain the upper hand. If that were to happen, we would have a change of heart; we would again enjoy sinning. Dominated by the old Adam, we would no longer sin "against our will." But our Christian will, renewed by the Spirit, now delights in God's holy Law, even under burdens, and is grieved by our ongoing sinning (see Galatians 5:16–17). The ongoing struggle of our Christian will against the old Adam is a cross because it is spiritually draining. If it were not for a constant flow of Gospel power through the Means of Grace, our faith would be completely exhausted.

Many churches today reject Scripture's clear teaching on original sin. Because they do so, they take a different view on the hardships of the Christian and his or her struggle against sin. For these people, the enemies of the Christian (the devil, the world, and our sinful flesh) are a bit farther removed, so the Means of Grace are less important or even dispensable. Although they proclaim that Christ came to save sinners (1 Timothy 1:15), the less they teach about and emphasize sin, the less they believe that people need the Gospel.

A CLOSER LOOK AT BAPTISM

In Baptism, God forgives all our sins for Christ's sake and gives us spiritual rebirth through His Word and Spirit. However, we remain sinners who continue to sin. Quite apart from any other suffering we may or may not have to endure as Christians, we can be certain of this struggle against sin, with its persistent failures.

At times these failures make one wonder: "After all these years of unsuccessfully fighting my sinful nature, what does God think about me? Is He still graciously disposed toward me despite my failure?" Baptism's promise declares: "Yes, for Christ's sake, God is still gracious to you, despite all your sins." This promise is spoken anew in the Divine Service when the called and ordained pastor, in Christ's stead and by His command, forgives you all your sins. We also recall God's promises made to us in our Baptism when we read, hear, or remember Bible passages that refer to this Sacrament.

Paul writes to Titus: "But when the goodness and loving kindness of God our Savior appeared, He saved us, not because of works done by us in righteousness, but according to His own mercy, by the washing of regeneration and renewal of the Holy Spirit, whom He poured out on us richly through Jesus Christ our Savior, so that being justified by His grace we might become heirs according to the hope of eternal life" (3:4–7). In this passage, the apostle clarifies that we are not saved, not even in part, based on our improvement in our battle against sin. We are saved by God's grace through faith in Christ alone, not by faith *and* love. Faith in the Gospel will show itself in our fight against sin. We will, by God's grace, make progress in this battle. While this is an indication of Christ dwelling in us through faith, under the close scrutiny of the Law this progress will appear insignificant, especially when considering original sin. Yet as Christ's baptized siblings, we strive to lead holy lives in the power of the Holy Spirit.

The Sacrament of Holy Baptism is itself embattled. Many churches misunderstand what Baptism is, does, and means. Some consider it to be merely a sign of faith; others teach that Baptism removes sin once but has no further relevance. Churches that do not teach the biblical doctrine of Holy Baptism deprive their people of the comfort that comes with the knowledge of what God gives in and through this Sacrament.

On the one hand, some churches minimize Baptism in favor of a personal feeling of faith and other compensating ideas that fill the void created by the need of a Christian to be certain of salvation. Under the fire of the Law, those who minimize the work of Baptism may make salvation doubtful as well: Did I really believe sincerely or have enough faith when I stepped forward to be baptized (and if I did, why do I doubt now)? At times, the teaching that Baptism brings eternal security (once saved, always saved) is brought forth to compensate for an incorrect understanding of this Means of Grace. But here, too, confidence is placed in "my faith" (back then), not "my Savior" (right now). Another typical compensation is to point to one's emotions, success, or happiness in life as indicators of being saved. This is a purely Law-based assurance (God justly rewards the good). This legalism and false assurance of salvation will break down under the trials and afflictions of the cross, as experience (and repeated Baptisms) clearly shows. If nothing else, all people must face their death and judgment (Hebrews 9:27–28).

However well one may do in this life, there always remains the specter of the next.

On the other hand, the Roman Catholic understanding of Baptism's removal of original sin does not adequately address the continuing power of the sinful nature in the life of the Christian nor the continuing benefit of and need for Baptism. In Roman Catholic theology, other sacraments, especially the sacrament of penance, are said to continue where Baptism presumably has left off. However, the Scriptures point to Baptism, and the promises God attaches to this Sacrament, as maintaining a significant role in our continuing struggle against sin and as the foundation of our sure confidence of salvation.

SPIRITUAL EXERCISES

◈ Review or commit to memory the section on Holy Baptism in Luther's Small Catechism (*Concordia*, pp. 339–40).

◈ Read and meditate on Romans 6:1–4:

> What shall we say then? Are we to continue in sin that grace may abound? By no means! How can we who died to sin still live in it? Do you not know that all of us who have been baptized into Christ Jesus were baptized into His death? We were buried therefore with Him by baptism into death, in order that, just as Christ was raised from the dead by the glory of the Father, we too might walk in newness of life.

◈ When failing in your battle against sin, comfort yourself with this reminder: I am baptized! Then rejoice in Christ's salvation given you in your Baptism once for all.

POINT TO REMEMBER

> We know that our old self ["old Adam"] was crucified with Him [Christ] in order that the body of sin might be brought to nothing, so that we would no longer be enslaved to sin. *Romans 6:6*

Cross and Sacrifice

The sacrifices of God are a broken spirit; a broken and contrite heart, O God, You will not despise. *Psalm 51:17*

Christians receive the blessings and benefits of the Sacraments, including Holy Baptism, because the One who instituted them made a tremendous sacrifice in order to bestow those gifts. Christ's suffering and death, His cross, is the all-availing sacrifice for the sins of the whole world. Yet through the gifts bestowed in Baptism, Christ's cross is also every Christian's example for self-sacrificial living according to God's will—in the context of personal vocations. Saved by Christ's sacrifice, we are called to offer sacrifices—ultimately ourselves and all that we have—to our Savior. But we need to develop the biblical understanding of sacrifice that distinguishes Law and Gospel and how it differs from the humanistic understanding of freedom prevalent in culture and church today. As the appropriate understanding of sacrifice takes over our lives, we are able to see our suffering as a sacrifice that is pleasing to our heavenly Father for the sake of Jesus Christ's all-availing sacrifice.

Consider an individual who chooses to leave career, family, and friends to serve his or her country in the military. Or consider a woman who leaves a flourishing career to raise children or to care for an ailing family member. Perhaps a man chooses to step off the fast track to be present with his family and better function as the head of his household. These may be difficult personal sacrifices, but we would all agree that the end results are beneficial to others. However, we also can quickly bring to mind people who sacrifice everything to "make it big" in life—selfishly stepping over others in their efforts to be first or the best. In the end such individuals may have the most toys, but will they have anyone with whom to share their successes? Clearly, what we choose to sacrifice, and for whom, indicates who or what is most important to us.

GOD'S SACRIFICE AND OUR SACRIFICES _____

Christ's sacrifice on the cross was not an accident of human history. The apostle Peter tells us that the coming of the Savior was planned by God before the foundation of the world (see 1 Peter 1:20); there was divine necessity behind it. The Son of God freely pledged Himself to die for sinful humankind even before humankind existed or had fallen into sin. His suffering and death was revealed when God told the serpent, "I will put enmity between you and the woman, and between your offspring and her offspring; He shall bruise your head, and you shall bruise His heel" (Genesis 3:15). Here in the Garden of Eden God makes the first promise of the Savior, a promise that would be proclaimed by God's prophets (see, for example, Isaiah 53:5–7) and recorded in God's written Word. The sacrificial rites of the Old Testament foreshadowed Christ's sacrifice, which was fulfilled during His earthly life, death, and resurrection.

As Christ had to suffer, so, too, must Christians suffer. In fact Paul tells Timothy that "all who desire to live a godly life in Christ Jesus will be persecuted" (2 Timothy 3:12). The fallen world cannot peacefully coexist with the members of Christ's Body, the Church, just as it could not coexist in peace with Christ. The world's alienation from God expresses itself in hostility toward God, God's Son, God's messengers (prophets, apostles, pastors), and God's people. They are strangers in this world. Christ has called His disciples out of this world, the kingdom of darkness, into His kingdom of light (see John 15:19).

Jesus told His disciples: "In the world you will have tribulation" (John 16:33). The apostle Peter tells his readers not to be "surprised at the fiery trial when it comes upon you to test you" (1 Peter 4:12). We will have tribulation in this world and suffer many things because we honor God's name by teaching His Word rightly and living our lives according to it. But in the same breath as He acknowledges the suffering we will face, Jesus says, "But take heart; I have overcome the world" (John 16:33). Peter, too, completes his reference to trials by inviting his readers to "rejoice and be glad when His [Christ's] glory is revealed" (1 Peter 4:13). Just as Christ suffered and was glorified, so we, as members of His Body, will suffer and be glorified. Suffering as a Christian does not drive the Spirit away; it is therefore not a sign of God's wrath! Indeed, like poor, ulcerous Lazarus, we may be dear to God in the midst of our suffering (Luke 16:20–22). Like Christ, we suffer because we are God's children. We can "rejoice in our sufferings" (Romans 5:3; see also Colossians 1:24; 1 Peter 4:13) because we know that we are joined to Christ.

When we consider the phrase "God's will" we often think only in terms of the Ten Commandments: thou shalt and thou shalt not. However, we also meet God's will in this world as it allots us hardships and suffering in the context of our vocations (see, for example, 1 Peter 2:18–21). Enduring these God-given sufferings is a form of doing good, following Christ's example. It is therefore a form in which we, in response to Christ's sacrifice, offer ourselves and all that we have as a sacrifice. But Christian sacrifices are not atoning sacrifices to gain or merit forgiveness; they are eucharistic sacrifices made in thanksgiving and praise for the forgiveness given in the Gospel for Christ's sake and received through faith. Lutheran reformer Philip Melanchthon explored the two kinds of sacrifice in the Apology of the Augsburg Confession:

> Now the rest are eucharistic sacrifices, which are called sacrifices of praise (Leviticus 3; 7:11[–18]; Psalm 56:12). These are the preaching of the Gospel, faith, prayer, thanksgiving, confession, the troubles of saints, yes, all good works of saints. These sacrifices are not satisfactions for those making them, nor can they be applied to others to merit the forgiveness of sins or reconciliation by the outward act (*ex opere operato*). They are made by those who have been reconciled. These are the sacrifices of the New Testament, as Peter teaches, "a holy priesthood, to offer spiritual sacrifices" (1 Peter 2:5). Spiritual sacrifices, however, are contrasted not only with those of cattle, but even with human works offered by the outward act, because *spiritual* refers to the movements of the Holy Spirit in us.[3]

What is this working of the Spirit? The gift of the Holy Spirit through the Gospel brings forth all sorts of good fruits (see Galatians 5:22–23). In Galatians 5:6, Paul teaches that faith is active in love, and in his Epistle to the Romans, the apostle also calls love "the fulfilling of the law" (13:10). We tend to consider love to be an active fruit of the Spirit—we show it through actions and words, just as we do joy, kindness, goodness, and self-control. We can consider "love" to be the summary of faith's fruits brought about by the Holy Spirit. But one fruit seems out of place in the list: patience. It would appear to be passive, especially in the context of patience in suffering. Yet this, too, is a form of loving God. Since patience is not "active" in the narrow sense of the word, we can call it "passive love."

No matter how impressive the sacrifice (including severe suffering), it is not pleasing to God unless it is offered in love (1 Corinthians 13:3). Indeed, from love flows much that can be identified with faith in Christ (1 Corinthians 13:4–7). In other words, a sacrifice is pleasing to God only when it is offered without the sinful intention of appeasing God through it, of working out one's own forgiveness apart from Christ. This intention is only "put to death" by faith in the Gospel, that is, by trusting that we are at peace with God for the sake of Christ's once-and-for-all sacrifice in His life and His death on the cross.

---

3 Ap XXIV [XII] 25–26; *Concordia*, p. 224. For the full discussion of the two types of sacrifice, see Ap XXIV [XII] 19–43; *Concordia*, pp. 222–28.

THY WILL BE DONE

We live in a democratic culture that highly values personal independence, individual freedom, self-realization, and self-determination. Anything that restricts these "rights" is viewed negatively. We want to be in charge of our lives from cradle to casket. However, in the Third Petition of the Lord's Prayer, Christians pray to their heavenly Father that His will, not ours, be done. How do we resolve this tension?

In much of contemporary Christianity, society's love of freedom expresses itself in the teaching that man is free to "choose" to follow Jesus. Upon careful examination, this is actually a claim that we can free ourselves from the kingdom of the devil and join the kingdom of God, as if both were human organizations or clubs. If, for argument's sake, we accept this thinking, we would have to believe that the contest between the devil and us is winnable on our part, however much or little we might credit God. If, however, God is a mere partner in our salvation, we might wonder: If we can beat the devil, what prevents us from creating a pain-free paradise on earth? What stops us from being masters of our destiny?

The simple answer is: God's will prevents us. Our own mortality is sure evidence of this (Genesis 3:19). Full holiness implies that we become free of death's curse and of all infirmity. What we must conclude is that, if the curse is still in force, so is the sin and rebellion that is expressed in the very fiber of our being. Regarding the fundamental aspects of human existence, such as life and death, we remain utterly passive (see Psalm 49:7; Matthew 5:36). When we try to grasp power over these fundamentals, we reject the creative and sustaining role of God and become full of pride and tempted to destroy God-given life for the sake of sinful plans. And God resists the proud (see James 4:6; 1 Peter 5:5; cf. Proverbs 3:34). In everyday terms, while our love toward our neighbor is *active,* our will in conversion is *passive.* Christ uses the analogy of birth (see John 3:1–8) to illustrate this in His discussion with Nicodemus. We do not conceive ourselves; rather, we *are conceived.* In the same way, we do not give birth to ourselves; we *are birthed* by our mothers. Here it is the actions of another that count.

In suffering, we likewise are to remain passive. Think of yourself as a patient in a hospital. You depend on others to feed, wash, clothe, and medicate you. That is not an easy thing to do; being active and productive all the time is what we are taught. Suffering, especially when we are in a situation in which we cannot free or help ourselves, reminds us that God takes care of us even without our active involvement—even when we sleep! And this is most apparent when we consider that "God, being rich in mercy, because of the great love with which He loved us, even when we were dead in our trespasses, made us alive together with Christ" (Ephesians 2:4–5). And God daily renews this life in us through His Means of Grace. When we see Christ as the patient Lamb of God who does not take matters into His own hands but commends Himself to the Father who judges justly, then we see that the Christian's right and privilege is to suffer with Jesus. A life of "soft clothing" (Matthew 11:8) is not that of Christ's disciples who follow their Savior in the context of their vocations. Human "rights" such as the right to have an abortion, to marry someone of the same sex, and to experiment on human embryos reflect *humanism*, not Christianity. Christians following their servant Lord focus on serving their Creator and their fellow creatures, not on serving themselves. This means that Christians will choose the difficult, narrow path instead of the wide, smooth road (Matthew 7:13–14). For them, the heavenly reward surpasses all suffering here (1 Corinthians 2:14, 4:17; 2 Thessalonians 1:5).

In an early sermon on the Third Petition of the Lord's Prayer, Luther asserted that it is good when our will (or our planning) does not come to pass. In comparison to God's plans, which are always for our good, the apostle James refers to human beings as "mist" and calls us to see boasting in our selfish plans as nothing but the highest form of arrogance (see James 4:13–15).

Luther clearly understood from God's Word that our sinful flesh goes against God's will. It does not desire God's will, but rather hates and rejects it at every turn. When He prevents our sinful desires from coming to fruition, God is guiding us to conform to His will, to let go of our ideas and to adopt His. In our blindness, we sometimes believe we are the lords of our lives; yet in the blink of an eye we realize that we are not in charge and that our plans are nothing when compared to God's might. This is a humbling experience of God's will (Law). The old Adam in us will forever rebel against God's will—we want our own way. Yet the new Adam, the baptized child of God, does indeed pray: "Thy will be done." God is not an obscure force of nature that plays dice with our lives. For us, God is the loving, wise Father. His will, whatever He may ordain, is best. And because we know hardships do not come from some anonymous fate, then we can pray to our gracious God and Father who gave them to us, trusting that He knows us well and means well for us.

PATIENT SUFFERING
AS "SPIRITUAL WORSHIP"

Most people worship some supreme being or spiritual force. Many are very dedicated, sincere, and even intense in their worship life. They take great pains (literally!) to make sacrifices of one kind or another to please or appease the god(s) of their religion. For example, some people pray for hours or make dangerous or costly pilgrimages. People of all religious beliefs spend significant sums of money to buy the latest spiritual self-improvement material that promises a successful marriage or career or a victorious life.

Such is the strenuous and impressive worship practiced by the religions of the world. Yet at its core Christian worship does not consist of doing this or that great feat in God's honor. At its heart, Christian worship is not giving to God through works but receiving from God through faith what He gives for Christ's sake through the Gospel in Word and Sacraments. The Gospel of Jesus Christ, not a set of religious and moral laws, is at the heart of our lives as Christians. Worship "in spirit and truth" (John 4:24) is primarily the passivity of faith in the Gospel, not the ensuing activity of love. We are declared righteous; we do not justify ourselves.

If passive faith is the "highest worship,"[4] then patiently bearing God's will (e.g., in a nursing home) is also a high form of love because it so closely reflects the role of faith in justification: purely passive and receptive, receiving the good things God gives. Suffering belongs to those things God gives through which He works for our good. We do not receive the blessings of the cross won by Christ apart from the painful experiences of the cross in our own lives.[5] We receive both faith and suffering passively.

When we bring to mind an "active" or "exemplary" Christian, we may think of a Christian athlete who points to heaven or prays before or after an important game. Such individuals are lauded for their active demonstrations of faith. We probably overlook the woman who suffers financially to care for her infirm husband, the parents who patiently yet invisibly suffer at the hand of a wayward child, or the widower who suffers lonely days in the nursing home. Because these Christians do not seem to be actively living out their faith, we may not consider them to

---

4   See Ap V (III) 33 [154]; *Concordia*, p. 106.
5   See Matthew 10:37–39; Luke 9:23; 14:27. See also LC I 42 (*Concordia*, p. 363) and FC SD XI 49 (*Concordia*, p. 609).

be exemplary. However, great things are taking place. By God's grace, Christians are "doing" patience. This makes suffering and temptation the touchstone that reveals genuine faith, not a means for material gain or personal recognition.

Obviously, apart from Christ neither faith nor love saves us. We are saved through faith in Christ alone. And while it might be surprising to say that faith does not save us, the statement is true when we consider that faith always must have an object. Faith in Christ saves because of what it receives, namely, Christ and His saving benefits. Love is the Gospel-motivated response of the believer, accomplishing the "good works, which God prepared beforehand, that we should walk in them" (Ephesians 2:10). This includes patience under the cross.

SPIRITUAL EXERCISES

❖ Identify the hardships you are currently experiencing in your life that are not the result of your active sin. Ask God to help you view your hardships as ordained by His will. Rejoice in being counted worthy to offer such a high sacrifice of praise to God.

❖ Meditate on the hymn "What God Ordains Is Always Good" (*LSB* 760). How does this hymn point you to God's sure promises found in His Word?

❖ Pray that God would open your eyes and your heart to the suffering of someone you know and that He would give you the courage and resources to provide help and comfort. Begin now as God's royal priest (1 Peter 2:9) to petition the Lord in prayer on behalf of this person.

POINT TO REMEMBER

I appeal to you therefore, brothers, by the mercies of God, to present your bodies as a living sacrifice, holy and acceptable to God, which is your spiritual worship. *Romans 12:1*

Temptations
and Other Afflictions

Consider that—according to the Scriptures—it is not at all difficult
to be converted. But to remain in a converted state—that is difficult.
C. F. W. Walther[6]

As baptized Christians, we know that we will suffer in our vocations.
We have learned that enduring this suffering is a gracious gift whereby
God allows us to worship Him by resisting the power of sin in our
lives and passively enduring life's hardships. Yet how do we deal with
the practical situation in the thick of the action? We do not know how
we will suffer or when. Undoubtedly this uncertainty is at the core
of attempts to impose hardships on ourselves, as if we could thereby
bribe or encourage God to keep the real thing away from us. We fear
we might not be able to withstand when tempted. For the baptized
members of the Body of Christ, there is no need to bargain with God
or to fear. Instead, every day we confidently commend into His hands
our bodies and souls and all things. For we have the promise that we
shall rise to life everlasting just as Christ is risen from the dead.

In our culture, *temptation* is most commonly understood to mean
the invitation to act on our sexual desires or to indulge in food or drink.
However, the devil, the world, and our sinful flesh tempt us in every
aspect of our lives.

GOD'S BAPTIZED CHILDREN ARE TEMPTED ___

Immediately following His Baptism by John, where He had been
revealed to be God's own Son, Jesus was "led up by the Spirit into the
wilderness to be tempted by the devil" (Matthew 4:1). Jesus is tempted
three times based on His hunger, His physical vulnerability, and His
lack of political or earthly glory (Matthew 4:1–11). Each of these
temptations reflects an aspect of Christ's humiliation, the fact that as
the incarnate Son of God, Jesus "made Himself nothing" (Philippians
2:7). He concealed His glorious form in the meekness and humility of
human flesh. Only rarely did Jesus use or display His divine attributes
while on earth—and never for His own good, but only to heal and save
others. Christ's humiliation, which made these temptations by the devil

---

6   Walther, *Law and Gospel: How to Read and Apply the Bible,* 413.

possible, was the necessary presupposition for His work as Savior: only the Son of Man in His humiliation could be obedient to His Father and die on the cross (see Galatians 4:4; Ephesians 2:14; Philippians 2:6–8; Hebrews 2:14–18).

Twice Satan introduces his tempting words by saying, "If You are the Son of God . . ." (Matthew 4:3, 6). Jesus was tempted by those same words again when He was hanging on the cross and the crowds mocked Him (see Matthew 27:40). In each instance, Christ was tempted to lay aside His humble state and reveal fully His divine glory. If He had done so, Jesus' work of salvation would have become impossible because He would not have been following His Father's will.

Satan might also tempt you by playing your high spiritual status as a child of God against your humble life of patient service and even suffering here on earth. The devil may ask, "Don't you deserve better? If you are God's child, shouldn't you have an easy life, one filled with good things and not these trials? Shouldn't others be serving you?" Think about when success as a Christian gets boiled down to one's status in the congregation or the community and the deference that others "ought to show."

But that is not the path Christ followed. He was and is all about serving, not being served (Matthew 20:28). He is our gracious God who stoops down in human flesh to serve us. Moreover, His service does not stop at the cross. Through our Baptism, Christ enables us to serve God and our neighbor humbly, according to God's unchanging commandments, even under our crosses. Toward the end of His ministry on earth, Jesus told His disciples about the suffering and death that was to come. But Peter took Jesus aside and said, "Far be it from You, Lord! This shall never happen to You" (Matthew 16:22). Like all human beings, Peter here displays a natural understanding of what God is, does, and how He should fare on earth (if He ever cared to come down). According to Peter, God does not suffer, so if Jesus is God's Son (which Peter had just confessed; see Matthew 16:16), He ought not to suffer either. But it is precisely on the cross that Jesus is triumphant for us over sin, death, and the devil.

In each of the temptations, Jesus defeats Satan with God's Word. Thus we have an example of how to deal with a tempter: use the "sword of the Spirit" (Ephesians 6:17), lest you be deceived by the devil as Eve was in the Garden of Eden. During temptation, we can appeal to no higher power than God's almighty Word, and Jesus has shown us that it is sufficient. To use this sword skillfully requires practice, that is, we are to study and learn this Word and apply it to our life and experience, always rightly distinguishing between Law and Gospel in order to hear God's words of reproof and of comfort in proper context.

In the devil's final temptation of Jesus in the wilderness, Satan wanted Jesus to bow down to him in exchange for "all the kingdoms of the world and their glory" (Matthew 4:8). This was a direct assault on the First Commandment: "You shall have no other gods before Me" (Exodus 20:3). Yet all temptations actually attack the First Commandment because it is the backbone of all the other commandments. When we do not look to God—Father, Son, and Holy Spirit—for all good things in this life and the next, then all other steadfastness and discipline will be of no avail. But being weak without God's help does not excuse us from asking God to empower us to resist temptation. We cannot claim to be believers in Christ when we simply give in to temptations. Even if we stumble, we are called and enabled through Baptism to fight the good fight, not to act as if temptations had a greater power or importance than the one true God. Jesus' explanation of the parable of the soils (Matthew 13:18–23) shows that we ourselves are to blame if the Word does not take root in us. The power to overcome temptation can come only from outside of us, from God's Word itself. We are to blame for unbelief; God is honored for our faith and perseverance.

ORIGINS OF TEMPTATIONS

If we are called to fight the good fight, who and what opposes us? Satan certainly is an important tempter. But he is by no means the only source of temptations. In the Large Catechism, Luther discusses the Sixth Petition of the Lord's Prayer and distinguishes temptations of the flesh, the world, and the devil. He even goes so far as to correlate various stages and vocations in life to temptations of the flesh (the young), the world (the old), and the devil (all who deal with God's Word).

Jesus' parable of the soils in Matthew 13 helps us to summarize the sources of temptation as Luther did. The devil snatches the Word out of man's heart, which is inclined to be hard and resistant to God's Word. The sinful nature is too shallow to allow the Word to take root and weather the scorching heat of persecution for the sake of the faith. The world has so many cares, or interesting things, to lay on our weak shoulders that the Word becomes an afterthought or is perceived as an additional burden. In a sense, this parable applies the account of Jesus' temptation to us: Jesus did not have a sinful nature that would resonate with the world. So only the essential conflict between Satan and God remains. As far as we are concerned, a couple more players remain on the field (flesh and world), but the ultimate battle is still between God and the devil. Giving in to self and world is always giving in to the devil. There is no neutral ground.

EMBRACING OR AVOIDING AFFLICTION _____

We may suffer afflictions because of our sin, yet the cosmic warfare between God and the devil and the sources of temptation also suggest that we will suffer even when we avoid temptation. Affliction hurts. It is that simple. That is why human nature seeks to avoid suffering and pain. Affliction seems unnatural because it truly is. In the beginning, there was no hardship on earth. However, Scripture teaches us that afflictions are now part of our natural lives in body and soul—we are not in Paradise anymore (Genesis 3:16–19, 23–24). Afflictions are also part of our lives as Christians—we are not yet in heaven (see Romans 8). In this life, we cannot avoid pain.

To be sure, Scripture does not advocate suffering for its own sake, nor does God's Word encourage people to seek out suffering. In fact, when the early Church was persecuted in the Roman Empire, the pastors of the Church discouraged Christians from actively seeking martyrdom. Yet they did not shrink from unavoidable suffering in the context of their vocations. A pleasant life in this world, tempting as it may be, is not a primary goal for Christians. Not only Christ but also the apostles showed this in the pattern of their lives.

Paul had to endure many hardships in life because of his vocation as an apostle of Jesus Christ. (He did not go around volunteering his services and then get into trouble; Paul did what God had called him to do.) Therefore, the trouble that comes with our vocations in church, home, work, and state, we endure for the sake of our neighbor and in the certain hope that these hardships will not be endless. Because God has established limits to the troubles we face, we do not need to seek to escape them prematurely, as if a life of hardship were not a life worthy of God's children. But we also need not take the whole world and its misery on our shoulders. That is God's work (John 1:29). God has reduced the world into little pieces that fit with our vocations. When we fail in our vocations, the Law will drive us to the Gospel, where we are forgiven for trying to "do it all" and sent back out to serve God and neighbor.

Paul writes beautifully of his faith in the resurrection of the body in 1 Corinthians 15. This faith in the resurrection afforded Paul an imperishable hope that is placed outside this world of death and decay, changes and chances. This faith mightily comforted Paul in his trials, which at times might have seemed endless and certainly beyond his weak powers of endurance. The resurrection Gospel reminds us that afflictions are not endless. God will bring them to an end. Just as a miserable life makes a life without misery very desirable, so trials on earth make faith in the resurrection more precious. In a sense, this reveals a Law/Gospel relationship: just as the Law shows us our sins, which makes the Gospel of forgiveness precious, so hardships in this life make "the life of the world to come" and the promises concerning that life very precious.

SPIRITUAL EXERCISES

◈ Meditate on Luther's explanation to the Sixth Petition of the Lord's Prayer in the Small Catechism (*Concordia*, p. 337). Notice how we pray for God's strength and help in our battle against the devil, the world, and our sinful nature.

◈ Study the hymn "I Walk in Danger All the Way" (*LSB* 716). Reflect especially on stanza 5, which points us to the wounds of Christ as our "hiding place" from Satan's power.

◈ Ponder Luther's Table of Duties in the Small Catechism (*Concordia*, pp. 346–48), confessing your responsibility for the suffering you have caused yourself and others. Trust in God's promise of forgiveness (1 John 1:8–9) and in the comfort God gives us amid our suffering (2 Corinthians 1:3–7) through our Savior, Jesus Christ.

POINT TO REMEMBER

But in fact Christ has been raised from the dead, the firstfruits of those who have fallen asleep. *1 Corinthians 15:20*

Our Cross with God

Truly, You are a God who hides Himself, O God of Israel, the Savior.
Isaiah 45:15

Various crosses—the battle against sin, disease, struggles at work, difficulties at home, and even challenges in our church community—sometimes make it difficult to believe in our gracious God. God's mercy and grace frequently may appear to be hidden in our lives. We wish God would reveal Himself clearly and deliver us (or at least get us "over the hump") so that we could "see and believe." We might also long to be vindicated before others who tease or simply ignore us because of Christ and His Word. We may long to say, "See, I was right after all."

However, God does not usually reveal Himself in this way. We do not have any promise to see God with our physical eyes before Christ's glorious return on the Last Day to judge the living and the dead. What we do have, though, is His Gospel. Christ hides Himself from natural investigation. Those who find God through logical pursuits do not find grace; rather, they encounter the holy, condemning voice of the Law that both orders the stars in their courses and curses mankind for straying from God's intended plan. Christ wants to be found where He is gracious: in Word and Sacrament. In these Means, He comforts us as we follow Him by bearing our cross. The orthodox Lutheran theologians speak of the water, bread, and wine (the "signs") *meeting* the Word according to the mandate and institution of Christ. We say that "under" these signs is the triune God and the body and blood of Christ. The signs are united with the God whom they both signify and truly offer. God is there present in a sacramental manner for the blessing of His people. There we receive the forgiveness of sins, the indwelling of Christ, and the strengthening of the new life in Christ.

While this manner of hiding and revealing is for our spiritual good, our reaction to it may be one of frustration on account of our own sin and desire to control.

HIDDEN FROM THE EYE, REVEALED TO FAITH

We sometimes are frustrated with God. Not only does He, for our good, prevent our plans from coming to pass, but also He hides Himself (except for the Means of Grace, which are where He wants to be found). God may not remove the thorn in the flesh; rather, He tells us,

"My grace is sufficient to you, for My power is made perfect in weakness" (2 Corinthians 12:9). The everlasting Gospel to the saints who suffer here (Revelation 14:6–13) may sound like God saying, "Buck up," to those who suffer persecution for Christ's name (Matthew 5:11). Yet the fact remains that troubles, persecution, and even death here are pleasant by comparison to everlasting hell. We cannot understand this by our natural powers, but God in His gracious Word has revealed this glimpse of reality to provide context.

Tornadoes, hurricanes, earthquakes, cancer, and accidents can kill. These all exist according to the inscrutable will of God who has called the very cosmos to be His agent of wrath against our inherited and actual sin (Genesis 3). Part of God's hiding involves His determined action to kill sin in us because sin is utterly and constantly opposed to Him; there can be no truce. That is the Law in full force, and God will carry out His wrath against sin to its fullest extent. So God allows His right hand, as it were, to work independently of His left. God will only let Himself be found, captured, touched, tasted, eaten, and drunk where the promises that lead you to heaven are located. The saints are called to persevere because heaven will repay infinitely for all earthly suffering (Mark 10:29–31).

Romans 1:18–25 illustrates a double blind of sorts that Luther also engaged in his writings. Human sin twists the created gifts given by God, causing the natural law impulse for people to worship God to be transferred to the worship of fellow creatures (such as extraordinary animals and people)! By turning away from worship of the Creator to the worship of creatures, people turn in on themselves. This breaking of the First Commandment results in God's wrath and moral confusion imposed by God as punishment. God uses sin and its consequences to punish sin, allowing His immediate presence to become "hidden" to those in such rebellious states. Yet some broken knowledge of God and morality is left, even among unbelievers, because God's Law, which is hardwired into us, has not completely been erased by sin. The various non-Christian religions bear witness to this. They make man's temporal efforts and achievements the basis of salvation; they only know the Law (and that imperfectly), but not the Gospel. They worship idols, not the one true God: Father, Son, and Holy Spirit.

The world does not want the God who comes in grace because grace is exclusively on God's terms. Our imperfect natural knowledge of the Law, combined with our sin, leads us falsely to believe that we can manipulate God by using the Law. That is why the Gospel must be proclaimed on the sole basis of God's revealed Word. The Gospel is utterly unlike the Law in its expectations and operation. In Jesus Christ, the Creator humbled Himself by becoming a human creature. Even though the world engages in creation-worship, it missed the Creator in human flesh because it expects great power and majesty. Instead of standing out as Creator by His stature or power, Jesus presented Himself in flesh and blood in order to be subject to God's wrath on the cross. Yet this was not the same kind of "hiding" on God's part that was discussed previously. Christ set aside the power and majesty that are His forever in order to save us, but He was not emptied of His divine attributes when He was poured out as a sacrifice for us. His strength was shown in human weakness, so that in our weakness we find strength in Him. The "Law presence" of Jesus was hidden in order that His "Gospel presence" might be revealed (cf. Matthew 20:28; Revelation 1:17–18). The failure to discern God in Jesus is entirely the work of human sin: "The light shines in the darkness, and the darkness has not overcome it" (John 1:5).

Human eyes will not and cannot see with the sight of faith apart from God's gracious action. God opens blind eyes through the "unreasonable" message of a crucified God and Savior, which, in worldly terms, is offensive. God cannot suffer and be weak, let alone die as a criminal; only humans can do so, and only sinners deserve such a death. This message does not make sense to man's fallen, Law-bound reason, just as Jesus of Nazareth as God does not make sense. This is why the Gospel *is and remains* a mystery, not the fact that it is not known as a piece of information. Both incarnation and crucifixion are indeed foolishness to the natural man, that is, the unbeliever. There are no exceptions. People cannot be prepared for God's Word by human activities. It is God's Law leading to a realization of one's sin and God's wrath over sin that prepares hearts for the Gospel, which creates faith when and where it pleases God. The Word of God in Law and Gospel succeeds where it succeeds because the Holy Spirit is present in it and at work through it.

Suffering can prepare the unbeliever for God's Word in the same sense that a speeding ticket can: both suggest to us that we are neither immortal nor almighty. But both experiences have limits because God's Law has been obscured by human sin. Suffering can also cause one to resent God or seek to go it alone. Suffering needs the clarifying word of God's revealed Law to be driven home, that is, to work genuine repentance by showing the full extent of sin's damage in man (original sin). The Gospel "makes sense" only to the person who has recognized his or her utterly lost state before God and who has been given the supernatural gift of faith by the Holy Spirit through the Gospel.

God uses worldly folly because worldly wisdom has proved truly foolish since it does not recognize Him. In this way, God punishes and destroys disobedient wisdom and makes all people equal. We are saved not based on our wisdom, since no wisdom of the world can know the mind of God. Therefore we cannot boast about what is in us or in certain creaturely gifts that we possess. We can boast only in the Lord. Since the apparent foolishness of the message cannot make sense apart from the work of the Holy Spirit, its rejection by sinful human minds works like the Law. Those who account themselves wise discover that their proud nature must be humbled. If in their arrogance they walk away from God, they will indeed be humbled—whether or not they desire such humbling. Such contrite humility prepares us for the true wisdom of God. When someone is converted, it is not because of some special natural gift in the speaker or in the hearer. It is because of the Holy Spirit working through the Word itself.

Even after conversion, Christians still contend with the limitations of human thought and the sin that results when human reason is elevated to the same level as God's clear Word. Some refuse to acknowledge the divine power and presence that is in the elements of bread, wine, and water because God's Word has been added to them. They judge based on reason, that is, what they can experience by their senses or conceive in their minds. Some feel offended by a pastor who claims to forgive sin on the basis of his office as God's servant. Yet this, too, is not a mere human claim; it is done based on God's power in His Word, which is added to the human voice. Christ Himself instituted Absolution after His resurrection (see John 20:22–23). Also, through "mutual conversation and consolation,"[7] believers extend God's gracious Word of forgiveness for Christ's sake to each other.

The Means of Grace are very humble instruments of God's service among us to forgive us our sins. This makes them, like Christ's humiliation, easy targets for ridicule. Some Christian churches have allowed "reasonable" aspects of this ridicule to influence the ways in which they practice Baptism and Communion, as well as the style and content of preaching. Some teach that the Means of Grace are God-commanded ordinances that people ought to do instead of wonderful opportunities where God comes to and serves His people. Others view the Means of

---

7   SC III III IV; *Concordia*, p. 278.

Grace as merely symbolic human rites or activities. They obscure and may even disbelieve God's Word, which teaches that God *does* give His saving grace in Baptism and Holy Communion as Christ instituted them and in the Gospel purely proclaimed, read, shared, or remembered. These Christians are often influenced by Swiss reformer Ulrich Zwingli, who believed that the only way God acts is directly in a person's heart. John Calvin's understanding of eternal election to either heaven or hell provides the idea that believers simply will respond because of their calling. John Wesley and Jacobus Arminius believed that people are simply free to choose the good. The traditions that grew from the writings of these theologians see Christian sacraments as events in which some kind of power has to be added because the "real" meaning lies elsewhere. This makes sense to fallen human reason—after all, some people believe and others do not. Some people are effective preachers (such as Billy Graham, Joel Osteen, Rick Warren) and others are not. But this leads only to boasting in human qualities and qualifications; it does not give glory to God who has chosen to save through a foolish Word preached by foolish men (1 Corinthians 4:10).

Since the Savior and the means by which He has chosen to save His people appear vulnerable to ridicule, is it any wonder that we, who follow our Master with our own crosses, also find ourselves exposed to similar ridicule? Jesus was rejected often—does that mean He was not God in those instances? People are converted when and where it pleases God, but they are always converted by means of God's Word. As the Means of Grace do not look like God's chosen instruments, as Christ in His humiliation did not look like God's Son, so we, too, often do not look like God's children in this life. Suffering and hardships, as well as sin, can hide our true identity. But that does not mean we are not God's children when we suffer! We point to those weak things to proclaim the perfect strength of God. If and when we bear crosses, we can humbly wear our sufferings as badges of honor.

HIDDEN TO REMAIN HIDDEN

Christians are not on a quest to unmask God; rather, they remain content to let God be God on His own time and in His own way. During His earthly sojourn of humiliation for us, Christ's divine nature on earth was hidden in His human nature so He could take the humble road to the cross. The glorified Christ is certainly radiant and splendid in heaven (Revelation 1:12–20), yet we would be struck "as if dead"

(Revelation 1:17) were we to see that glory. For us, Christ hides His glorious yet awesome presence, though He still reveals Himself now under Law and Gospel, Word and Sacraments. This is for our good. In the Means of Grace, we can be certain that we will encounter our crucified and risen Savior with His gifts, even under the cross when we do not feel redeemed. At the same time, we are not consumed by the superabundant glory that is Christ's.

Our triune God is present not only in the Means of Grace. In fact, we encounter Him everywhere—at times for our good, as in the bounty of creation, and at times in a damaging, killing way, as in the little and big disasters of this life and world. On the positive side, which is often not acknowledged because it is less traumatic, we might see a bumper crop or a promotion or a healing against all odds. On the negative side, there might be the death of a child or seemingly endless trials and afflictions, as well as examples of unusual cruelty such as German concentration camps in World War II, the Stalinist Gulag, or the terrorist attacks of 9/11. In all these things, God is present in His unsearchable, divine wisdom. He even permits the existence of Satan, that creature of His who fell and has since caused many others to perish. Although God works through the joys and catastrophes of this life, God does not want to be found in them.

We are called to leave the hidden things hidden. We should not try to figure them out. In God's Word there might not be a satisfying answer to every question that is raised by hardship and cross-bearing. Jesus directs us to turn our eyes away from what we cannot fathom to the blessings that are ours by faith in the Gospel. Our many unanswered questions concerning God in this world might go unanswered—but God in Jesus Christ is present in the Gospel.

THE HIDDEN CHURCH

Christians suffer because we are baptized into Christ's suffering and death. Like our Savior, we are no more than strangers in this world. This is true for us individually; it is also true for Christ's Church on earth. The Church is not a place where we enjoy outward peace and harmony. In fact, the harshest conflicts of all arise in the Church. In the Church, the truth of God's indivisible Word, and with it eternal damnation and eternal salvation, is at stake.

In his 1539 treatise *On the Councils and the Church*, Luther counts cross-bearing as one of the marks of the true Church, that is, the Church that teaches God's Word in all its truth and purity and uses Christ's Sacraments (Baptism and Communion) rightly. The true Church is the Church hidden under the cross. Luther also notes that churches that take greater liberties when it comes to God's Word and Sacraments often prosper.

Difficult questions for Christians include: Why is there disunity in Christendom? Why do people not embrace the Gospel of salvation? Why is the full truth of the Gospel often persecuted and denied most vigorously in the Church? The short answer to all these questions is, of course, sin. But why does God not prevent sin from disrupting the Church? Through Moses, God warned the children of Israel that when false prophets came among them, these were tests "to know whether you love the LORD your God with all your heart and with all your soul" (Deuteronomy 13:3). And the apostle Paul pointed out that "there must be factions among you in order that those who are genuine among you may be recognized" (1 Corinthians 11:19). If false teachers proclaim their views in God's name—for example, preaching only the Gospel without calling people first to repentance, as did the false prophets in the days of Jeremiah—then God calls us to avoid them. But human nature wants to follow the majority, not adhere to the truth of God's Word. We want to walk by sight, not by faith. In other words, even in the Church, a realm that human reason says should be identified by harmony, the cross awaits us. After all, Jesus was rejected most fiercely by the religious leaders of the time. We live now in the Church militant; the Church triumphant in heaven is yet to come.

False teachers are popular because they speak nothing that is fundamentally opposed to the world, even when (or especially when) strict moral demands are made. The Law is no mystery to the world; the Gospel is. And yet the true Church does have God's solemn promises that it will not be conquered by all the hordes of Satan. Even this "little flock" is not without a helper, because the one true God, Jesus Christ, is its Shepherd. And He guides and protects us not from a distance, but He is presently governing His flock in and through His Word and Sacraments in the hands of His ministers, the pastors. These promises, not statistical charts, are our comfort under the cross in the Church until we are vindicated on the Last Day, when we will rise to life everlasting in heaven with all believers in Christ who have fought valiantly the good fight of faith on earth.

SPIRITUAL EXERCISES _____

◈ Resolve to arrive early for worship and to spend time in quiet reflection and prayer before and during the Divine Service (suggested Prayers for Worship are provided in the front flyleaf of *Lutheran Service Book*).

◈ The next time you visit someone in the hospital, take along a Bible and a hymnal in addition to cards and flowers. Use these books to comfort someone laboring under the cross.

◈ Meditate on the hymn "Thee We Adore, O Hidden Savior" (*LSB* 640). Contemplate the rich imagery of Christ providing us "living food" by giving us His body and His blood in the Sacrament.

POINT TO REMEMBER _____

For since, in the wisdom of God, the world did not know God through wisdom, it pleased God through the folly of what we preach to save those who believe. *1 Corinthians 1:21*

God Tests; the Devil Tempts

Thus the sailor at last still clings
To the cliff which was to destroy him.
Torquato Tasso (J.W. v. Goethe)[8]

Based on God's Word (James 1:13), in his Small Catechism Luther teaches: "God indeed tempts no one."[9] However, there are several passages in Scripture that speak about God testing His holy people, either individually or as a group. Does this mean there are two types of testing: one being done by the devil, the world, and our sinful flesh (temptation) and the other being done by God? Are these tests different, and, if so, how can we tell them apart? And if God tests us, where can we flee for refuge?

"GOD TESTED ABRAHAM . . ." _____

Perhaps the most famous of God's tests is His command to Abraham to sacrifice Isaac (Genesis 22). As human beings, we try to raise moral objections and we try to look at things logically, after all, why would

---

8   Translation by the author of this chapter.
9   *Concordia*, p. 337.

God now demand the life of the very child He had promised to Abraham and through whom God would establish His covenant (see Genesis 17:21)? Yet Abraham does not object to God's plan. Instead, the next morning Abraham gathers the wood and fire and the offering (Isaac) and heads out for the mountain.

According to the author of the Epistle to the Hebrews, Abraham "considered that God was able even to raise him from the dead" (11:19). The promise of the resurrection of the dead comforted and strengthened Abraham for the horrible task before him. The trial revealed that Abraham clung to God's promise by faith; he "feared the Lord," even above his beloved son. This faith made Abraham confident that he and the boy would return to the servants waiting at the bottom of the mountain. He did not worship Isaac as his idol, even though he loved him as his son.

As Abraham is ready to offer Isaac, the angel of the Lord halts the killing blow. And God provides the substitutionary ram (Genesis 22:13) for the sacrifice. This substitute points forward in time to Jesus Christ, the Lamb of God, God's own Son, the perfect Substitute whom the heavenly Father would sacrifice for the sins of the world. On His cross, Jesus took our place and suffered God's wrath for us. The God-man became our substitute. Isaac, the beloved son of Abraham, foreshadowed Jesus, the Father's beloved Son (Matthew 3:17).

Although the Lord's angel commends Abraham for his obedience, Abraham was not saved because he had passed this test. Holy Scripture clarifies that, concerning the promise of a son, Abraham "believed the LORD, and He counted it to him as righteousness" (Genesis 15:6). In all this, Abraham remained sinful by nature and at times he failed to believe in God. Therefore Abraham was unable to save himself. His astounding feat of obedience on the mountain was a direct fruit of his saving faith in the God who would provide (see Genesis 22:14). In addition to eternal salvation (which is by faith in the coming Messiah), God blesses Abraham and makes him the ancestor of the Messiah through whom the entire world would be blessed, that is, delivered from the curse of the Law (see Galatians 3:13–16).

Abraham trusted in God's promises: of a home in a new land, of a son, of a Savior. And God blessed Abraham. We, too, first need to believe in the Gospel, the good news concerning Christ our Savior from all sin, death, and the devil. As Paul writes: "For all the promises of God find their Yes in [Christ]" (2 Corinthians 1:20). The major distinction in God's Word is the distinction between Law and Gospel. The former promises certain death to the sinner; the latter promises life and salvation for Christ's sake. By the Holy Spirit's work through the Word, we believe the Law, that is, we accept its death sentence because of our sin. By the Holy Spirit's work through the Word, we believe the Gospel, that is, we accept God's judgment of "not guilty" because of the life, death, and resurrection of Jesus Christ. Compared to believing both the Law *and* the Gospel as God's Word, the rest of Scripture is actually easy to believe. Yet faith in Scripture's teaching is always brought about by the Holy Spirit, not by us. When we believe Scripture, we are dealing not with mere factual information (how the world was made or how long the flood lasted) but with how these facts are related to our salvation in Christ.

As "children of promise" (Galatians 4:28), we are the spiritual children of Abraham, related to him through faith in the same promise concerning the Messiah. We are begotten by the promise that our sins are forgiven. We are free from the curse of the law, and God's abundant blessing is ours for the sake of our substitutionary Lamb, Jesus Christ (Galatians 3:16, 26–29). Like Isaac, we will endure persecution from unbelievers. Flesh and spirit cannot be at peace, neither within (Galatians 5:17) nor without (Galatians 4:29). And we are always tempted to complete in the flesh what has been begun in us by the Spirit. We will always be tempted to slide back under the Law and make our salvation dependent on something we do in addition to what Christ has done— whether prayers, faith, devotion, suffering, or success in life.

GOD'S PURPOSE IN TESTING HIS SAINTS _____

Why does God test His saints? The scriptural answer is to reveal what is in our hearts. And this revelation is not for God, but it is for us. God's tests function like a mirror or, as we might also say, as the Law. They reveal what is inside of us. Upon examination, the natural human is governed by a basic logic: the good are rewarded and the bad are punished. This is the logic of the Law, which was implanted in man's heart from creation. It is the foundation of human society and of all world religions.

Many churches and books advertise Christianity as the best world religion, that is, the most reliable way to achieve worldly success and influence. But genuine Christianity is different. It teaches from God's Word that, just because we are saved and strive to follow the crucified Christ in all things, this does not mean things will work out in this life.

As we live under our crosses, it is a tremendous comfort to know that our salvation does not depend on either our holiness or on our success in life. We are free from the Law.

God's tests can take the form of abundant material or spiritual blessing: an abundant harvest, a long-awaited child (Abraham and Sarah!), even progress in conquering sin or adding new members to our congregation. If we were all spirit, such blessings would offer no challenge for us. We would receive them as what they are: undeserved gifts of our heavenly Father for Christ's sake. Such blessings would not come between us and God. God could withhold them at any time and we would still love and fear and trust in Him for the sake of the Gospel's gift of eternal salvation. At least in Genesis 22, Abraham was free from sinful attachment to the gifts of God: he loved Isaac, but he feared the Lord. In the freedom that comes with faith, Abraham was ready to give up this precious gift at the Giver's command, trusting that God would raise Isaac again.

When God initially promised him a son, Abraham boldly believed God's unreasonable, laughable promise concerning an heir (see Genesis 15). But Abraham later wavered because he looked away from God's promise to his own and to Sarah's advanced age. So Abraham sought other solutions and eventually had a son with Sarah's maidservant, Hagar (Genesis 16). Thus we see that just like us, Abraham was a sinner, who by nature doubted and rejected God's Word and promise. He was more impressed by God's gifts than by what he heard from God in His Word. Faith lives on God's Word of promise, which will sound particularly joyful, albeit unrealistic, in trials. If we turn away from the promises God makes in His Word, we go it alone and are lost.

Just as the Israelites were led into a desert hostile to life, so are we being tested by the hardships of this life. We see little of anything good except God's promise, so the question is: Will we cling to God and His promise, or will we doubt and rebel? And lest we think that testing comes only in the form of deprivation, testing also happens when we are blessed financially or otherwise. Such blessings can become our idols, or we can begin to think we deserve such blessings as a reward for our great work of believing—which is also a sin against the First Commandment as we place our work ahead of Christ's. God's purpose in testing is to lead us to know our hearts, to save us from spiritual arrogance, and to lead us to the unchanging Gospel to strengthen or renew our faith.

On the other hand, Satan's temptations always seek to separate us from the Gospel by leading us either into carnal security or into despair. *Carnal security* means that we are led not to repentance, but to belief that sin does not matter, since "God loves everybody just the way they are." *Despair* means that we are led to believe not that our sins are forgiven by God for Christ's sake, but that our sins are too serious to be forgiven. And Satan compounds this despair by leading us to believe that our difficult, humble life indicates that God has forsaken us. (Satan's temptations of Job were continued through the speeches of his legalistic friends!) Satan's temptations confuse Law and Gospel, while in His testing God properly applies the Law's mirror to lead sinners to the Gospel. God cannot lie or deceive; even when He tests us, He works for our eternal salvation.

"LEAD US NOT INTO TEMPTATION"— TEMPTATION AND PRAYER

Jesus Christ taught His Christians to pray: "Lead us not into temptation" (Matthew 6:13). But we are not asking God not to tempt us (the petition does not read, "Tempt us not"). Part and parcel of God's will for Christians to be under the cross is to strengthen our reliance on the unchanging Gospel in Word and Sacraments as compared with the perishing goods of this world, which include our own strength.

In this petition, we pray that God would protect us so that we are not deceived and misled from the Gospel "into false belief, despair, and other great shame and vice."[10] The "deceivers" are not just on the outside; we cannot blame it all on the devil. Our sinful nature remains one of his powerful allies as it contributes its powerful and confusing seductions.

Cross-bearing, including resisting multiple temptations, is hard work for our faith. We will start huffing and puffing. Where do Christians catch their breath from serving God and neighbor, including finding time for prayer? We catch our breath only in the Gospel. There the Holy Spirit breathes new life into our hearts; we then breathe out that same Spirit in prayer to our Father through His Son, Jesus Christ. But prayer is not some type of miracle drug that delivers from temptation and trial. It is not true that, if we pray sincerely enough or long enough, God will change His mind. Prayer cannot force God's hand. However, praying that the good and gracious will of our heavenly Father would

---

10 SC III; *Concordia*, p. 337.

be done expresses faith's passivity that looks to God's gracious activity and will for all good things.

SPIRITUAL EXERCISES

◈ When tested by God, turn to the Gospel and prayer.

◈ When tempted by the devil, turn to the Gospel and prayer.

◈ Meditate on the hymn "When in the Hour of Deepest Need" (*LSB* 615). Spend time laying all your woes (stanza 4) before God in prayer.

POINT TO REMEMBER

God is faithful, and He will not let you be tempted beyond your ability, but with the temptation He will also provide the way of escape, that you may be able to endure it. *1 Corinthians 10:13*

The Purpose of Our Cross

Christ will crown the cross-bearers.
Johann Sebastian Bach[11]

Today, as ever, suffering and hardship without limits are usually regarded as pointless. Certainly, we may believe that a certain degree of hardship builds character. But too much suffering seems to do the opposite. Experience teaches us that unbounded suffering destroys people, often in a senseless fashion. The cross, in whatever shape God might send it, hurts. But in the shadow of the cross, the light of the Gospel shines brightly. We have already seen that God sets limits around suffering in this life. Continuing in that line of thought, Luther pointed out that in afflictions we will realize how sweet the Gospel really is and become better theologians for it. The more the Holy Spirit is at work in us to strengthen and mature our faith, the clearer it becomes that God works good through bad all the time—He kills by the Law to make alive by the Gospel.

---

11 An inscription written beneath Canon BWV 1077. Translated by the author of this chapter.

THE IMAGE OF HIS SON

In Scripture, the "image of God" means that man looked like God spiritually, not physically. Therefore, Adam and Eve, who were created in God's image, knew God and His will perfectly and lived accordingly in relationship to Him and His creation. Theirs was "original righteousness": they did God's will with ease, by nature. After the fall, this image was lost. Original righteousness and natural integrity were lost and replaced by original sin and natural corruption. God's image was replaced by Adam's image.

God's image, lost in the fall, is restored in us through Baptism when original sin is not removed but is forgiven along with all other sins. This is when we are adopted as sons of God (Romans 8:15). The image of God is first restored by imputation as God declares us righteous and holy for Christ's sake. Through faith in Him, all knowledge and wisdom of God is ours. In the new heaven and the new earth, the image of God will be restored in full actuality and life because the corruption of original sin will have been removed at death or on the Last Day.

The image of the Son is not different from the image of God. The Son *is* God. Suffering helps shape this image as it trains us in Christlike patience and perseverance (Romans 8:29). In other words, what is imputed to us by faith also shapes our life. By faith in Christ, we are perfectly patient under our crosses because Christ's perfect patience is credited to us. Yet through the Means of Grace our lives now also can become Christlike and patient, though at times this might mean that we will look like the "man of sorrows" (Isaiah 53:3; John 19:5) before our bodies will be glorified like His. This is not a loveless search for apparent "Christian" glory (1 Corinthians 13:3), nor is it a way to earn merit before God. The power to be patient does not come from our suffering (or from following the examples of Christ and His saints) as if it were a payment based on the Law. Instead, the power to be patient comes as a free gift of the Gospel. When faith is exercised in love (including patience, the passive form of love) then there needs to be a source of faith, which is the Gospel in Word and Sacraments. Suffering causes us to despair of our own powers and seek refuge in God's strength, which is made available to faith in the Gospel.

In solidarity with all of God's creation, Christians suffer because our first parents, Adam and Eve, fell away from God and brought His deadly curse upon the entire world. Christ does away with this curse, and in the Gospel He brings us blessing. Yet this does not take away from the believer the temporal consequences of sin, including disease, failing families, hardships, and physical death. These afflictions shape our prayers; often we will lament and groan to God under the burdens we and fellow creatures bear. It is most important to remember that it is the Spirit who brings our prayers to God's throne; we do not have the power to do that. The Spirit is available only in the Gospel, which gives us rest from our labors and new breath to cry: "Abba, Father" (Romans 8:15; Galatians 4:6).

According to Hebrews 12:7, one purpose of affliction is discipline. Limited hardship can lead to a more responsible path. As we experience some of the temporal consequences of our sins, God reminds us of our sinfulness and sin's fruits. He thereby reminds us of our constant need for His forgiveness and thus keeps us close by the Gospel. When disciplined, we should seek God's forgiveness and the strengthening of our faith in the Gospel. Then our zeal is renewed to struggle against sin and to please our heavenly Father. Christ's righteousness and obedient endurance is already ours by faith, but our lives now ought to become more like His as well. By reminding us gently (when compared to eternal death in hell) of our ongoing need for forgiveness and by thus leading us to the Gospel, God works in us a greater outward conformity to Christ. God's discipline is a fruit of His love, whereas His punishment grows out of His wrath and therefore affects those outside of Christ. Yet God's punishment also seeks to lead the sinner to the Gospel.

God's grace is indeed sufficient for us because it forgives us all sin and offers the hope of resurrection and ultimate deliverance from all evil. Christians live by God's Word alone and thereby follow Christ's example. Obviously, what is true by faith in Christ is not yet fully evident in this life. Our faith is weak and it struggles against sinful unbelief. Christ's image is being shaped in our lives to conform us to Him more and more. Suffering aids in this process as it weans us from this perishing world and directs us to God's imperishable Word. The power to benefit from suffering in a godly manner comes from the Gospel alone.

REFRESHMENT UNDER THE CROSS: BAPTISM AND THE LORD'S SUPPER

Baptism holds the sure promise of suffering and cross-bearing with Christ. This promise is inseparably united with the promise conveying Christ's cross-earned forgiveness to you. However, this is not the full picture and comfort Baptism offers, for it also conveys God's sure promise that, as we have suffered here with Jesus, we will also live with Him in heavenly glory. So long as we live, Baptism's promise is there for us.

Baptism is by no means the only comforting "rod and staff" God provides for those traveling through life's dark valleys. The promises concerning our forgiveness in Christ, as we read them in Scripture and as they sound forth in the Divine Service, are important too. And we find the greatest comfort in the Lord's Supper. Here not only the promise of forgiveness is applied individually, but we are given the assurance that we are not alone as we walk by faith, and we are sealed to Christ by His very body and blood. The Lord's Supper is a saving foretaste of the endless marriage feast of the Lamb, while in this life the cup of salvation is tied to the cup first drunk by Jesus on the cross. Further, we enjoy earthly fellowship with other believers with whom we commune.

As Baptism has connected us to Christ's death and resurrection, we shall also be raised in glory with our Head, Jesus Christ. Here we suffer with Christ; in heaven we shall be glorified with Him. Whenever we remember our Baptism, this cooling breeze from eternity gives us new breath in the heat of the battle against sin, temptation, and despair. Christ describes His own suffering and death as a baptism, a submerging that kills. By God's grace, our suffering makes us more patient because it holds down the old Adam (who does not like to suffer) until he is finally destroyed in our ultimate suffering, that is, in physical death.

When Jesus instituted His Supper, He spoke of the future meal in heaven with those who would believe in Him on earth. A wedding supper awaits us after we have shared Christ's cups of pain and salvation here on earth in faith. In the new heaven and new earth we will have glorified bodies, like Christ's body following His resurrection. Christ Himself ate after His resurrection to prove to His disciples that He was not a ghost but their Savior who has not shed His human body. We, too, will have real, resurrected bodies that can eat and drink, even though they will not need food or drink. As a result, when we suffer in the body, when our bodies are disfigured by disease or accident, we can look forward to that day when our bodies will be made new.

COMFORT UNDER THE CROSS: PREDESTINATION

At times, God's saints undergo extreme trials. If such calamity strikes us, we might fear to lose faith and forsake our Savior. God's Word contains great comfort in this troublesome situation. First, it teaches that faith is not the same as frail human willpower or optimism. Faith is brought about and sustained exclusively by God the Holy Spirit by means of the Gospel in Word and Sacraments. Christian faith is faith in Christ as our one Savior from all sin, death, and the devil. Further, God's Word teaches that Christians are recognized by bearing their crosses patiently as they follow their crucified Lord; thus suffering is not a sign of being forsaken by God.

There also is Scripture's wonderful teaching on predestination or eternal election. This doctrine confirms that we are saved by God's grace alone, apart from anything in us (including happiness and prosperity). It teaches that before the world was even made, God chose to save us in Christ. He did so because of Christ's life and death and He effected it through the Gospel in Word and Sacraments. We will be saved indeed, even through many tribulations. We know that we are God's elect children by faith in the Gospel of Jesus Christ. Through the Means of Grace, God provides the strength we need to hold onto Christ by faith.

The doctrine of predestination teaches that God chose us in Christ before the foundation of the world (Romans 8:28–30). Furthermore, this doctrine specifies that this adoption and salvation through Christ takes place in time by means of the Holy Spirit creating faith through the Means of Grace. For those called according to God's eternal election, all things, even suffering, will work for our eternal salvation as we, according to our callings, lead holy lives. This will of God cannot be frustrated. The elect will be preserved unto eternal life. God will strengthen our faith through the Gospel, and by faith in the Gospel we will also know that we are God's saints who cannot be separated from His love in Christ because we are elected in Christ in eternity to be saved in time through God's Word.

Actual steadfastness in trial and under the cross gives evidence of the presence of God's Spirit in us. Therefore, it affords additional comfort under the cross because it shows to us that our faith is genuine and not a delusion.

SPIRITUAL EXERCISES _____

◈ Study and meditate on the following passages of Scripture, which teach your eternal predestination to salvation by faith in Christ's Gospel: Romans 8:18–39; 2 Peter 1:3–11; Ephesians 1:3–9, 11–14.

◈ Meditate on the hymn "If God Himself Be for Me" (*LSB* 724). Rejoice in the warm and bright confidence you have in the "sun that cheers [your] spirit," Jesus Christ (stanza 10).

◈ Listen to *St. Matthew Passion* by J. S. Bach. Follow the emotional arc of being deeply saddened by our readiness to run away with Christ's disciples, to being truly relieved from this sin because Christ willingly bore the cross for us, to being eager and ready to receive our cross out of the hands of our crucified and risen Lord.

POINT TO REMEMBER _____

For those whom He foreknew He also predestined to be conformed to the image of His Son, in order that He might be the firstborn among many brothers. *Romans 8:29*

Lutheran Teaching on the Cross

As outlined in the introduction to this chapter, the cross in the life of the Christian was discussed by the first Lutherans in the sixteenth century. In the Roman Church, self-imposed, self-chosen afflictions had become one of the ways people were taught to cooperate in their salvation. Lutherans rejected the idea that a person could cooperate in his or her salvation (either actively by doing good or passively by suffering evil) because pointing people to their works at this point confuses Law and Gospel. This confusion infringes on what Christ has accomplished by His active and passive obedience and makes man's salvation uncertain ("Have I suffered enough and with the right attitude?").

WE TEACH, BELIEVE, AND CONFESS—THE CROSS

Paul also says, "I discipline my body and keep it under control" (1 Corinthians 9:27). Here he clearly shows that he was keeping his body under control, not to merit forgiveness of sins by that discipline, but to keep his body in subjection and prepared for spiritual things, for carrying out the duties of his calling. Therefore, we do not condemn fasting in itself [Isaiah 58:3–7], but the traditions that require certain days and certain meats, with peril of conscience, as though such works were a necessary service. (AC XXVI 37–39; *Concordia*, p. 53)

God's precepts, and God's true service, are hidden when people hear that only monks are in a state of perfection. True Christian perfection is to fear God from the heart, to have great faith, and to trust that for Christ's sake we have a God who has been reconciled [2 Corinthians 5:18–19]. It means to ask for and expect from God His help in all things with confident assurance that we are to live according to our calling in life, being diligent in outward good works, serving in our calling. (AC XXVII 49; *Concordia*, p. 57)

The Ten Commandments require outward civil works, which reason can in some way produce. But they also require other things placed far above reason: truly to fear God, truly to love God, truly to call upon God, truly to be convinced that God hears us, and to expect God's aid in death and in all afflictions. Finally, the Law requires obedience to God, in death and all afflictions, so that we may not run from these commandments or refuse them when God lays them upon us. (Ap IV [II] 8; *Concordia*, p. 83)

The difference between this faith and the righteousness of the Law can be easily discerned. Faith is the divine service (*latreia*) that receives the benefits offered by God. The righteousness of the Law is the divine service (*latreia*) that offers to God our merits. God wants to be worshiped through faith so that we receive from Him those things He promises and offers. . . . For faith justifies and saves, not because it is a worthy work in itself, but only because it receives the promised mercy. (Ap IV [II] 49, 56; *Concordia*, p. 89)

Job is excused though he was not troubled by past evil deeds [Job 2:3–10]. Therefore, troubles are not always punishments or signs of wrath. Indeed, terrified consciences should be taught that there are more important purposes for afflictions [2 Corinthians 12:9], so that they do not think God is rejecting them when they see nothing but God's punishment and anger in troubles. The other more important purposes are to be considered, that is, that God is doing His strange work so that He may be able to do His own work, as Isaiah 28 teaches in a long speech. . . . Therefore, troubles are not always punishments for certain past deeds, but they are God's works, intended for our benefit, and that God's power might be made more apparent in our weakness. (Ap XIIb [VI] 61, 63 [158, 160]; *Concordia*, p. 181)

If we would be Christians, therefore, we must surely expect and count on having the devil with all his angels and the world as our enemies [Matthew 25:41; Revelation 12:9]. They will bring every possible misfortune and grief upon us. For where God's Word is preached, accepted, or believed and produces fruit, there the holy cross cannot be missing [Acts 14:22]. And let no one think that he shall have peace [Matthew 10:34]. He must risk whatever he has upon earth—possessions, honor, house and estate, wife and children, body and life. Now, this hurts our flesh and the old Adam [Ephesians 4:22]. The test is to be steadfast and to suffer with patience [James 5:7–8] in whatever way we are assaulted, and to let go whatever is taken from us [1 Peter 2:20–21]. (LC III 65–66; *Concordia*, p. 416)

To feel temptation is, therefore, a far different thing from consenting or yielding to it. We must all feel it, although not all in the same way. Some feel it in a greater degree and more severely than others. For example, the young suffer especially from the flesh. Afterward, when they reach middle life and old age, they feel it from the world. But others who are occupied with spiritual matters, that is, strong Christians, feel it from the devil. Such feeling, as long as it is against our will and we would rather be rid of it, can harm no one. For if we did not feel it, it could not be called a temptation. But we consent to it when we give it the reins and do not resist or pray against it. (LC III 107–108; *Concordia*, p. 421)

The act or ceremony is this: we are sunk under the water, which passes over us, and afterward are drawn out again. These two parts, (a) to be sunk under the water and (b) drawn out again, signify Baptism's power and work. It is nothing other than putting to death the old Adam and effecting the new man's resurrection after that [Romans 6:4–6]. Both of these things must take place in us all our lives. So a truly Christian life is nothing other than a daily Baptism, once begun and ever to be continued. For this must be done without ceasing, that we always keep purging away whatever belongs to the old Adam. . . . This is Baptism's true use among Christians, as signified by baptizing with water. Therefore, where this is not done, the old man is left unbridled. He continually becomes stronger. That is not using Baptism, but working against Baptism. (LC IV 65, 68; *Concordia*, pp. 429–30)

WITNESS
We Share Our Faith[1]

A s Lutherans, we affirm that sharing our faith with others is an integral part of our Christian existence in this world. This activity remains with us even as the Church enlists certain individuals for outreach projects close to home or overseas. In this chapter, we hope to encourage among Lutherans a broader commitment to share their faith in whatever callings the Lord has placed them.

What motivates Christians to share their faith? Would it not be better to remain silent and leave it to experts such as the pastor or elders? Paul reminded the congregation in Ephesus that they who were once in darkness were now "light in the Lord" (Ephesians 5:8). Paul did not mean to suggest a passive existence as a believer in Christ. Rather, he encourages the Ephesians as they live their lives as children of light (verse 8). Just as a flashlight brings light to darkness, Christians also light up the world around them through their witness and exemplary lifestyle. This concept of "light" should sound familiar. In the Sermon on the Mount, Jesus called His disciples to be salt and light to the world so that through their good deeds people might come to praise God in heaven (Matthew 5:13–16).

Our world desperately needs to hear about our Christian faith and see it at work. We have been given new and eternal life through Christ's death on the cross and His resurrection. Filled with the joy of our own

---

1   Adapted from *The Lutheran Spirituality Series: Witness*, written by Klaus Detlev Schulz, edited by Robert C. Baker. Copyright © 2007 Concordia Publishing House.

salvation (1 Peter 2:9), we are enabled to share the Good News about what Christ did, not only for us but also for others (John 3:16). Wherever and whenever the opportunity arises for us to witness about Christ to those who are without our Savior, we do so without compulsion but joyously and voluntarily, enabled by the new life granted by the Holy Spirit.

To an extent, Jesus serves also as our example. He alone is our righteousness and has attained our right standing before God. But just as Jesus' attitude was oriented toward the spiritual well-being of His human creatures, so we, too, willingly and voluntarily embrace sharing our God-given faith with others.

In order that our light might never go out but instead enlighten the world around us, our faith needs to be nurtured through regular attendance at church, where we receive the Word and the Sacraments. Baptism gives us our birthright as God's children, and His Word and Christ's Supper strengthen and nourish our faith for an active witness. We do not witness to our faith in order that we might gain glory for ourselves, but that all glory may be given to Christ, our Lord (Philippians 2:10–11).

Salvation to the Ends of the Earth

The noblest and greatest work and the most important service we can perform for God on earth is bringing other people, and especially those who are entrusted to us, to the knowledge of God by the holy Gospel. *Martin Luther*[2]

In today's hectic world, with numerous pressing needs and endless responsibilities, we sometimes forget that many people do not know Christ. Our horizon needs to be expanded and our awareness of others heightened. That is why we begin this chapter on witnessing our faith by looking first at the Old Testament. There we read about God's creation of the world and His establishment of the nation of Israel. There we also learn that God's purposes for humanity extend through Israel

---

2   Ewald M. Plass, comp., *What Luther Says* (St. Louis: Concordia, 1959), 958 (no. 3010).

to people of many races and social settings—to all "Gentiles." He is the one true God, who rules over all creation and who is intent on bringing His salvation to the entire world. Our witness builds on the understanding that we have an obligation and privilege to bring God's fallen human creatures back to their Creator: Father, Son, and Holy Spirit.

When we lose sight of the needs of others, we can begin to refocus by reestablishing our priorities—both at home and at work. Quite often this is a time-management issue. For anything we consider worthwhile—whether relationships, job performance, or volunteer activities—we simply have to make the time.

GOD OF ALL NATIONS

In the Old Testament, we learn that Israel understood herself as God's nation, for whom He performed His wonderful and mighty deeds. God's covenant relationship with the people of Israel prefigures Christ's special relationship with the new Israel, Christ's Church. God rescued the Israelites from bondage under the heavy hand of Pharaoh. He also did not forsake His people even after their exile in Babylon. With Ezra and Nehemiah, the remnant returned to the land and Israel was restored as a nation once again.

God revealed His will to His people through Moses on Mount Sinai. While the Israelites strove to follow God's will and Law, many times they were unsuccessful. They did not always succeed in demonstrating a holiness separate from all other nations, even though God commanded Israel repeatedly not to mingle with them (see Deuteronomy 4:32–34; Nehemiah 13:23–27). Nevertheless, on some occasions, outsiders were received into Israel's midst upon fulfillment of certain conditions. For example, when the Israelites left Egypt, some Egyptians who sought protection from the plague (Exodus 9:20) joined the Israelites in their exodus (Exodus 12:37–38). Later, Joshua commanded that Rahab and her family be welcomed into the Israelite camp following the destruction of Jericho because of her protection of the spies (Joshua 6:25). Foreigners were assimilated into Israel after being circumcised. It also was expected that they would follow the Law. These same conditions were placed on Jewish proselytes up till the early New Testament period (consider the story of Peter and the God-fearer Cornelius in Acts 10). The point is that the Israelites had other people come into their midst who were not directly of their biological descent.

But no sooner did God dramatically rescue His people than they participated in idolatrous worship. God's Old Testament people often sinfully and selfishly turned away from Him. This is seen clearly in the golden calf apostasy, which consisted not only in the worship of false gods (Exodus 32:4, 8) but also in the blending of pagan worship with the worship of the one true God (Exodus 32:5). At times, Israel focused on her own special rights at the expense of seeing herself as God's holy nation and a blessing for all other nations. However, God always showed patience with His nation, even after the incident of the golden calf. This reveals that God rebukes and punishes sin and then forgives the repentant sinner.

In the Old Testament, we see that God is the only God of the entire world. The narrative of creation shows us a God who created the universe and everything in it (Genesis 1:1). This is the earth on which all nations live, not just the nation of Israel. Yahweh is the only God; therefore, He is Lord of all creation (Isaiah 45:18).

God does not ignore the nations who reject Him as God either through their worship or through their moral misconduct. The story of Sodom and Gomorrah is a powerful lesson (see Genesis 18:16–19:27). It shows both how God judges sin that is too grievous to tolerate and how He listens to the fervent prayers of believers who beg for mercy for those who do not deserve it.

GOD'S SALVIFIC WILL

God's desire to extend His salvation to all nations is beautifully expressed in Isaiah 49:6: "I will make you as a light for the nations, that My salvation may reach to the end of the earth." The phrase "to the end of the earth" means that God's desire is to save all nations. God uses a similar expression when He calls Abraham and promises that in him "all the families of the earth shall be blessed" (Genesis 12:3; cf. Exodus 19:5–6). Through Abraham and ultimately through his Seed, Jesus Christ, God's blessings will extend to all nations. The prophet Isaiah announces that "the time is coming to gather all nations and tongues. And they shall come and shall see My [the Lord's] glory" (66:18).

The references to "salvation" and "blessing" in Genesis 12:3 and Isaiah 49:6 are best interpreted through what Christ has done for us on the cross. When Abraham was called to be a blessing, he was also blessed by God with a wealthy life with numerous animals and servants. Eventually he was blessed with the child of promise, Isaac. However,

God's blessings are more than temporal blessings. Christ as Savior brings eternal life, and that is the fuller understanding of "blessing" in the Old Testament. Abraham's faith was reckoned to him as righteousness (Romans 4). That righteousness is the same for all people. The Church is the place where the blessings of salvation are bestowed, that is, where the forgiveness of our sins, life, and salvation are distributed. Our witness to those outside the Church can, when God wills, be the prelude to them receiving these blessings within the Church as baptized believers and within your congregation as members.

GOD USES PEOPLE SUCH AS ABRAHAM AND JACOB

God used His prophets and messengers to share His will with the people of Israel and the neighboring nations. Isaiah 49:6 speaks of the Suffering Servant (Jesus Christ) becoming the light for the nations. Through the Suffering Servant and through individuals such as Abraham (Genesis 12:14–16), Jacob (Genesis 35:2), and each of us, God enlightens people outside of Israel. Luther notes:

> He [God] chases them back and forth not only for their sake, in order to prove their faith, but also so that they may be useful to other people. Abraham certainly could not remain silent, and he did not consider himself unfit to preach to the people of God's mercy. . . . God acts in wonderful ways on earth; he sends apostle and preacher to people before they themselves perceive or in anyway think about it.[3]

Next to Abraham and Jacob, Jonah, the prophet to the Gentiles in Nineveh, may come to mind. Recalling these biblical individuals helps us see how God's plan to bring salvation and reconciliation to the nations takes on human flesh through real people.

Light is a common theme in Scripture, and it helps us to visualize our own witness. Light means safety and order in contrast to danger and chaos. Jesus Himself tells us: "You are the light of the world. . . . Let your light shine before others, so that they may see your good works and give glory to your Father who is in heaven" (Matthew 5:14, 16).

---

3   Volker Stolle, *The Church Comes from All Nations*, trans. by Klaus Detlev Schulz (St. Louis: Concordia, 2003), 16.

SPIRITUAL EXERCISES _____

◈ Meditate on each stanza of "The God of Abraham Praise" (*LSB* 798). Give thanks to God that, through Holy Baptism, you have been grafted into Christ and thus are an heir to the promises God made to Abraham.

◈ In thanksgiving to God for His mercy extended to the Gentiles through faith in His Son, Jesus Christ, read Romans 3:21–5:11.

◈ Commit to memory Luther's Table Blessings in the Small Catechism (*Concordia*, p. 345). Pray them before and after meals.

POINT TO REMEMBER _____

I will bless those who bless you, and him who dishonors you I will curse, and in you all the families of the earth shall be blessed. *Genesis 12:3*

Rooted in Christ's Ministry

After we have learned to know God in His Son and have received the forgiveness of sins and the Holy Spirit, who endues hearts with joy and with the peace of soul by which we look with contempt on sin and death, what remains to be done? Go, and do not be silent. You are not the only one to be saved; the remaining multitude of men should also be preserved. *Martin Luther*[4]

Those who wonder what to witness about need only look to Jesus as the content of their message. We cannot speak of the Church's witness to the world without being reminded that the Lord Jesus Christ prepared the way for us to do so. Our witness is anchored in His ministry on earth that continues through His Church. We can trace the wonderful deeds of God through His Son, Jesus Christ, whom He sent to preach, teach, heal, raise, and absolve. Through Jesus' life, death, and resurrection He reconciled the world to Himself. The exemplary life Jesus lived on our behalf, His sufferings and death on the cross for our forgiveness, and His glorious resurrection for our justification are the

---

4   Plass, *What Luther Says*, 960 (no. 3019).

content of our message. While many will be saved by this Gospel, others will take offense at what we say (1 Corinthians 1:23).

JESUS CHRIST SENT TO THE WORLD _____

In the Old Testament, we read about God sending prophets to the world. Motivated by His love for the entire world, God sent His Son so that no one would perish (John 3:16). Thus we call Jesus "the Sent One" from God, and when Jesus spoke of His ministry on earth, He often referred to Himself as being sent by the Father. In a similar way, Christ sent His apostles to continue His ministry of preaching the Word. The Church today—including all believers—is sent as well. The Greek word used for God's sending of Jesus is rendered into Latin as *mission*, which is the same as our English word *mission*. *Mission* simply means "sending." The motif of "sending" is found throughout the Gospel of John and many other books in the Bible.

According to Galatians 4, Jesus was "born under the law" for us (verse 4; see additional legal language in John 3:16–17, which includes words such as *perish* and *condemn*). Christ came into this world to redeem those "under the law" (Galatians 4:5), which should be explained in two ways. First, Christ came to this world to obey the Law in everything it demands. We were obliged to fulfill it, but because we could not, Christ came in our place as a perfect fulfillment of what God desires from us. Second, the Law is a curse over all those who fail to fulfill it. That curse is the wrath of God. Jesus also came to the world to bear the full brunt of God's wrath toward us on the cross. Only Christ could fulfill the Law's demands, and He was the only human who could bear the curse of the Law that was directed against all humanity. Christ's ministry, His perfect, obedient life, and His bitter sufferings and death were performed on our behalf (vicariously) so that we are redeemed and "receive adoption as sons" (Galatians 4:5). And with the Holy Spirit who has been sent into our hearts, we are able to cry "Abba! Father!" (verse 6).

With Christ's coming and fulfillment of the Law, our relationship with the Law has changed. The Law's condemnation over all believers has been removed. That does not imply that we are no longer obedient to the will of God as expressed in His Law. In fact, Galatians 5:13–14 summarizes many laws into one commandment, the law of love, which we are obligated to obey. As we obey the Law, we do so not with the intention of fulfilling it in order to earn God's salvation. That would make us slaves of the Law. The Law has already been accomplished for us through Christ's perfect life and His vicarious death on the cross. He lived and died on our behalf. Rather, we follow the Law out of gratitude, because God desires it according to His immutable will.[5] The Law no longer separates believers as Jews were once separated from Gentiles (Galatians 3:28). Through faith in Christ, all are one in Christ. Therefore, Christians should not set up human laws that bar others from membership in Christ's Church.

HERE AM I!

We defined the word *mission* as "sending." And when we consider this word, it may bring to mind exotic places and faraway lands—not a personal or local effort to share the Good News. In the Old Testament, God called numerous people to speak for Him. Among the most famous callings are of Moses and Isaiah, but they represent two different responses. Moses expresses concern that he is not qualified to speak for the Lord: "Who am I that I should go to Pharaoh and bring the children of Israel out of Egypt?" (Exodus 3:11). On the other extreme, after he has been purified by the coal from the altar of the Lord, Isaiah answers boldly, "Here am I! Send me" to the Lord's question, "Whom shall I send, and who will go for Us?" (Isaiah 6:8).

Many years later, God sent His only Son, Jesus, to the world, but with more power and authority than the prophets (Matthew 12:41; John 12:45; Hebrews 1:1–2). Jesus not only says what God wants Him to say, but His person and His work also are integral parts of what He says. Jesus speaks with authority and demonstrates that the kingdom of God has come in His person (Mark 1:15). His preaching disclosed the will of God. He heals, forgives sins (Mark 2:5), and interprets the Law of the Old Testament (Mark 2:23–28; 7:15).

Obviously, there are differences between the sending of Christ (and His apostles) and our sending. Christians today are not eyewitnesses. Rather, we rely on the written testimony of what the apostles and others saw, heard, or wrote (Luke 1:1–4). The difference between our mission and Christ's mission certainly includes the fact that Christ as God's Son, and the apostles by Christ's blessing, performed miracles. In contrast, our witness relies on the power of God's Word and our prayers for those who are ill and in need of healing. Nevertheless, the goal of our mission is the same: to proclaim salvation through Jesus Christ.

---

5   See FC SD IV 16; *Concordia*, p. 549.

MANY ROOMS, ONE SAVIOR

Scripture frequently attests that Christ is the only way to salvation, so that all those who believe in Him will be saved (John 3:14–18; 11:25). This salvation is extended to all, since there are many rooms in the Father's house (John 14:2). Among other biblical metaphors, Jesus describes Himself as the Good Shepherd, who laid down His life for the sheep. He also has many other sheep who are not yet of His fold (John 10:11–16). In Galatians 4:4–7 Paul refers to those outside of Christ as "slaves," whereas in Christ believers are "sons" and "heirs" of God's kingdom. Through Christ, we find ourselves in a large family to which all who have faith in Christ belong.

The Church as a building with many rooms is a powerful and inviting biblical image, as is the description of believers as children of the same heavenly Father. All Christians are one in Christ and stand equally as sons and daughters before God their Father (Galatians 3:27–28; 4:6). This unique God-given relationship helps us interact with other members of Christ's Body.

SPIRITUAL EXERCISES

◈ Meditate on the hymn "Dear Christians, One and All, Rejoice" (*LSB* 556).

◈ Commit to memory Galatians 4:4–5:

> But when the fullness of time had come, God sent forth His Son, born of woman, born under the law, to redeem those who were under the law, so that we might receive adoption as sons.

Rejoice that not only did Christ through His sacrificial death upon the cross satisfy God's demand for justice for you, but He also fulfilled the Law in the flesh for you.

◈ Ask God to soften your heart toward those in your circle of relationships who do not yet know Jesus or who are unbaptized. Pray daily for them. Ask God to grant you the opportunity, the courage, and the words to speak to them about your Savior.

POINT TO REMEMBER

> For God so loved the world, that He gave His only Son, that whoever believes in Him should not perish but have eternal life. For God did not send His Son into the world to condemn the world, but in order that the world might be saved through Him. *John 3:16–17*

Follow Me

> We live on earth for no other purpose than to be helpful to others. Otherwise it would be best for God to take away our breath and let us die as soon as we are baptized and have begun to believe. But He lets us live here in order that we may lead other people to believe, doing for them what He has done for us. *Martin Luther*[6]

Jesus sent His apostles from Jerusalem as witnesses to Judea and Samaria, and finally to the ends of the earth. The scope of their mission was outwardly focused. We call that the centrifugal motion of the Gospel. That is, the Gospel moves out from a central point to other locations. Luther compared this centrifugal aspect of the Gospel with a pebble falling into the water and causing waves in an outward, concentric motion.[7] Today, we need to see Jerusalem, Judea, Samaria, and the ends of the earth in our own context.

During His earthly ministry, Jesus sent out His disciples to the cities and villages of the land of Judea (see Luke 10). Then before He ascended to heaven, Jesus announced the Great Commission (Matthew 28:18–20; Mark 16:15–16; Luke 24:45–49; John 20:19–23). From these passages, the Church is commanded to preach and teach the Gospel of the forgiveness of sins in Christ alone and to baptize in the name of the triune God. The disciples did these activities under the authority of Jesus Christ. They were ambassadors in Christ's stead (2 Corinthians 5:20), having been sent into a world where no geographic boundaries apply.

Contemporary Christians, as members of a congregation, support this Great Commission when they enlist individuals to carry out the functions of preaching, teaching, and baptizing. Additionally, all Christians support this mission through their own witness within their own vocations. Every Christian has been called through Baptism to be a disciple of Christ, and sharing one's faith has a lot to do with understanding oneself as a disciple. Our Baptism affects our relationships with other Christians and with unbelievers. The secular world would have us focus on becoming rich in terms of assets or status. Such aspirations can get in the way of committing oneself to the task of witness and to living the Christian life. But as Christians share their faith, the Holy Spirit comes to their assistance and works faith in the hearts of those who hear their words about Jesus.

---

6   Plass, *What Luther Says*, 961 (no. 3021).
7   See Stolle, *Church Comes from All Nations*, 24–25.

LEAVE THINGS BEHIND AND ENDURE _____

Just as the call to repent and be baptized once went out through John the Baptist and Jesus Christ, and just as Christ called out to Levi, the son of Alphaeus (Mark 2:14), or to Philip to "follow Me" (John 1:43), Christians also are called through repentance and Baptism to follow Christ and become His disciples. The response is an act of obedience, and since Jesus calls, the Christian follows at once, as Levi did. By profession, many of Jesus' disciples were fishermen, and they were called by Christ to be "fishers of men."

Jesus made radical demands upon His first disciples, such as leaving behind all possessions and taking only a few things on their way (Matthew 10:9–10). This indicates that nothing should get between the disciple and Christ in terms of things that may distract us from our call. The willingness of Jesus' followers to share the Gospel is also to be motivated by love for the Lord (John 14:24), which allows them to make important adjustments to their lives without feeling coerced into doing so.

The story of Zacchaeus (Luke 19:1–9) demonstrates vividly how someone who is in the company of Jesus and believes in Him relates to his belongings and alters his moral standards. Previous to his meeting with Jesus, Zacchaeus was a dishonest tax collector. But when Jesus called him down from the sycamore, Zacchaeus's perspective changed. He announced, "Behold, Lord, the half of my goods I give to the poor. And if I have defrauded anyone of anything, I restore it fourfold" (Luke 19:8). Parting with half of one's property in response to the gift of faith may seem an exaggeration, but our thankfulness for forgiveness and eternal life knows no bounds. Paul and many other apostles and disciples left everything in order to follow Christ. Such choices were not made by human will, but they are brought about by the Holy Spirit at work in the heart of the forgiven and justified sinner to earnestly desire a change of life that reflects the change of heart.

Being justified before God by His grace through the gift of faith in Christ impacts one's relationship to the world and demands a lifestyle of nonconformity. Paul says that we are "to present [our] bodies as a living sacrifice" (Romans 12:1). This implies that everything we do should be done without blemish and fault and with total devotion to the cause of witness. Christians should exercise their minds and hearts in searching God's will recorded in Scripture, and then act according to it. In other words, being a Christian impacts every facet of one's life; it is holistic by implication.

The Lord who sends us has also left Himself as an example. Because we may suffer for being witnesses of Christ (1 Peter 2:21), Christians should be prepared to patiently endure the consequences of sharing their faith with others. We may be rebuked, discriminated against, or otherwise persecuted. While Scripture records only the martyrdom of Stephen (Acts 7:54–60) and James (Acts 12:2), reliable church histories note that Peter, Paul, and James, the brother of our Lord, were also martyred for the sake of Christ.[8] But in all our sufferings for the faith, we have the sure promise of Jesus: "Be faithful unto death, and I will give you a crown of life" (Revelation 2:10).

COME AND SEE

Even before the Great Commission, we see Jesus' disciples sharing their faith. For example, after Jesus called him, Philip went to find his friend Nathanael. And he shared the good news: "We have found Him of whom Moses in the Law and also the prophets wrote" (John 1:45). Although Nathanael doubted Philip's words, Philip invited his friend to "come and see" (John 1:46). The Samaritan woman by the well also invited her neighbors to "come and see" (John 4:29) Jesus at the well, who promised her water that would quench her thirst eternally (see John 4:13–15). We cannot invite people to come and see in quite the same way as Philip or this Samaritan woman could, but we can invite friends and family members to attend church with us. In the company of God's people, they will hear Jesus Christ proclaimed and see Him come to us in the Sacrament. He is present in Word and Sacrament to forgive, strengthen, encourage, and enable for service.

FROM JERUSALEM TO THE WORLD

In His final words before ascending into heaven, Jesus told His followers that they would be His witnesses "in Jerusalem and in all Judea and Samaria and to the end of the earth" (Acts. 1:8). The use of Jerusalem, Judea, and Samaria provides three significant dimensions in terms of scope of this witness: geographic, ethnic, and theological. Geographically

---

8   For information about other martyrs of the Church, such as Perpetua and Felicitas, see Ruth Tucker, *From Jerusalem to Iran Jaya* (Grand Rapids: Zondervan, 2004), 32–34.

and ethnically, Jerusalem was the place where Jesus finished His earthly work and where the remnant Jews would live, continuing to await their Savior. Judea-Samaria harkens back to the entire house of Israel under one king (Ezekiel 37:15–22), and it encourages the apostles to share the Gospel to the entire Israelite nation. Finally, the "ends of the earth" (Isaiah 49:6; Acts 13:47) means that the Gospel should reach all nations. Theologically, the Jewish nation would be in need of salvation just as all the "nations" (the Gentile world) would need to hear the Good News of salvation in Jesus Christ. If all of us could look back far enough, we would discover ancestors who knew nothing of God or of Christ. Thank God for the Gospel that was preached and shared to those who came before us and to us as well!

Today we do not necessarily need to think only in terms of geographic areas where we can share the message of salvation, but we can think also in terms of local situations. Are there local immigrant populations who may need to hear the Gospel? What about your next-door neighbor? How can you and your congregation reach out in your community to share the love of Jesus with the homeless, the elderly, people suffering from AIDS, or the poor? Christian care and Christian witness go hand in hand.

SPIRITUAL EXERCISES

◈ The *Evangelical Dictionary of World Missions*[9] notes that about 150,000 Christians are being martyred annually. By 2025, that figure is expected to increase to 600,000 Christian lives lost each year. Meditate on the hymn "Saints, See the Cloud of Witnesses" (*LSB* 667). Ask the Lord to give grace and strength to all who suffer or who are martyred in His name.

◈ Memorize Luther's explanation to the Second Petition of the Lord's Prayer (*Concordia*, p. 333).

◈ Pray the hymn "Take My Life and Let It Be" (*LSB* 783/784) with the request that God grant you the wisdom and strength to use you for His purposes.

POINT TO REMEMBER

But you will receive power when the Holy Spirit has come upon you, and you will be My witnesses in Jerusalem and in all Judea and Samaria, and to the end of the earth. *Acts 1:8*

---

9   Scott Moreau, gen. ed., *Evangelical Dictionary of World Missions* (Grand Rapids: Baker, 2000).

Witness Boldly

The Lord wants to say: You have received enough from Me—peace and joy and everything you ought to have; personally you need no more. Therefore work now, look at what I have done, and imitate it. My Father has sent Me into the world for your sake alone, in order to help you, not to benefit Myself. This I have done; I have died for you and have given you all I am and have. Therefore you should think and act in like manner. Henceforth spend your lives serving and helping everyone; otherwise you would have nothing to do on earth, for through faith you have enough of everything. Therefore I send you into the world as My Father has sent Me, that is, that every Christian may instruct and teach his fellow man also to come to Christ. *Martin Luther*[10]

It is important that we see the connection between our faith, heart, confession, and lifestyle (see Matthew 12:34; 15:18–19; Romans 10:9–10). Our justification leads to a sanctified life. As we discuss the call to witness in this world, Scripture reminds us that our lives as Christians are a complete package. In Christ, God gives us not only the right faith but also the right attitude and a willingness to witness. Finally, God also gives us the ability to say the right things. Faith is a God-given gift; it is trust in Christ alone. But faith in Christ cannot be divorced from a confession of Christ, which is expressed clearly and truthfully according to Scripture. One leads to the other. In addition, Scripture provides many examples of how such a confession is made. Most important, our witness of Christ comes from a joyful heart. This is not a "fuzzy" or "good" feeling about something, but Christian joy is an explicit sense of gratitude for what Christ has done for us.

Many Christians may not be able to "feel" joy at any particular moment, but they possess it nevertheless. The joy that we are talking about here is joy over *Heilsgewissheit,* that is, certainty concerning one's own salvation in Christ and being possessors of it. Christians may trust in the promises that God makes in His Word. Their sins are forgiven in Christ, and they are God's children.

CONFESS CHRIST WITH A BOLD HEART _____

The faith in our hearts and the confession of our lips are intimately connected. Although faith is God's gift of grace and is passively received,

---

10 Plass, *What Luther Says*, 960 (no. 3017).

it does not remain silent. Faith speaks about our Savior. Paul states that "the word is near you, in your mouth and in your heart (that is, the word of faith that we proclaim)" (Romans 10:8). Our witness flows naturally and without coercion from our hearts when they have been renewed by God's powerful Word. In his preface to Paul's Epistle to the Romans, Luther gave this well-known description of such an active faith:

> O it is a living, busy, active, mighty thing, this faith. It is impossible for it not to be doing good works incessantly. It does not ask whether good works are to be done, but before the question is asked, it has already done them, and is constantly doing them. . . . For through faith a man becomes free from sin and comes to take pleasure in God's commandments.[11]

In a sermon, a pastor once scolded his congregation members for the empty pews, which he said were a result of their failure to witness to others. That comment might have used fear and frustration to motivate the members to witness. In Scripture, and from Luther, we see that faith speaks from the heart, and not just from the mind. Because many evangelism programs have a tendency to be legalistic, we need to be aware that our motivation to share Jesus' love for others comes from His love for us. Such love flows from a righteous faith and thus takes pleasure in the will of the Lord. Luther's comment about an active faith sounds almost too good to be true, but a Christian can only do a God-pleasing work such as witness if he or she trusts in God.

When we think about the first confession of faith made in the New Testament, we naturally think of Peter. When Jesus asked him, "Who do you say that I am?" Peter replied, "You are the Christ, the Son of the living God" (Matthew 16:15–16). Our Lord praised the confession Peter made as one that was revealed to Peter by God the Father. That is, Peter's faith and confession did not arise out of his own natural ability to reason or to believe. Rather, both faith and confession were for him (and for us) gifts of the Holy Spirit through God's Word.

But as we all know, Peter was very human. Despite making such a beautiful (and the "first") confession, he later denied Jesus (see Matthew 26:69–75; Mark 14:66–72; Luke 22:54–62; John 18:15–18, 25–27). And later, the apostle Paul rebuked Peter concerning a false understanding of justification (see Galatians 2:11–21). If the doctrine of justification is misunderstood, then it will impact the behavior of Christians toward

---

11 AE 35:370, 371.

others. We have freedom in our witness to become "all things to all people" (1 Corinthians 9:22), provided we do not sacrifice the Gospel or the doctrine of justification.

The early Church confessed its faith in sometimes unique ways. During periods of persecution, some Christians used the nonverbal sign of a fish (ΙΧΘΥΣ in Greek) to indicate that the confession of Peter was also their own. (ΙΧΘΥΣ = Jesus [Ι]; Christ [Χ]; God's [Θ]; Son [Υ]; and Savior [Σ].) We, too, must be prepared to give an answer as Peter did. In worship, Christians confess the Apostles' Creed, which can serve as a basic diagram of the Christian faith that can be used to help formulate your own words when sharing your faith with others.

MAKE KNOWN GOD'S GREAT DEEDS _____

Romans 10:8–10 speaks of a confession of faith made from the heart. Peter speaks of our proclamation, as God's royal priests, about His glorious deeds, "the excellencies of Him who called you out of darkness into His marvelous light" (1 Peter 2:9). Here, Peter uses the Greek word *euangelizein*, which means "speaking the Good News."[12] Proclaiming the excellencies of God includes the joyful praises all Christians offer to God for what He has done for their salvation, as well as for the gifts of faith, love, and hope (1 Corinthians 13:13) that He continues to give to us through preaching, teaching, Baptism, and the Lord's Supper. Such proclamation occurs both during the Divine Service and outside the church setting. Such proclamation must be undergirded by honorable conduct (1 Peter 2:12).

In 1 Thessalonians, we glimpse the communal dimension of sharing our faith and making God known to others. Paul praised the Christians of Thessalonica for communicating their Christian faith in nonverbal and verbal ways in an alien environment that rejected the faith in the triune God. He wrote, "You became an example to all the believers in Macedonia and in Achaia. For not only has the word of the Lord sounded forth from you in Macedonia and Achaia, but your faith in God has gone forth everywhere, so that we need not say anything" (1 Thessalonians 1:7–8). This passage illustrates that the Church does not exist in a vacuum. Neighbors and community members will have opinions about "your" church.

---

12   The words *evangelist* and *evangelism* come from this Greek word. For similar Bible passages that use *euangelizein*, see Acts 14:21 and Romans 1:15.

DEFEND THE FAITH WITH CONFIDENCE _____

The apostle Peter writes that we should be "prepared to make a defense to anyone who asks you for a reason for the hope that is in you" (1 Peter 3:15). Some may think that "to make a defense" means that something is wrong with our faith and that we should apologize for it. The word *defense*, however, simply means to persuasively argue our faith when it is attacked or slandered. This would include patiently answering questions that others have about our Christian beliefs. As we speak of Jesus Christ, people may have misconceptions about His virgin birth, His miracles, or that He is God in human flesh. As Peter notes, we should at all times defend our faith with "gentleness and respect" (verse 15).

Later in the same Epistle, Peter tells his readers that they should "not be surprised at the fiery trail when it comes upon you to test you" (1 Peter 4:12). Suffering for the Christian faith might come across as out of touch with reality in view of a society that is, in comparison to many countries, quite tolerant of religious beliefs. Yet Christian suffering can be subtle, such as increasingly negative portrayals of our faith by some media or subtle forms of discrimination at work when someone openly prays to God before a meal or reads the Bible on break. Suffering for our faith in the West pales in comparison to the suffering of Christians in some Asian, African, and Middle Eastern countries.

Scripture passages also encourage us to be prepared to explain our faith to others. Two Christians, Priscilla and Aquila, when they heard Apollo speak in the synagogue, "took him and explained to him the way of God more accurately" (Acts 18:26). For the sake of our witness, we should always be on our best behavior and be prepared to speak about our faith (Colossians 4:5–6). Thus we become apologists for the Christian faith, people who are able to defend their faith with arguments that are logical and understandable. Although we may doubt our worthiness and ability to engage in sharing the faith—after all, isn't that why we have pastors and missionaries?—we know that God speaks through the weak and makes their witness strong. In every witnessing encounter, there is someone "behind the scenes": the Holy Spirit. And the Lord acknowledges every confession before His Father in heaven (Matthew 10:32–33). There is much comfort in reading that Paul did not use "lofty speech or wisdom" when he preached Christ crucified. Instead, Paul spoke "in weakness and in fear and much trembling" (1 Corinthians 2:1, 3). Nevertheless, his words demonstrated the Spirit's power (verse 4). As weak as our words about Jesus are, we, too, rely on the Holy Spirit for the power to make them take root in the heart of those who hear them.

The fear of rejection is perhaps the foremost reason Christians do not engage in witness. The human tendency to take rejection personally keeps many from speaking confidently about their faith. But those who reject the Gospel we present are not rejecting only us or the words we say, they are rejecting the Lord (Luke 10:16). People may think they are hearing only us talking when we share the Good News of our Savior, but behind our faithful witness stands the Son of God and the Holy Spirit. God's Word is never spoken in vain when it is spoken for the love and benefit of others. God's Word does not return empty (Isaiah 55:10–11). Although the rejection of God's Word spoken by us is the rejection of the very source of living faith, we do not know at what point the Holy Spirit might produce Christian faith in those who appear to reject the Word, yet in some way are listening to us (see Romans 10:14–17). Thus we keep on speaking the Gospel, trusting the Lord to use our words according to His gracious will and timing.

SPIRITUAL EXERCISES

◈ Pray the hymn "Come, Holy Ghost, God and Lord" (*LSB* 497), asking for the Spirit's presence and help as you share the Good News of Jesus with family members, friends, co-workers, and even strangers.

◈ Memorize Hebrews 13:15–16:

> Through Him then let us continually offer up a sacrifice of praise to God, that is, the fruit of lips that acknowledge His name. Do not neglect to do good and to share what you have, for such sacrifices are pleasing to God.

◈ Consider Luther's words on who should hear the Gospel:

> What is the Gospel but the sermon that Christ gave Himself for us that He might save us from sin, that all who believe this might certainly be saved in this manner, and that thus sinners, despairing of their own efforts, might cling to Christ alone and rely on Him? This is a very lovely and consoling declaration and readily enters such hearts as are despondent about their own efforts. Therefore the word "evangel" means a sweet, kind, and gracious message which gladdens and cheers a sorrowful and terrified heart.[13]

---

13 Plass, *What Luther Says*, 562 (no. 1706).

POINT TO REMEMBER _____

But what does it say? "The word is near you, in your mouth and in your heart" (that is, the word of faith that we proclaim); because, if you confess with your mouth that Jesus is Lord and believe in your heart that God raised Him from the dead, you will be saved. For with the heart one believes and is justified, and with the mouth one confesses and is saved. *Romans 10:8–10*

Go Where?

Nothing but faith is needed to be saved, to give God the honor due Him and to accept Him as my God, confessing that He is just, true, and merciful. Such faith sets us free from sin and all evil. If I have thus given God His due, I live the rest of my life for the benefit of my neighbor, to serve and to help him. The greatest work that follows from faith is that with my mouth I confess Christ, sealing that confession with my blood and, if it is so to be, laying down my life for it. Not that God needs this work. But I am to do it that my faith may thereby be proved and known, that others may likewise be brought to believe. Then other works follow; they must all be directed toward serving my neighbor. *Martin Luther* [14]

For many people, jobs or professions are simply ways to earn money. But Christian witness exists precisely in those callings where we as Christians serve our neighbors. Pastors, theologians, and other church workers cannot be expected to be experts in all the various professions of the world or to have exposure to them. Therefore, lay Christians are "frontline" representatives of Christ and His Church in the world. When Christians strive to perform their duties well, when they excel in collegiality and in loving service to their neighbor, their witness to Christ is credible.

Christians contribute toward furthering God's kingdom through their own witness and lifestyle in their vocations. The arena of their witness is wherever God chooses to place them: in the family, at work, on the streets, in restaurants, in malls, on airliners, and in all the other places where they go about their daily activities. This is a fundamental Lutheran insight. Christians do not lead a life of seclusion from the world and neighbor, as monasticism and fundamentalism demand.

----

14 Plass, *What Luther Says*, 960–61 (no. 3020).

Rather, Christians are pointed to a life in the world and to a neighbor whom they will serve in word and deed. The Church of Christ is always a Church for the world. For this reason, congregations should help their members take their sending into this world seriously and not restrict their time with endless church activities.

In Luther's day, the religious (that is, those who had taken vows to live in Roman Catholic religious orders) set themselves apart in order to merit a right standing before God or in order to please Him. Ironically, today some Christians isolate themselves from the world for the same reasons by shopping only at Christian bookstores, purchasing only from Christian retailers, listening only to Christian music, and, if possible, avoiding most if not all contact with unbelievers. While Christian books, products, music, and so on are God's good gifts that may edify and encourage His people, they can become idols when we believe that their use puts us in God's good graces. We are to serve our neighbor in love, even our sinful neighbor, just as Christ came to serve sinners, including us.

WHO IS MY NEIGHBOR?

Jesus responded to the question Who is my neighbor? with the parable of the Good Samaritan (Luke 10:25–37). The hero of Jesus' parable is the Samaritan who comes to the aid of the injured man when both a priest and a Levite (fellow countrymen) pass by. Samaritans were despised by the Jews for establishing alternative worship sites in the northern heights away from Jerusalem. The point of the parable is that our neighbor is anyone who needs our loving attention and service. The neighbor is not only the person who belongs to the "family of believers" but also those who hate us and persecute us for our faith (Matthew 5:43–45). Thus their need for help extends beyond the physical situation that we can see with our eyes, but is a spiritual need that can be addressed only with the balm of the Gospel.

A Christian's relationship to God is defined by faith. But with a neighbor, the Christian's relationship is defined by his or her deeds done to the neighbor in love. The apostle James uses even stronger language, calling those whom we are called to help "brother or sister" (James 2:15). But the use of *brother, sister,* or *neighbor* refers not only to those whom we like but also to our enemies. If a Christian fails to respond when a neighbor (or a sibling) is in need, the Christian's sincerity or his or her faith may be called into question. Therefore Christians should not delay service, lest integrity be questioned.

In his treatise *On the Freedom of a Christian*, Luther discusses our Christian standing before our neighbor. We should use our freedom not as a license to serve ourselves, but as an opportunity to surrender ourselves in service to our neighbor. In this treatise, Luther draws inspiration from Philippians 2:3–11 (see also Ephesians 5:1–2), in which Paul presents Christ's sacrificial giving of His life to the neighbor. This should also form our attitude:

> "I will therefore give myself as a Christ to my neighbor, just as Christ offered himself to me; I will do nothing in this life except what I see is necessary, profitable, and salutary to my neighbor, since through faith I have an abundance of all good things in Christ."

> Behold, from faith thus flow forth love and joy in the Lord, and from love a joyful, willing, and free mind that serves one's neighbor willingly and takes no account of gratitude or ingratitude, of praise or blame, of gain or loss. For a man does not serve that he may put men under obligations. He does not distinguish between friends and enemies or anticipate their thankfulness or unthankfulness, but he most freely and most willingly spends himself and all that he has, whether he wastes all on the thankless or whether he gains a reward.[15]

Philippians 2:3–11 underscores that Christians look to Christ as their Savior and as an example for their own faith and life. Because, as Luther notes, we have an "abundance of all good things in Christ," Christians are rightly motivated to help their neighbor just as Christ helps us. When we are motivated to witness by the Law, we do so motivated by guilt, and our witness is no longer a good work in the eyes of God. When we are motivated by the Gospel, we are set free to be who God has called us to be in Christ and we do good deeds willingly and without coercion. Christians should never be told that God will send people to hell because the Christians did not witness or did not witness enough.

IN FAMILY AND SOCIETY

While many Christian families consist of biologically related father, mother, and children, many others do not. In some cases, Christian families include adopted or extended family members. Regardless of how the Christian family looks, God has placed each member into

---

15 AE 31:367.

the family to serve one another in love. Paul describes the interaction among Christian family members in Ephesians 6:1–4. Each member is called to treat the other with the appropriate respect. Children are to obey their parents and they are blessed for doing so (verses 1 and 3), and parents are to bring their children up "in the discipline and instruction of the Lord" (verse 4).

Christians also belong to God's spiritual family. This fact casts a special light on our relationships with our biological family. At times, that relationship needs to be addressed or rearranged (Mark 3:31–35). It may even lead to separation (Luke 12:52). This division in our biological family may be a result of the Gospel and our confession of it or of our membership in a church. Non-Christians may live together with Christians in the same family. The Gospel may positively affect the life of the family so that non-Christian family members may be brought to faith. In other situations, the Gospel may cause divisions and rifts in the family.

In addition to family, God places Christians in another arena of service: society. Although we Christians have already become inheritors of a spiritual citizenship (Ephesians 2:19), we cannot withdraw ourselves from our roles as citizens in this world. We should submit ourselves to "the governing authorities. For there is no authority except from God" (Romans 13:1). As Christians, we see our vocation in this world as a means to uphold and support society and government. The demand for obedience to the civil authorities (Romans 13:1; 1 Peter 2:13–14) finds its place in the Fourth Commandment. Luther makes that connection beautifully by broadening "parents" to include teachers and rulers—a typical hermeneutical approach Luther adopts for many of the commandments. We have no intentions of rebelling against our authorities, provided they allow us to continue with our witness to others. Should we be prohibited from speaking our faith, we would be compelled to obey God rather than people and to continue our Christian witness (Acts 5:29).

BEARING THE CROSS AS GOOD EXAMPLES

Christians should see themselves as salt that permeates the world and as a light to all people (Matthew 5:13–16). That light shines forth through exemplary conduct so that those who are illumined by our words and deeds may give glory to God in heaven. This doxological and ethical motive, which calls us to a missionary lifestyle, is affirmed by the apostle

Peter: "Keep your conduct among the Gentiles honorable, so that when they speak against you as evildoers, they may see your good deeds and glorify God on the day of visitation" (1 Peter 2:12). Christians should be concerned about expressing appropriate behavior before unbelievers so that they might come to faith through hearing the Gospel. While a few employers and organizations prohibit or restrain the free exercise of sharing our Christian faith, we should actively look for opportunities to witness when and where we are allowed. When we live a morally upright lifestyle; when we are kind, generous and fair; and when we treat others with respect, then colleagues, classmates, team members, and others will want to know why. Nonverbal communication is nevertheless communication, and as our actions are joined with our words, the Lord receives praise (1 Peter 2:9; 3:15). Being good examples to others has a lot to do with refraining from some or many things occurring in the world around us (Colossians 3:1–11).

The message about Christ crucified and resurrected for the forgiveness of our sins does not always find open hearts and minds. The Gospel can be and is rejected by many people. The apostle Paul testifies to this by saying that the message of Christ crucified is "a stumbling block to Jews and folly to Gentiles" (1 Corinthians 1:23). But we can trust that the Lord will use our words and deeds as He wills to accomplish His purposes.

SPIRITUAL EXERCISES

◈ Meditate on the Ten Commandments to prayerfully discern where you have not fulfilled your duties in your vocation as parent or spouse, employer or employee, friend or neighbor, student or citizen, and so forth. Confess your sins to God, knowing that He has forgiven you through His Son, Jesus Christ (1 John 1:9). If there are sins that trouble you deeply, make an appointment for private Confession and Absolution with your pastor, so that you may hear from the Lord's called and ordained servant that your sins are forgiven through Christ's blood.

◈ Reflect on how Luther extols good works toward our neighbor that are motivated by God's love for us in Jesus Christ:

> A legalistic teacher of the Law enforces his restraints through threats and punishments. An evangelical preacher of grace invites and incites by pointing to the goodness and mercy which God has shown to men, for he wants no work which flows from an

unwilling spirit and no service which is wrung from a sullen heart. He wants glad and cheerful service to God.[16]

◈ Pray the hymn "How Clear Is Our Vocation, Lord" (*LSB* 853).

POINT TO REMEMBER

So, brothers, in whatever condition each was called, there let him remain with God. *1 Corinthians 7:24*

The Hub of Christian Life and Witness

The godly rejoice when the Gospel is widely spread, many come to faith, and Christ's kingdom is increased in this way. *Martin Luther*[17]

Certain airports today are designated as a "hub" for all incoming and outgoing flights of a particular airline. At this hub, the airline concentrates its cleaning and repair facilities, meal preparation services, training centers, and more. It allows the airline to consolidate its forces in preparation for meeting the needs of travelers.

In the same way, the congregation is a hub for us Christians and for all those who will come to know Christ through our witness. In our church, God's Word and Sacraments strengthen us so that we can live a life out in the world. We return to our church for further strengthening. Since Christians very often stand alone as an outpost in this world, the communal life at church is crucial. Our spiritual hub, the congregation, also becomes the hub for all newcomers as they are assimilated and become members of it. Thus the church plays the central role in our Christian witness. As we share our faith with others, we make the church an integral part of our message.

In the Large Catechism, Luther calls the Church our "mother."[18] While Christians are at times alone in the world, through the Word and water of Holy Baptism the Holy Spirit gives birth to new believers and brings them into God's family. The Church serves her divine Husband,

---

16 Plass, *What Luther Says*, 1512 (no. 4893).
17 Plass, *What Luther Says*, 959 (no. 3013).
18 LC II 42; *Concordia*, p. 403.

Jesus Christ, by serving her children. Through Word and Sacrament, the Church supports, strengthens, disciplines, and nourishes them. No witness can therefore exclude the reality of the Church.

NOW WHAT?

Christians share their faith in a world that is pluralistic in its religious beliefs and practices. As they share their faith, they should be mindful of the question people sometimes ask: "Brothers, what shall we do?" (Acts 2:37). Peter responded by saying, "Repent and be baptized every one of you in the name of Jesus Christ for the forgiveness of your sins" (verse 38). This question and answer demonstrates that every witness should point to repentance and Baptism and, ultimately, to the community in which the Sacrament of Baptism is administered. It is important to note that when repentance and Baptism are separated, they can be mistakenly understood as activities human beings perform based on their own logic, reasoning, or decision.

In view of the central article of justification, all references to our salvation should be carefully explained when we witness to others. This is perhaps especially the case with terms such as *accepting* and *saving yourself*. The Greek text in Acts 2:41 conveys in both cases a much less active understanding. In our English Bibles, Acts 2:40 is rendered as "Save yourselves from this crooked generation." Yet the Greek verb is actually passive and is best translated as "be saved." In the same way, the best translation of Acts 2:41 is "so those who *received* [Peter's] word," rather than the word *accepted* that is used in many English translations. The appropriate use of such passive verb constructions highlights the divine monergism—that God does the work of salvation.

The life of the Church has a lot to do with those whom Peter identified as having been "far off" (Acts 2:39) yet who have now have been "added" to the congregation (verse 41; cf. verse 47). Again, note that the verb *added* is passive; God alone adds people to Christ's Body, the Church. Through Baptism and through His Gospel, God made us members of His household. Since the Gospel and not the Law is the means by which we were added, clearly Gentiles can be added to the Church along with the Jews. In Christ, both those who are far (the Gentiles) and those who are near (the Jews) are united into one Body (Ephesians 2:11–18). As would be made clear in Peter's vision and his witness to Cornelius, the prohibitions to abstain from certain foods and the command to be circumcised no longer apply (see also Ephesians 2:15).

ENABLED FOR WITNESS

Today, being added to the Church is often understood as a process of assimilation. Newcomers may have come to your church based on the invitation or witness of a church member. Then the pastor and other lay leaders may provide catechetical instruction that leads to Baptism and/or a public reception of the new member. At this public rite, new members confess their faith before the congregation and are welcomed into fellowship, at which point they are able to participate in Holy Communion. In addition, the newcomer may be introduced to the activities of the church (Bible classes, small-group activities, or opportunities for service).

Many activities taking place in churches nurture faith and prepare members for witness. Peter's audience on Pentecost, after repenting of their sins and being baptized, "devoted themselves to the apostles' teaching and the fellowship, to the breaking of bread and the prayers" (Acts 2:42). Today, the Word is still preached and the Sacraments still administered because these Means of Grace sustain the life of the congregation. Because these precious Means are intended by our Lord for the entire world, the congregation should promote a missionary culture that informs and encourages Christians to serve their neighbors in love as Christ's witnesses. This may occur through instruction in Bible class or sermons, through literature, through presentations made by missionaries, through visual reminders at church, and by the example of the pastor himself.

All that we receive as Christians prepares us to witness. Preaching, teaching, catechetical instruction, the study or memorization of the creeds, participation in the Divine Service, the reception of the Means of Grace, hymns and spiritual songs, and so on provide us the biblical and spiritual content of our witness. Our own story of God's grace in our lives in good times and in bad times personalizes our witness. Some congregations celebrate a Mission Sunday as an opportunity to share work being done around the world or in their own backyard. Such a celebration also communicates ways in which members can support mission activity through their prayers and offerings. Other congregations offer evangelism weekends or courses to help members gain confidence in sharing their faith.

The Word of Christ dwells richly among Christians when they come together and sing psalms, hymns, and spiritual songs with gratitude in their hearts to God (Colossians 3:15–17). Whatever Christians do in word and deed, it should be done "in the name of the Lord Jesus, giving thanks to God the Father through Him" (Colossians 3:17). God's forgiveness of our sins through His Son, Jesus Christ, is the goal of all liturgy and worship, which yields itself in thanks and praise.

The early Church followed an important sequence that we might consider: outreach (witness), which led to instruction (catechesis) and participation in worship (liturgy). The liturgical life of the first Christians (Acts 2:46–47) was meant for those who had already been added to the body of believers. Thus the primary witness took place outside the worship life of the community. This is because the purpose of a congregation's liturgical or worship life is to receive the gifts that God delivers in the Means of Grace, His Word and Sacraments. Style and custom change over time and space and are reflected in different approaches to music, architecture, and decorative artwork. Nevertheless, how we worship—that is, our demeanor and practices in the Divine Service—does convey to visitors what we believe is happening in worship. The inescapable result of worship practices is that they teach.

TO THE GLORY OF GOD

Everything that Christians do sheds light on themselves and their God. Thus people may not simply judge us based on what we have said or done, but they also may judge God based on what we have said or done. Thus all our words should be spoken as if they are the words of God "in order that in everything God may be glorified through Jesus Christ. To Him belong glory and dominion forever and ever. Amen" (1 Peter 4:11).

The Lord laid down the important principle that it is not what enters the mouth but that which comes out of it that becomes destructive (see Matthew 15:11). This points to the tongue as an important organ that indeed may destroy our relationship with others and with God (see James 3:6). Yet without the tongue, Christian witness would look different. So Christians should strive toward improving their witness, not by refraining from speaking but by listening first and then expressing their words to others. The tongue should be used to focus on glorifying God with every word that leaves the mouth.

As individuals and as a Church, we must always be prepared for the Last Day, when Christ will return as judge. We share the Gospel with the goal that people may one day stand before God's throne, guiltless because of the blood of Christ. Every aspect of a congregation's life should point to Jesus Christ as the world's only Savior from sin. It should emphasize that Jesus will return to judge the world. Through Christ's death and resurrection, God has already declared all people not guilty. On the Last Day, all people will declare Him Lord, but only those who have confessed Him as Savior here in this life will enjoy eternity with Him. We pray that those who hear the Good News will bow before Christ as Savior in humble faith, because on the Last Day those who did not believe in Him will bow before Him as strict judge. God's grace and compassion in Christ for us are what motivate and enable us to bear witness to Him.

SPIRITUAL EXERCISES

◈ Commit to memory Luther's explanation to the Third Article of the Apostles' Creed (*Concordia*, p. 330).

◈ Meditate on the following hymns:

"May God Bestow on Us His Grace" (*LSB* 823/824)
"Hark, the Voice of Jesus Crying" (*LSB* 826)
"We Are Called to Stand Together" (*LSB* 828)
"Spread the Reign of God the Lord" (*LSB* 830)
"On Galilee's High Mountain" (*LSB* 835)

◈ When you pray "Thy kingdom come," ponder Luther's words in his Large Catechism concerning the kingdom of God going throughout the world: "We pray that it may go forth with power throughout the world [2 Thessalonians 3:1]. We pray that many may find entrance into the kingdom of grace [John 3:5], be made partakers of redemption [Colossians 1:12–14], and be led to it by the Holy Spirit [Romans 8:14], so that we may all together remain forever in the one kingdom now begun."[19]

POINT TO REMEMBER

And whatever you do, in word or deed, do everything in the name of the Lord Jesus, giving thanks to God the Father through Him. *Colossians 3:17*

---

19 LC III 52; *Concordia*, p. 414.

Lutheran Teaching on Witness

SALVATION TO THE ENDS OF THE EARTH

It is not God's will that anyone should be damned, but that all people should be converted to Him and be saved eternally [2 Peter 3:9]. . . . Out of His immense goodness and mercy, God provides for the public preaching of His divine eternal Law and His wonderful plan for our redemption, that of the holy, only saving Gospel of His eternal Son, our only Savior and Redeemer, Jesus Christ. By this preaching He gathers an eternal Church for Himself from the human race and works in people's hearts true repentance, knowledge of sins, and true faith in God's Son, Jesus Christ. By this means, and in no other way (i.e., through His holy Word, when people hear it preached or read it, and through the holy Sacraments when they are used according to His Word), God desires to call people to eternal salvation. He desires to draw them to Himself and convert, regenerate, and sanctify them. (FC SD II 49–50; *Concordia*, p. 529)

---

1. The human race is truly redeemed and reconciled with God through Christ. By His faultless obedience, suffering, and death, Christ merited for us the righteousness that helps us before God and also merits eternal life.

2. Such merit and benefits of Christ are presented, offered, and distributed to us through His Word and Sacraments.

3. By His Holy Spirit, through the Word, when it is preached, heard, and pondered, Christ will be effective and active in us, will convert hearts to true repentance and preserve them in the true faith.

4. The Spirit will justify all those who in true repentance receive Christ by a true faith. He will receive them into grace, the adoption of sons, and the inheritance of eternal life [Galatians 3:19].

5. He will also sanctify in love those who are justified, as St. Paul says (Ephesians 1:4). (FC SD XI 15–19; *Concordia*, p. 605)

JUSTIFIED FOR CHRIST'S SAKE, THROUGH FAITH

Our churches teach that people cannot be justified before God by their own strength, merits, or works. People are freely justified for Christ's sake, through faith, when they believe that they are received into favor and that their sins are forgiven for Christ's sake. By His death, Christ made satisfaction for our sins. God counts this faith for righteousness in His sight (Romans 3 and 4 [3:21–26; 4:5]). (AC IV; *Concordia*, p. 33)

So that we may obtain this faith, the ministry of teaching the Gospel and administering the Sacraments was instituted. Through the Word and Sacraments, as through instruments, the Holy Spirit is given [John 20:22]. He works faith, when and where it pleases God [John 3:8], in those who hear the good news that God justifies those who believe that they are received into grace for Christ's sake. This happens not through our own merits, but for Christ's sake. (AC V 1–3; *Concordia*, p. 33)

KEEP PROCLAIMING THE WORD

First, his words say this: the name of the Lord will be great. This is accomplished by the preaching of the Gospel. Through this preaching, Christ's name is made known and the Father's mercy, promised in Christ, is recognized. The preaching of the Gospel produces faith in those who receive the Gospel [Romans 10:17]. (Ap XXIV [XII] 32; *Concordia*, p. 226)

Without any doubt God also knows and has determined for everyone the time and hour of his call and conversion. But this time has not been revealed to us. Therefore, we have the command always to keep proclaiming the Word, entrusting the time and hour ‹of conversion› to God (Acts 1:7). (FC SD XI 56; *Concordia*, p. 610)

VOCATION
God Serves through Us[1]

In making conversation with a new acquaintance, one of the first questions we often ask is, "What do you do?" We would be surprised if someone answered, "Well, I do a lot of things. I sing in the shower. I eat sushi. I mow my lawn every Saturday. And I watch a lot of television." That is not the kind of answer we would be expecting. What we really meant to ask was, "What do you do for a living? What is your job?"

We tend to think that, in large part, a person's job defines who that person is. In describing ourselves, we might even say, "I *am* an auto mechanic." "I *am* an engineer." "I *am* a teacher." Those who do not get paid for their work, such as homemakers, full-time students, or retirees, may feel out of sync with such an approach. Why? Because a person's job serves as an indication of his or her status in the world.

Vocation, however, includes more than just one's occupation. According to an individual's many callings in life, a person may be a husband or a wife, a father or a mother, a son or a daughter, a friend, a neighbor, a citizen, an employer, a mentor, a volunteer in the community—the list goes on and on.

Scripture and the Lutheran Confessions proclaim and teach the true meaning of vocation. As children of God, we not only have a place in God's heavenly kingdom, but we also have been given a new status here in God's earthly kingdom. How do we balance this dichotomy? Christians are faced with many questions about living a Christian life in

1   Adapted from *The Lutheran Spirituality Series: Vocation*, written by Chad E. Hoover, edited by Robert C. Baker. Copyright © 2007 by Concordia Publishing House.

a secular world: How can I live a Christian life in a secular workplace? Is my job, which is not directly affiliated with the Church, God-pleasing? How can I balance my calling as a Christian with my calling as a citizen of this community?

This chapter will examine these questions from a distinctly Lutheran perspective. The richness of the Gospel will be extolled as we explore this doctrine of vocation—a Christian's service to others and their service to us in this world.

God's Gifts through Vocation

I believe that God has made me and all creatures. He has given me my body and soul, eyes, ears, and all my limbs, my reason, and all my senses, and still preserves them. In addition, He has given me clothing and shoes, meat and drink, house and home, wife and children, fields, cattle, and all my goods. He provides me richly and daily with all that I need to support this body and life. He protects me from all danger and guards and preserves me from all evil. He does all this out of pure, fatherly, divine goodness and mercy, without any merit or worthiness in me. For all this I ought to thank Him, praise Him, serve Him, and obey Him. This is most certainly true. *Martin Luther* [2]

In the late 1980s, the world was instructed in the philosophical wisdom of Bobby McFerrin with his catchy little tune "Don't Worry, Be Happy." In it, McFerrin warns against worry because when we do, we "make it double." In contrast, Jesus instructed His disciples, "Do not be anxious about your life, what you will eat, nor about your body, what you will put on" (Luke 12:22). Jesus is not denying the presence of trouble in our world. He is not suggesting, as McFerrin does in his ditty, that we are not to worry because if we would stop worrying, everything would be fine. Rather, Jesus is telling us not to worry because our Father knows what we need. Even amid trouble (caused by sin in the world), God is in control and provides for us in this life.

---

2   SC II; *Concordia*, p. 328.

GOD PROVIDES ALL THAT IS NEEDFUL _____

Human beings have been given a special place of authority over the rest of God's creation (see Genesis 1:26–28). In Luke 12:23–28, Jesus illustrates the heavenly Father's care for humankind by showing His great care and provision for objects of lesser value (birds and flowers) within His creation. Jesus teaches us that we do not need to worry about the daily needs of this life because through His goodness and mercy, our heavenly Father provides for our needs in great abundance.

How do we know—especially amid sickness, suffering, and death—that God will provide for our daily needs? We can trust God only because we have been given faith. Apart from the gift of faith, we cannot believe that "life is more than food, and the body more than clothing" (Luke 12:23). Despite our distressing circumstances, God's Word of promise sustains us. This is something that the world cannot give; only Christ gives us the strength to see through our hardships.

In his explanation of the First Article of the Apostles' Creed, Luther includes a lengthy list of God the Father's good gifts. We summarize this list when we pray in the Lord's Prayer: "Give us each day our daily bread" (Luke 11:3). God provides bread through the work of the grocer, who sells the bread to us. But before that, God provided flour for the baker, and before that, seed for the farmer. Although God could miraculously provide daily bread for His creation as He did for the Israelites in the wilderness (see Exodus 16), He chooses to meet our earthly needs through the vocations of others. God even uses unwilling, unknowing, or unbelieving servants to carry out His work. We may have an unbelieving doctor, attorney, or electrician, for example, who nevertheless performs his or her services for us and does them well.

More important than earthly clothing, food, or drink, God clothes believers with Christ and His righteousness (Galatians 3:27; Philippians 3:8–9) and grants us the forgiveness of sins and eternal life in His kingdom through faith in His name (Luke 24:46–47; John 3:16; Acts 2:38–39). The First Article gifts that God gives us are here today but gone tomorrow. They are good gifts, but they are temporary. They wear out. They rot and decay. Faith, however, is the God-given gift (Ephesians 2:8–9) that apprehends Christ's saving work and that opens eternal life to all believers. God grants and strengthens this gift of faith through the Gospel and the Sacraments.

Ultimately, all good gifts are from God. Whether people realize it or not, God has blessed His entire creation with many gifts. Without

God's sustenance, life on this earth would cease to exist. Although sinful humans do not always perfectly trust in God's provision for their needs, God does not cease to provide for His creation. His provision for the needs of body and life are not dependent upon faith. God "makes His sun rise on the evil and on the good, and sends rain on the just and on the unjust" (Matthew 5:45). In his explanation of the Fourth Petition of the Lord's Prayer, Luther writes, "God certainly gives daily bread, even without our prayer, to all wicked people; but we pray in this petition that He would lead us to realize this and to receive our daily bread with thanksgiving."[3]

GOD'S GIFTS TO YOU
AND THROUGH YOU _____

> What else is all our work to God—whether in the fields, in the garden, in the city, in the house, in war, or in government—but [means] by which He wants to give His gifts in the fields, at home, and everywhere else? These are the masks of God, behind which He wants to remain concealed and do all things. . . . We have the saying: "God gives every good thing, but not just by waving a wand." God gives all good gifts; but you must lend a hand and take the bull by the horns; that is, you must work and thus give God good cause and a mask. *Martin Luther*[4]

Luther described the various occupational roles—parents, farmers, laborers, soldiers, judges, retailers, and the like—as being "masks of God" (*larvae Dei*). This phrase describes the means God uses to work on our behalf and to show Himself while remaining hidden. A mask hides someone's face. If a person's vocation is a mask of God, then God is hidden but is still at work on our behalf. He is not seen in the work, but He is there nonetheless.

The purpose of our vocation is to serve our neighbor. School-work, a daily nine-to-five job, or chores around the house can at times seem frustrating, pointless, and exhausting. However, as a new creation in Christ, our works have been sanctified; that is, they are continually made clean by His Holy Spirit. No matter how mundane or ordinary the work, it has meaning and significance because God is working through the believer's vocation for the benefit of his or her neighbor.

---

3   SC III; *Concordia*, p. 335.
4   AE 14:114–15.

THE GOSPEL CHARACTER OF VOCATION _____

The doctrine of vocation is a great comfort for the Christian. Although vocation is an exercise of God's Law, it is very much driven and enabled by the Gospel. Because of sin, we all fail in our vocations, but God is continually with us, offering us the forgiveness of sins through Christ. He serves others through us despite our failures. Ultimately, we cannot take credit for the good works that we do because they are God's work.

Apart from Christ, we could do nothing because we were dead in our trespasses and sins. Anything that does not proceed from faith is sin (Romans 14:23). Our union with Christ gives us everything! He has freed us from the bondage of our sin, and He gives us the power to truly serve our neighbor and do good works. Furthermore, because God has promised to provide for our bodily needs, we are free to serve our neighbor without worry for ourselves.

At times, we may question our place in God's kingdom. Perhaps it seems that we are always letting God down. Maybe we have not been faithful witnesses or humble servants in all areas of our lives. Thankfully, our relationship with God is not dependent upon our works; it is dependent upon God and His promises to us in Christ. In terms of our salvation and our place in God's everlasting kingdom, we have a guarantee signed with the blood of Christ and sealed with the gift of the Holy Spirit (see Ephesians 1:7–14).

SPIRITUAL EXERCISES _____

◈ List the many ways that God is serving you through the vocations of others. Meditate on Psalm 145, thanking God for each of these gracious provisions.

◈ Identify your many vocations and relationships with others, as Luther teaches in the section on Confession in the Small Catechism: "Consider your calling according to the Ten Commandments, whether you are a father, mother, son, daughter, master, mistress, or manservant or maidservant. Consider whether you have been disobedient, unfaithful, or slothful? Consider whether you have grieved anyone by words or deeds, whether you have stolen, neglected, wasted, or done other harm."[5] Confess your sins privately to God; to your neighbor, if you have harmed him or her; or if your conscience is troubling you greatly, confess to your pastor, and receive the forgiveness of Christ.

---

5   SC V; *Concordia*, p. 341.

◈ Read Matthew 6:1–34 and reflect on this passage in light of the previous discussion in this chapter. Reflect on the section on the Lord's Prayer in Luther's Small Catechism (*Concordia*, pp. 331–38).

POINT TO REMEMBER

Your Father knows what you need before you ask Him. *Matthew 6:8*

Faith, Love, and the Christian Life

Therefore faith always justifies and makes alive; and yet it does not remain alone, that is, idle. Not that it does not remain alone on its own level and in its own function, for it always justifies alone. But it is incarnate and becomes man; that is, it neither is nor remains idle or without love. Thus Christ, according to His divinity, is a divine and eternal essence or nature, without a beginning; but His humanity is a nature created in time. These two natures in Christ are not confused or mixed, and the properties of each must be clearly understood. . . . Just as I am obliged to distinguish between the humanity and the divinity, and to say: "The humanity is not the divinity, and yet the man is God," so I make a distinction here and say: "The Law is not faith, and yet faith does works. Faith and works are in agreement concretely or compositely, and yet each has and preserves its own nature and proper function." *Martin Luther*[6]

In his first Epistle to the Thessalonians, Paul commended these new Christians for their "work of faith and labor of love," which served as "an example to all the believers in Macedonia and in Achaia" (1:3, 7). So, too, our union with Christ is made evident by "faith working through love" (Galatians 5:6). A proper view of the nature and role of faith and love in the Christian life is necessary to understand the doctrine of vocation.

In our world, the word *faith* is typically defined as confidence in oneself, in another person or group, or in a particular outcome. For example, "I have faith in you, Jimmy! You can beat that nasty habit." The word *love* is used flippantly in our culture: "I love sports!" "I love

---

6   AE 26:272–73.

cookies!" "I loved that movie!" "I love you, man!" But *faith* and *love* are essential words in any discussion of God and the Christian life. Faith (trust in Christ's saving work for us) works through love—and when we see these works, we say that faith is "alive." But the connection between faith and works is always made through the Gospel.

FAITH WORKING THROUGH LOVE _____

Apparently from out of the blue, God calls Abram to pick up stakes and head to the land of Canaan. What is more, God promises, "I will make of you a great nation, and I will bless you and make your name great, so that you will be a blessing" (Genesis 12: 2). However, apart from God's promise, there was little reason for Abram to believe that he would become the father of a great nation. After all, he had no children. But in faith, "Abram went, as the LORD had told him" (Genesis 12:4). There was nothing in Abram himself that would allow him to believe anything God was promising. Abram did not choose God, but God chose him. Despite the incapacity of Abram's sinful flesh, God gave him faith to believe the promise, and Abram's faith was credited to him as righteousness (see Genesis 15:6; Romans 4:1–12; Hebrews 11:8–12, 17–19). The same gift of God-given faith in Christ as our Savior connects us with Christ and all other believers.

Just as Paul writes to the Galatians, God gives all believers the gift of faith through hearing the Gospel, not by observing the works of the Law (see Galatians 3:1–9, 14). Receiving the Holy Spirit and faith through the proclamation of the Gospel and through Holy Baptism is the beginning of the Christian life. Paul reminds the Galatians that the Christian life is not only begun in the Holy Spirit, but it continues day by day in God's grace. Works of the flesh, as Paul calls them, do not in any way bring a person into a closer relationship with God.[7] However, the Gospel, which we have received through faith, both motivates and enables us to do good works, or acts of love for the benefit of our neighbor.

Sadly, some Christians are taught that Old Testament believers were saved by their works, by the many ways they kept the Law. But this is not true. Like us, God saved them by His grace, through faith without works, though faith is always accompanied by good works.

---

7   Consider Luther's words: "But the Holy Spirit has called me by the Gospel, enlightened me with His gifts, sanctified and kept me in the true faith" (SC II; *Concordia*, p. 330).

Faith precedes action in the Christian life. The writer to the Hebrews records in chapter 11 the number of things that Abraham did by faith, including obeying, traveling to Canaan, and offering Isaac (11:8–12, 17–19). These things did not save Abraham or cause God to declare him righteous. Rather, Abraham's faith saved him and that resulted in good works.

In his Epistle, James uses the example of Abraham to illustrate how faith results in obedience to God (see James 2:14–26). James does not deny the necessity of faith. The well-known saying is true: "We are saved by faith alone, but faith is never alone." James's message is God's Word, and it is consistent with the whole of Scripture. However, James reminds his readers that true faith is active in works. If good works are absent, then where is the faith? Is it dead? It would certainly appear so. Love for God and love for your neighbor naturally flow from a heart of faith.

Christians are made clean not because they bear fruit; they are made clean through the grace of God and the power of the Holy Spirit. Faith is a prerequisite for any and all good works. For apart from being connected to Christ (the Vine), we (the branches) cannot do anything (see John 15:1–8). Christians abide in the love of Christ so we can serve our neighbor with that same love. Without Christ as the life-giving source, our good works would wither away and die, just like a branch that has been cut off from a vine. The vine is the source of life for that branch. Without it, the branch cannot live.

In Matthew 25:31–46, Jesus describes the end times and the manner in which He will judge the nations. Jesus says that those on His right, the sheep (the righteous), did everything perfectly in the eyes of the Father. They fed the hungry, gave drink to the thirsty, welcomed the stranger, clothed the naked, and visited the sick and those in prison (verses 35–36). These sheep have not kept God's Law perfectly, but Jesus does not enumerate their sins. After all, He has kept God's Law perfectly for them and for all people—thereby giving significance to the relatively menial acts of love and charity that are recorded. Through faith, the sheep did indeed do good works.

On the other hand, those on the left, the goats (the unrighteous), did not bear any fruit. Jesus says, "I was hungry and you gave Me no food, I was thirsty and you gave Me no drink, I was a stranger and you did not welcome Me, naked and you did not clothe Me, sick and in prison and you did not visit Me" (Matthew 25:42–43). But is it really true that no one in this group ever did anything "good"? From a human perspective, there probably were good actions, but the Father does not recognize these works because they have not proceeded from faith. Although unbelievers may reach out to others with seeming charity, without faith their works are sin (Romans 14:23).

THE PLACE OF GOOD WORKS IN THE CHRISTIAN LIFE

Centuries ago, the Lutheran confessors wrote: "It is God's will, order, and command that believers should walk in good works. . . . Truly good works are done not by our own natural powers, but in this way: when a person is reconciled with God through faith and renewed by the Holy Spirit."[8] Paul writes that a person is "created in Christ Jesus for good works" (Ephesians 2:10).

Although unbelievers do "civil works" (external works that appear to be good), without faith in the crucified and resurrected Savior, God does not consider them to be good works at all.[9] Works done without faith are impure because they do not flow from regenerate hearts, that is, hearts that have been regenerated by God. On this point Scripture is clear: "For whatever does not proceed from faith is sin" (Romans 14:23).[10]

Good works are *not* necessary for salvation, but they *are* necessary.[11] However, good works apart from Christ are not good works at all. Just as it is impossible for a banana tree to grow oranges, it is impossible for an unbeliever to produce good works. If you want oranges, you need an orange tree. If you want to produce good works, you must be in Christ, who is the source of true goodness.

LIVING THE FAITH

The apostle James writes: "If a brother or sister is poorly clothed and lacking in daily food, and one of you says to them, 'Go in peace, be warmed and filled,' without giving them the things needed for the body, what good is that? So also faith by itself, if it does not have works, is dead" (James 2:15–17).

---

8 FC SD IV 7; *Concordia*, p. 547.
9 See Ap V [III] 9–10 [130–131]; *Concordia*, p. 103.
10 For further information about this point, read FC SD IV; *Concordia*, pp. 546–52.
11 See AC VI (*Concordia*, pp. 33–34); Ap V (III) 1–4 [122–125] (*Concordia*, p. 102); FC Ep IV (*Concordia*, pp. 482–84); FC SD IV (*Concordia*, pp. 546–52).

The apostle John writes very explicitly concerning what love is, namely, Christ laying down His life for us on the cross (see 1 John 3:16–17). We show love in a similar way by our willingness to lay down our lives for our brothers and sisters. We may say, "I love you," but even more than mere words or feelings, our actions show others the love of Christ that abides in us.

Although as redeemed children of God, we desire to do all things to the praise and glory of His name, we encounter countless obstacles as we attempt to live the faith. These obstacles are the result of Satan, the world, and our flesh trying to cut us away from the true Vine, Jesus Christ. Also, we will fail to do all things to the glory of God; this is unavoidable. The only reconciliation we have with God comes through the blood Christ shed upon the cross. God forgave our sins for Christ's sake, and through the Gospel and the Sacraments, God applies Christ's atonement and perfect life to us. We are cleansed and reconciled with God the Father. However, a Christian is not alone in this world. The Holy Spirit works through our pastors, teachers, congregation members, and Christian family and friends to encourage us in living the faith. Paul tells us that "speaking the truth in love, we are to grow up in every way into Him who is the head, into Christ" (Ephesians 4:15). As we challenge one another in the Body of Christ to continue walking in our vocations, the Spirit is there to strengthen our faith and to bless us with His good gifts through the "mutual conversation and consolation of brethren."[12] He has promised to build up the Body of Christ, "until we all attain to the unity of the faith and of the knowledge of the Son of God" (Ephesians 4:13).

SPIRITUAL EXERCISES _____

◈ Review Luther's explanations to the Fourth through the Tenth Commandment (*Concordia*, pp. 320–26). Note especially how he presents both the prohibitions ("You shall not") and the prescriptions ("You shall") in each commandment. For example, not only do we not murder our neighbor (the Fifth Commandment), but we also "help and befriend him in every bodily need."[13]

◈ Meditate on the hymn "I Know My Faith Is Founded" (*LSB* 587). Focus especially on the second stanza:

> Increase my faith, dear Savior,
> For Satan seeks by night and day

---

12 SA III IV; *Concordia*, p. 278.
13 SC I; *Concordia*, p. 321.

To rob me of this treasure
And take my hope of bliss away.
But, Lord, with You beside me,
I shall be undismayed;
And led by Your good Spirit,
I shall be unafraid.
Abide with me, O Savior,
A firmer faith bestow;
Then I shall bid defiance
To ev'ry evil foe.

◈ List the ways 1 Corinthians 13:4–8a describes that you can express your faith in love to others. Rejoice that God expresses His love and service to you in a similar manner through Jesus Christ, His Son.

POINT TO REMEMBER

Truly, I say to you, as you did it to one of the least of these My brothers, you did it to Me. *Matthew 25:40*

Spiritual Living in an Unspiritual World

Thus a Christian man who lives in this confidence toward God knows all things, can do all things, ventures everything that needs to be done, and does everything gladly and willingly, not that he may gather merits and good works, but because it is a pleasure for him to please God in doing these things. He simply serves God with no thought of reward, content that his service pleases God. On the other hand, he who is not at one with God, or is in a state of doubt, worries and starts looking about for ways and means to do enough and to influence God with his many good works. He runs off to St. James, to Rome, to Jerusalem, hither and thither; he prays St. Bridget's prayer, this prayer and that prayer; he fasts on this day and that day; he makes confession here and makes confession there; he questions this man and that man, and yet finds no peace. He does all this with great effort and with a doubting and unwilling heart, so that the Scriptures rightly call such works . . . labor and sorrow. And even then they are not good works and are in vain. *Martin Luther*[14]

---

14 AE 44:27.

How are Christians different from everyone else? Our world, and even some Christian denominations, see Christianity as a religion of morality. In other words, some Christians strive to live under the Law of God, seeking to earn His favor. This is impossible. Christianity and morality are not synonymous. If they were, then there would be many unbelievers who are "better Christians" than many of us. Holding to a particular set of moral standards is not what makes a person a Christian. Rather, what makes someone a Christian is repentant faith in Jesus Christ. We would certainly expect Christians to live morally upright lives, have compassion for those in need, rally for worthwhile causes, and so on. However, it is not the works they do that actually make them Christians. These good works are the fruits of faith, which flow from a heart that has been regenerated by the Holy Spirit through the Gospel. Some Christians think that good works are not at all necessary in the Christian life. This is a mistake as well.

IN THE WORLD, BUT NOT OF THE WORLD

In His High Priestly Prayer, Jesus says that His followers "are not of the world" (John 17:14). He also says that His disciples (and ultimately all Christians) will be hated by the world because they are not of the world, just as He is not of it. Jesus prays for His disciples to remain in the world, however, so that they can be sent into it with the Good News of Christ (verse 18). This apostolic word must be proclaimed so that the benefits of Christ's life, death, and resurrection will be spread throughout the world. Although we struggle in this sinful world, we remain in it for the sake of those who have not yet heard the Word of life. For we know that faith comes through hearing the Word about Christ (see Romans 10:13–17).

Christ came to earth with one mission: to redeem God's fallen creation and bring it back into a right relationship with Him. He did not accomplish this mission by being part of the world and following its logic, but by following the Father's plan to be the perfect atoning sacrifice for the sins of the world. Christ sanctifies Himself, that is, He dedicates Himself to this task of salvation, so that we are cleansed of our sinfulness and accepted by God on account of Christ. His Word is truth, and it is the Holy Spirit working through this Word who sanctifies us (John 17:17–18). Sanctification is the ongoing process of repentance, forgiveness, and renewal in the Christian life. It is accomplished through the work of the Holy Spirit, who continually does for us through God's Word of truth.

Sinful humanity is dead in its trespasses and sins. The right relationship between God and humankind was destroyed in the fall. However, God loves fallen human beings despite our sinful rebellion against Him. He is gracious and merciful, and through faith He has restored us to Himself and made us alive in Christ. Because of this, Paul says that God has "raised us up with Him and seated us with Him in the heavenly places in Christ Jesus" (Ephesians 2:6).

Having been redeemed by God through the shedding of Christ's blood on the cross, what are Christians called to do in this world? While Ephesians 2:8–9 is often trumpeted by Lutherans as the best definition of *grace*, verse 10 makes very clear that God has even more in store for His chosen people: "For we are His workmanship, created in Christ Jesus for good works, which God prepared beforehand, that we should walk in them." Paul also writes to the Romans that Christians are to "present [our] bodies as a living sacrifice . . . to God, which is [our] spiritual worship" (12:1). We are not to be "conformed to this world, but be transformed by the renewal of [our] mind, that by testing [we] may discern what is the will of God, what is good and acceptable and perfect" (verse 2). Christians are called to do good works in this world, to serve the neighbor with the love of Christ, and to submit to the authorities that God has established.

The apostle Peter tells us that we are to "be subject for the Lord's sake to every human institution," whether as rulers or subjects (elected officials or citizens) or as masters or servants (employers or employees) (1 Peter 2:13; cf. 1 Peter 2:13–25). All earthly authorities derive their power from the ultimate authority of God, who rules over all things (see Romans 13:1–2). Therefore, submission to these earthly authorities is also submission to the greater authority of God. These authorities have been established by God to serve us. Whereas Christians are called to be loving and merciful in their interpersonal relationships, governmental authorities have a God-given mandate to enforce the law and punish evildoers (see Romans 13:4).

There have been corrupt leaders and governmental systems throughout the history of the world, and there always will be. In the words of the Lutheran Confessions: "It is necessary for Christians to be obedient to their rulers and laws. The only exception is when they are commanded to sin. Then they ought to obey God rather than men (Acts 5:29)."[15] In Acts 5:29, when the disciples were forbidden by law to preach the Gospel, they answered, "We must obey God rather than men." Luther believed that when it was necessary to disobey the authorities, Christians should be willing to accept the punishment and face martyrdom rather than obey a godless law. As citizens and Christians, we have the duty to speak out against the murder of unborn children, embryonic stem-cell research, homosexual marriage, and other godless laws or practices.

In John 18:33–38 and 19:9–12, Jesus distinguishes God's kingdom of grace from God's rule through earthly government, which at that time and place was represented by Pontius Pilate. In John 18:36, Jesus tells Pilate, "My kingdom is not of this world." If God's kingdom were simply an earthly one, then Christians would have no hope! For an earthly king to be humiliated and crucified, as Jesus was, would have been a disgrace. The cross is foolishness to the world, but it means life and salvation for those who believe in Christ (see 1 Corinthians 1:18–25). In John 19:11, Jesus tells Pilate, "You would have no authority over Me at all unless it had been given you from above." Truly, Pilate had no power to condemn Jesus to death. As Jesus says, "For this reason the Father loves Me, because I lay down My life that I may take it up again. No one takes it from Me, but I lay it down of My own accord" (John 10:17–18). Jesus laid down His life willingly. Through faith in Him, we have access to His kingdom of heaven on earth so that we will live and reign with Him into the fullness of everlasting life.

LIVING IN TWO KINGDOMS

For the Christian, a proper distinction between God's earthly governance and His heavenly governance must be maintained. God rules and reigns over both kingdoms, but He does so in different ways. As part of God's creation, we hold citizenship in His earthly kingdom and are subject to God's Law. As God's new creation in Christ, we are subjects under God's Gospel and hold citizenship in His heavenly kingdom as well.

In the earthly realm, God deals with His whole creation according to His Law. One must work in this world in order to achieve. One must obey earthly authorities (Fourth Commandment). God preserves all people with the blessings of His creation, but this world will fade away. The gifts given here do not last. In the heavenly realm, God operates

---

15 AC XVI 6–7; *Concordia*, p. 40.

under the principle of grace according to His Gospel. We do not rely upon our works for citizenship in His kingdom. Rather, God makes us His own through faith in His Son. God not only preserves the Christian in this life but also provides salvation and eternal life in this never-ending kingdom.

There is danger in confusing these two kingdoms. For example, if we were to teach that Christian parents should not punish their children for misbehavior (instead, they should be forgiving and loving as God is forgiving and loving), consider the chaos that would ensue in the home and in society. But it is equally incorrect and confusing to say that absolutely no one in the maximum-security wing of a state prison is a Christian because they have been convicted of such heinous crimes. We are not the judge of what is in a person's heart in terms of their faith.

Confusion of the two kingdoms is really a confusion of God's Law and Gospel. In this world, parents should discipline their children because that is the job that God has given them to do. Furthermore, if someone breaks the law of the land, they should be brought to justice through the legal system. However, just because someone has been found guilty in a court of law does not mean that he or she stands guilty before the throne of God. There is a completely different standard in the heavenly kingdom, a standard that does not depend upon one's own works or efforts but upon Christ's actions. And Christ's perfect life and death are accounted to us through repentant faith. The thief on the cross was rightly punished according to the current law of the land, administered by the Romans. Nevertheless, that day he joined Christ in paradise, even as our Savior promised (Luke 24:39–43).

WILL THIS WORLD EVER CHANGE?

Thirty years ago, a famous Coca-Cola jingle suggested that the world could sing in "perfect harmony." This message of peace struck such a chord that the song became a pop hit when it was recorded as a single in 1971. Although well-intentioned, the aspiration to reach perfect harmony in this present, fallen world is both unrealistic and a denial of sin. People keep expecting that this world will change, but it never will. In fact, one could argue that the world has become even more disconnected and out of harmony than it once was. However, it is important to note that sin is sin, and humankind is no more sinful today than it was in the past. But today it seems that sin in the world goes largely unchecked.

In 2 Corinthians 4:8–18, Paul clarifies that Christians in this world will be afflicted, perplexed, persecuted, struck down, dying. But Paul proclaims that "this light momentary affliction is preparing for us an eternal weight of glory beyond all comparison" (2 Corinthians 4:17). Although it may be unseen at the moment, we share in this glory with Christ. As Christians in this world of sin, we fix our eyes upon Christ and the glory promised to us for His sake.

SPIRITUAL EXERCISES

◈ Use the service of Morning Prayer (*LSB*, pp. 235–42). Note how this service ascribes praise to God both as our Savior and as the Provider of our daily needs.

◈ Christ serves us in His Word and Sacraments. Review the First Commandment through the Third Commandment and their explanations in Luther's Small Catechism (*Concordia*, pp. 317–19). Give thanks to God— Father, Son, and Holy Spirit—for His precious name and His Holy Word.

◈ Review the Fourth Commandment and its explanation in Luther's Small Catechism (*Concordia*, p. 320). Note that the authority God gives to fathers and mothers also extends to all earthly authorities. Pray that the Holy Spirit would guide you to identify any sin in your life so that you may repent of it, receive forgiveness, and strive to obey all those whom God has placed in authority over you.

POINT TO REMEMBER

For by grace you have been saved through faith. And this is not your own doing; it is the gift of God, not a result of works, so that no one may boast. For we are His workmanship, created in Christ Jesus for good works, which God prepared beforehand, that we should walk in them. *Ephesians 2:8–10*

Vocation
in the Christian Home

When I have this righteousness within me, I descend from heaven like the rain that makes the earth fertile. That is, I come forth into another kingdom, and I perform good works whenever the opportunity arises. . . . If I am a father, I rule my household and family, I train my children in piety and honesty. . . . In short, whoever knows for sure that Christ is his righteousness not only cheerfully and gladly works in his calling but also submits himself . . . to everything else in this present life—even, if need be, to burden and danger. For he knows that God wants this and that this obedience pleases Him. . . .

The Spirit is whatever is done in us through the Spirit; the flesh is whatever is done in us in accordance with the flesh and apart from the Spirit. Therefore all the duties of Christians—such as loving one's wife, rearing one's children, governing one's family, honoring one's parents, obeying the magistrate, etc., . . .—are fruits of the Spirit. *Martin Luther*[16]

A child's first teachers are his or her parents. However, many parents today feel ill-equipped to teach their children about the Christian faith. Sadly, it appears that even some Christian churches are incapable of aiding parents in this task. There has been a general decline in Christian and family values in Western culture over the last fifty years. Standards of community and morality that the Church has proclaimed as godly and that even unbelievers long considered to be good for society have been displaced by an unrelenting search for immediate self-gratification in many aspects of life. These developments have much to do with the overwhelming disconnect between churches and families today. If churches fail to engage families, they are labeled cold and distant. If the churches engage family life any more than expected, they can be accused of being meddlesome. God created us not to be isolated; rather, He has made us a family and a community and has turned our eyes toward one another. Through His Word, God helps us face cultural and technological challenges to our Christian lives. He has given specific vocations, duties, and responsibilities to those in the family to govern the household and to nurture one another for service within the home and to the neighbor—as well as to teach the faith.

---

16 AE 26:11–12, 217.

GOD-GIVEN ROLES WITHIN THE HOME _____

A new vocation arises within the Christian home when God joins a man and a woman together in marriage. When God created Adam and Eve, He gave them the divine command to "be fruitful and multiply" (Genesis 1:28). In reading Genesis 2, more detail is given concerning the relationship between the man and the woman. God created the woman to be a "helper fit for the [man]" (Genesis 2:18), in other words, for *companionship*. When Adam awoke and saw Eve, his wife, he loved her in a way that could not be replicated by anything else in God's new creation. It was an intimate, deeply personal love that Adam and Eve had for each other. Furthermore, a man and a woman *complete each other*. Jesus reiterates this truth in Matthew 19:5: "Therefore a man shall leave his father and his mother and hold fast to his wife, and the two shall become one flesh" (cf. Genesis 2:24).

Christians are called to serve their neighbors, and a person's closest neighbors are others within the home. Paul writes that believers are to submit to one another "out of reverence for Christ" (Ephesians 5:21). In terms of the home, God instituted marriage; therefore, husbands and wives have God-given offices with God-given duties. And when God defines our roles in marriage, then husbands and wives are freed from worrying about their own needs being met and are protected from the fear that their spouse may seek to dominate. In Ephesians 5, Paul could have used any analogy to illustrate the relationship between husband and wife. However, he uses the correlation between our Lord and His Church to show the great significance of the marriage relationship. Paul specifies that wives submit to their husbands "as to the Lord" (verse 22), and husbands "love [their] wives, as Christ loved the church" (verse 25), that is, sacrificially. The husband, who is the head of the home, is analogous to Christ, who is the Head of the Church. Paul compares the wife to the Church, which is the Bride of Christ. Therefore, just as the Church submits to Christ, a wife submits to her husband. Likewise, just as Christ offered Himself entirely for the benefit of the Church, so, too, does a husband offer himself sacrificially for the benefit of his wife.

When children enter the picture, vocation within the home expands. The apostle Paul emphasizes that a major component of vocation in parenthood is raising children "in the discipline and instruction of the Lord" (Ephesians 6:4). But parents are not the only ones with God-given duties and responsibilities. The Fourth Commandment (the first of the commandments that deal with our relationships to others) proclaims that we are to honor our fathers and mothers. God calls children to obey their parents. In Paul's charge to parents recorded in Ephesians 6, another role for children within the home is implicit—children are to learn from their parents. Not only do children learn basic social skills in the home, but they also learn the Christian faith.

At times, raising children can be incredibly frustrating, though it can also be incredibly rewarding. God has given both fathers and mothers authority over their children. However, parents should not abuse their duties or position of authority. Children need discipline and love. When parents are firm but loving and willing to teach, they will help to shape their children and prepare them for adulthood. A father (or mother) who is overbearing or antagonistic toward his children is not fulfilling the duties that God has given him. A father (or mother) who continually frustrates his children is not providing for them the environment that God wills for bringing up a child in the faith.

God gives children special status within the family. Inspired by the Holy Spirit, Solomon proclaims in Psalm 127 that children are a blessing from God. But Solomon is quick to point out the necessary foundation for the home: "Unless the LORD builds the house, those who build it labor in vain" (Psalm 127:1). A home established upon the foundation of Christ is built upon an eternal source. A home without a biblical foundation is ultimately empty, because all the material things gathered within it will not last into eternity. Unfortunately, in the homes of unbelievers, even the relationships that the family members have established with one another will not last. As believers, we have the comfort and joy of knowing that together we make up the Body of Christ. The relationships that we have with other believers here on earth, including especially those in our home, will last into eternity.

TREASURING CATECHESIS

> Train up a child in the way he should go; even when he is old he will not depart from it. *Proverbs 22:6*

Parents have a God-given duty to instruct their children in the faith. That is why many of the Six Chief Parts in Luther's Small Catechism begin with the phrase "As the head of the family should teach it in a simple way to his household." The Small Catechism helps parents teach the faith by giving them a ready-made devotional guide that is based upon the Word of God. Luther's carefully crafted words and rhythmic writing will put the faith on the tongue of each child who is exposed to the catechism. The repetition of the text benefits children, encouraging them to learn it by heart. Although they may not fully understand everything in the Small Catechism, it is better to give children a faith to grow into than a faith to grow out of. Parents also will find their own faith strengthened through this continual review of the Small Catechism.

Parents have the primary responsibility to instruct their children in the Christian faith: the content of God's Word, the specific details of Bible stories, the specifics of the faith as found in the Small Catechism, favorite Christian hymns, the prayers of God's people. As other Christian individuals such as pastors and teachers interact with our children, they build on the foundation established by parents in the home.

DISTINCTION BETWEEN OFFICE AND PERSON

> To the position of fatherhood and motherhood God has given special distinction above all positions that are beneath it: He does not simply command us to love our parents, but to honor them. Regarding our brothers, sisters, and neighbors in general, He commands nothing more than that we love them [Matthew 22:39; 1 John 3:14]. In this way He separates and distinguishes father and mother from all other persons upon earth and places them at His side. *Martin Luther*[17]

It could be argued that if parents are doing their job, their children will not always like them. Whether or not children "like" their parents has little to do with whether or not they should obey them. Children do not like to be disciplined, but parents must discipline their children so that they learn right from wrong. Children can and should honor their father and mother, even if they consider them to be a little old-fashioned or embarrassing. There is a distinction between the duties that a parent has and the actual person. Parents are entrusted by God with the care of their children. This is the office they hold within the home, and it should be held in the highest regard. It is indeed a great blessing for children both to honor *and* to enjoy their parents, though for many this may not occur until children reach adulthood.

As we read earlier, a father's authority is based upon the authority that Christ has given. When James and John came to Jesus requesting places of honor and authority next to Him, Jesus told them that they were not to seek honored positions to lord authority over anyone;

---

17 LC I 105; *Concordia*, p. 371.

instead, they were to be servants to all (see Mark 10:35–45). In the same way, parents have positions of authority, but they also can lovingly serve their children while maintaining the authority that God has given them in the home.

SPIRITUAL EXERCISES

◈ Have regular devotions with your spouse or family. (If you are single or an empty-nester, consider inviting a relative, friend, co-worker, or neighbor to join you.)[18]

◈ Pray the following hymns, noting how each extols the blessings God gives through spouse, family, children, and vocation:

"Oh, Blest the House" (*LSB* 862)
"Our Father, by Whose Name" (*LSB* 863)
"Lord, Help Us Ever to Retain" (*LSB* 865)
"Lord Jesus Christ, the Children's Friend" (*LSB* 866)
"Let Children Hear the Mighty Deeds" (*LSB* 867)
"How Clear Is Our Vocation, Lord" (*LSB* 853)
"Lord, Help Us Walk Your Servant Way" (*LSB* 857)

◈ Learn Ephesians 5:1–2 by heart.

POINT TO REMEMBER

Unless the LORD builds the house, those who build it labor in vain.
Psalm 127:1

Christianity in the Workplace

Therefore, if we recognize the great and precious things which are given us, as Paul says [Rom. 5:5], our hearts will be filled by the Holy Spirit with the love which makes us free, joyful, almighty workers and conquerors over all tribulations, servants of our neighbors, and yet lords of all. For those who do not recognize the gifts bestowed upon

---

18 *The Lord Will Answer: A Daily Prayer Catechism* (St. Louis: Concordia, 2004) is a good resource that takes you through each section of Luther's Small Catechism with short devotions for each day of the year. A more structured resource based on the liturgy and appropriate Scripture readings is *Treasury of Daily Prayer* (St. Louis: Concordia, 2008).

them through Christ, however, Christ has been born in vain; they go their way with their works and shall never come to taste or feel those things. Just as our neighbor is in need and lacks that in which we abound, so we were in need before God and lacked his mercy. Hence, as our heavenly Father has in Christ freely come to our aid, we also ought freely to help our neighbor through our body and its works, and each one should become as it were a Christ to the other that we may be Christs to one another and Christ may be the same in all, that is, that we may be truly Christians. *Martin Luther*[19]

Christians are engaged in the culture, involved in the fabric of society. That means Christians go to the movies, eat at local restaurants, and cheer on their favorite team at the ballpark. Christians also hold a vast assortment of occupations. Maybe your hairdresser is a Christian, or perhaps the pizza delivery person, or even the mayor. Think about your own place of employment. Many workplaces have Christians and non-Christians working side by side doing the same or similar jobs. Any work that benefits others can be done to the glory of God. However, "jobs" that go against God's will and do not uplift humanity cannot be done for the glory of God and should not be done by Christians. And non-Christians, of course, should not serve as Christian pastors or called church workers.

RELATIONSHIPS IN THE WORKPLACE

Christians in the workplace may find themselves in positions of authority or they may serve in positions under the authority of another. Paul does not say in Ephesians 6:5–8 (or elsewhere in his Epistles) that working under the authority of another is a shameful or degrading position. A Christian should serve his or her master (a vocation that would be the equivalent of today's boss, supervisor, or crew leader) with "fear and trembling" (Ephesians 6:5) and not for the sake of appearance or to move up the corporate ladder. Submission in the workplace is submission to Christ. Paul expresses here that a person's earthly master is to be obeyed as one would obey Christ. But because of our sinful nature, struggles between supervisors and employees are prevalent in nearly every place of work. However, Christians offer a positive witness when they continue to fulfill their duty even when they suffer mistreatment or work under harsh or abusive supervisors. In all such situations,

19 AE 31:367–68.

they work patiently and through proper channels for the resolution of the situation for their own benefit and the benefit of their employer.

Paul tells supervisors: "Do the same to them," meaning carry out your duties regarding your employees with the same "fear and trembling." He also adds: "And stop your threatening" (Ephesians 6:9). Those in positions of authority give the sinful flesh an opportunity to poke up its ugly head and take advantage of those under their authority. Paul reminds masters that their authority comes from God, who is Lord over all, including themselves *and* those under them. Therefore, a superior office does not give a person license to be disrespectful to others or lord authority over anyone. A person can be in a position of authority and still be a servant to all. When an employer treats his or her employees with respect, that respect is easily reciprocated. This makes the workplace more pleasant and productive.

Paul notes that "there is no partiality" with God (Ephesians 6:9; cf. Luke 1:51–53; Acts 10:34–35, 44–48; Galatians 3:26–29). But if God does not play favorites, than why do we have distinctions within earthly relationships? Such distinctions among our earthly vocations prevent chaos in the world. But when we stand before God, there is not master or slave, supervisor or employee, boss or errand person, for we are all heirs of His heavenly kingdom. There is no partiality with God—He loves us and saves us all the same!

In Matthew 20:1–16, Jesus tells the parable of the laborers in the vineyard. The master hires groups of workers at specific times during the day. With the first group, which was hired early in the morning, the master negotiated the typical payment for a day of labor. With groups hired later in the day, he said he would pay "whatever is right" (verse 4). At the end of the day, every worker received the same amount of money—a denarius, the amount for a day of labor. This parable illustrates Paul's statement that there is no partiality with God. Although some of the workers in the parable worked only one hour, they were paid the same as those who had worked all day. In our world, this would be an unfair practice that would not be allowed by any labor union. This arrangement works for the kingdom of heaven, however, because our reward is not based upon our own labors but upon the labors of Christ. The compensation, so to speak, that we receive in Christ is the same for everyone, no matter who they are or how long they have been Christian. Our salvation is based upon the generosity of our heavenly Father and the gifts He bestows in and through Christ. He holds nothing back. Through Jesus' life, death, and resurrection, He has given all things to those who believe in Him. It is God's grace.

But this model would not work in the world (nor does our Lord intend it as anything other than a description of the kingdom of heaven). Because of our sinful nature, people need to be motivated by the Law to go to work. If employees know that they will be paid the same no matter what time they show up for work, how inclined would they be to put in a full day? While a Christian ought to have a higher work ethic than that, the sinful nature corrupts even the best of intentions.

WORKING IN A SECULAR ENVIRONMENT ____

Living our Christian lives in the workplace begins with receiving Christ's gifts in the Divine Service. But attending church should not become one more item on a long list of things to do each week. The Christian life is about *being* before it is about *doing*. Our faith is fed through worship. We need the refreshment and encouragement that the Holy Spirit provides us through the Gospel and the Sacraments to strengthen us for the daily grind. All week long, we are working to fulfill our vocations in this world, but in worship we receive from Christ a glimpse of our eternal inheritance. Further, we rejoice in the fact that we can rest in His work for us. Worship strengthens us so that we can go out into the world with the assurance of Christ's forgiveness and be equipped for service to our neighbors in the workplace (and elsewhere). Despite the struggles and difficulties in this life, our faith keeps us going and provides hope for us as we look forward to the fullness of the life that awaits us (see Romans 8:18–28).

WORSHIP BEYOND THE SANCTUARY _____

Peter writes: "Always [be] prepared to make a defense to anyone who asks you for a reason for the hope that is in you; yet do it with gentleness and respect, having a good conscience, so that, when you are slandered, those who revile your good behavior in Christ may be put to shame" (1 Peter 3:15–16). Although applicable to many situations in life, Peter's words hold great significance for the workplace. Through their vocation in the workplace, Christians may have more access to nonbelievers than a pastor does. When Christians and non-Christians work together and get to know one another, friendships, bonds, and trust may be formed, resulting in opportunities to share Christ. This is why worship and study of God's Word is so important, because the workplace provides opportunities for effective evangelism.

What are some effective ways for a Christian to live the Christian life in the workplace? We can adopt the catchphrase of Popeye, "I am what I am!" Our Christianity is a large part of who we are. However, we do not have to talk about our faith all the time or beat people over the head with it. Be a Christian, and people will know you are a Christian. Do what is expected of you in the workplace, be respectful and obedient to your employer, be courteous and respectful to your co-workers, and do not pilfer your employer's goods or time. After relationships have been formed with your co-workers, they are more likely to come to you and inquire about your faith. As Peter writes in his Epistle, be prepared to give an answer, do not pursue arguments, and be of service to your co-workers by treating them with the love and respect of Christ.

SPIRITUAL EXERCISES

◈ Pray for your co-workers, for your supervisor(s), or for those under your supervision throughout the workday. Pray that you would be faithful in your duties, rendering service to your neighbors in the workplace as you would to the Lord.

◈ As you rest from your labors this week, meditate upon Psalm 92 and rejoice in the labors of God's hands for His people. May this encouraging Word rejuvenate you as you enter into His harvest field each day.

◈ Review the Second Article of the Apostles' Creed and its explanation in Luther's Small Catechism (*Concordia*, p. 329). Marvel at the work of Christ on our behalf. Trust not in your own work for salvation but only in the merits of our Lord.

POINT TO REMEMBER

For You, O LORD, have made me glad by Your work; at the works of Your hands I sing for joy. *Psalm 92:4*

Freedom of the Christian

A Christian is a perfectly free lord of all, subject to none. A Christian is a perfectly dutiful servant of all, subject to all. These two theses seem to contradict each other. If, however, they should be found to fit together they would serve our purpose beautifully. Both are Paul's own statements, who says in 1 Cor. 9[:19], "For though I am free from all men, I have made myself a slave to all," and in Rom. 13[:8], "Owe no one anything, except to love one another." Love by its very nature is ready to serve and be subject to him who is loved. So Christ, although he was Lord of all, was "born of woman, born under the law" [Gal. 4:4], and therefore was at the same time a free man and a servant, "in the form of God" and "of a servant" [Phil. 2:6–7]. *Martin Luther*[20]

Luther points out the paradoxical nature of the Christian life: Christians are both lords and servants, freemen and slaves. Luther admits that these two ideas seem to contradict each other, but he assures us that both are based upon the clear teaching of Scripture. Christian freedom means that we are freed from the condemnation of God's Law. However, we are still bound to keep the civil laws that have been enacted for the sake of good order in the world. The distinction between the two kingdoms helps us understand the paradoxical nature of the Christian life because it distinguishes between God's mode of operation in one kingdom versus the other (earthly kingdom = Law; heavenly kingdom = Gospel).

SLAVES UNTO RIGHTEOUSNESS _____

In the Epistle to the Galatians, Paul warns the believers not to compromise the truth of God's Gospel. He writes: "For freedom Christ has set us free" (Galatians 5:1), and he goes on to explain that Christ has freed us from spiritual slavery and fulfilled for us every obligation to the Law. If the Galatians instead agree with those who are insisting that Christians must be circumcised to be saved, they will again place themselves in bondage. If our place in God's kingdom comes through keeping the Law, then we are no longer free but slaves to the Law. This is a serious problem, because the Gospel cannot be robbed of its sweetness and still be Good News.

Although God no longer counts our sins against us, Paul warns Christians not to indulge the sinful nature (Galatians 5:15). Christians continue to have an obligation to love one another through Christian service, not in order to earn salvation but because salvation has already been given as a gift. Also, sin always has consequences, including the power to tear down and destroy in the temporal realm. Paul tells his readers that the flesh (our corrupt sinful nature) fights against the

---

20 AE 31:344.

Holy Spirit, who dwells within us (Galatians 5:17). A Christian is at the same time sinner and saint. The sinful nature and the Spirit are contrary to each other. There is a constant struggle within the Christian's own person—between the sinful self and the renewed self in Christ. Whereas the sinful nature seeks after its own pleasures, the new person in Christ seeks to do the will of God.

Because we are in Christ, our sins no longer have the power to separate us from God. He cleanses us. But we still struggle with the sinfulness of our flesh, which seeks ways to abuse the freedom that we have been given in Christ. In selfish sinfulness, we take advantage of God's grace and neglect the needs of others.

Christians have been set free by Christ, but under some circumstances they may choose not to exercise their freedom. There may be certain times when the exercise of those freedoms would not be appropriate. Paul tells the Corinthian Christians that "all things are lawful, but not all things are helpful . . . not all things build up" (1 Corinthians 10:23). Not everything is beneficial, and exercising one's freedom could cause offense to a Christian with weaker faith. We may have a full understanding of what our freedom in Christ means, but others may not. If our demonstration of Christian freedom causes others to sin or to question their own faith, it would be best to refrain from such an action.

The difference between this admonition and Paul's warning to the Church in Galatia is that of motivation. Out of Christian love, a person might choose not to exercise Christian freedom because he or she is free to do it and free not to do it. It is truly a matter of freedom and choice. However, because it was a serious violation of an article of faith, it would not have been a matter of Christian freedom for the Galatians to succumb to those mandating circumcision as entry into the Church. In a situation such as this, it is important for the sake of the Gospel not to compromise, give in, or allow others to make legalistic demands that could damage faith.

In Galatians, Paul boldly asserts that Christians are freed by Christ. In Romans 6:15–23, he declares that Christians are slaves to righteousness. How is this possible? Just as Paul says, "When you were slaves of sin, you were free in regard to righteousness" (Romans 6:20), the reciprocal is also true. When you are slaves to righteousness, you are freed from the control of sin! Once Christ cleanses you of your sinfulness, He also makes you righteous. Therefore, becoming a slave to righteousness is the natural consequence of being freed from sin.

The designation of "slave to sin" or "slave to righteousness" comes as a result of who your master is. If your master is sin, you are a slave to sin. If your master is Christ, you are a slave to righteousness. Jesus says, "No one can serve two masters, for either he will hate the one and love the other, or he will be devoted to the one and despise the other. You cannot serve God and money" (Matthew 6:24). Our lives in Christ are defined by our master. We have been given a new status—slaves to righteousness. As such, serving others with the love of Christ is simply what we do according to our new nature in Christ. This gives vocation its Gospel character.

FREED TO SERVE

The forgiveness that Christ so freely gives has set us free to serve our neighbor. All concerns that we may have about our own salvation have been alleviated by the words and work of our Savior, who for the joy that was set before Him endured the cross (Hebrews 12:2). Indeed, it is for freedom that Christ has set us free!

Not only have we been freed from sin, which ensures our eternal salvation, but we have been freed to do good works. Before our union with Christ, our sinful nature defined who we were and what we did. Since our master was the sinful flesh, we were enslaved to sin, unable to do anything good in the eyes of God. As Jesus explains to Peter by way of parable in Matthew 18:21–35, since we have been freed from such a huge debt, we have been given the ability and the responsibility to forgive those minor debts our neighbor owes us.

The ultimate goal of evangelism is to tell the Good News of Christ's forgiveness. Christianity would be no different than any other world religion if it were based upon human works. Although our sinful pride may enjoy trying to keep the Law, thus earning our righteousness, this is not comforting at all. When we become aware of sin (through the Law), there is only one way to be relieved from that burden. The Gospel tells us of Christ's salvation, which is a free gift, with no strings attached.

THE REALITY OF SIN

Good works are not necessary for salvation, but they are necessary.[21] Although Christians daily battle the sinful flesh, we rejoice with Paul, who wrote: "I have been crucified with Christ. It is no longer I who

---

21 See AC VI (*Concordia*, pp. 33–34); Ap XIIb (VI) 77 [174] (*Concordia*, p. 183).

live, but Christ who lives in me. And the life I now live in the flesh I live by faith in the Son of God, who loved me and gave Himself for me" (Galatians 2:20).

In Romans 7:14–24, Paul points out that we do the very things we do not want to do and are unable to do the good things we desire. These struggles trouble us because, as redeemed children of Christ, we do not want to sin against God or against our neighbor. As Christians, we agree that the Law is good, as Paul explains in Romans 7, and so we desire to follow it. In our struggle with sin, we cry out with Paul, "Wretched man that I am! Who will deliver me from this body of death? Thanks be to God through Jesus Christ our Lord!" (Romans 7:24–25). The struggles between the old self and the new self are evidence that our faith is alive. It is evidence that the Holy Spirit is working in our lives, convicting us of our sins and driving us to repentance. These struggles should not concern us in regard to our salvation; we should never think that they come as a result of our lack of faith (see Romans 8:1–4).

Since we will never reach a point in our earthly lives when we no longer struggle against the sinfulness of our flesh, it would be very alarming indeed if we were to become so complacent in our sin that we were not at all troubled by it. If we thought we could go on sinning without any regard for God's Law, this would be evidence that faith is dead. We have a continual need to confess our sins before God our Father and receive the forgiveness that Christ freely offers.

Paul proclaims: "There is therefore now no condemnation for those who are in Christ Jesus" (Romans 8:1). Our connection to Christ through faith—brought about through the Gospel and the Sacraments—is the means by which we receive the forgiveness of sins that Christ won for us on the cross. Christ is our only hope and source of good works, just as He is our only hope and source of the forgiveness of sins and eternal life. To God alone be all praise and glory!

SPIRITUAL EXERCISES

◈ Meditate on the hymn "Salvation unto Us Has Come" (*LSB* 555). Note how Law and Gospel are distinguished, how Christ's work for us is exalted, and how the fruit of good works is portrayed as evidence of a living faith.

◈ In consideration of Paul's words in 1 Corinthians 10:23–11:1, analyze your attitude and actions to see if your exercise of your Christian freedom has caused offense to your neighbor. With the Holy Spirit's guidance, confess where you have sinned, and look for ways to serve that person in love. Rejoice that God has forgiven your sins for Christ's sake.

◈   If you have not already done so, commit to memory Luther's explanation
of the Third Article of the Apostles' Creed (*Concordia*, p. 330).

POINT TO REMEMBER

But thanks be to God, that you who were once slaves of sin have
become obedient from the heart to the standard of teaching to which
you were committed, and, having been set free from sin, have become
slaves of righteousness. *Romans 6:17–18*

Lutheran Teaching on Vocation

Our churches teach that this faith is bound to bring forth good fruit
[Galatians 5:22–23]. It is necessary to do good works commanded by
God [Ephesians 2:10], because of God's will. We should not rely on
those works to merit justification before God. The forgiveness of sins
and justification is received through faith. The voice of Christ testifies, "So you also, when you have done all that you were commanded,
say, 'We are unworthy servants; we have only done what was our
duty' " (Luke 17:10). The Fathers teach the same thing. Ambrose says,
"It is ordained of God that he who believes in Christ is saved, freely
receiving forgiveness of sins, without works, through faith alone."
(AC VI; *Concordia*, pp. 33–34)

Our churches teach that lawful civil regulations are good works of
God. They teach that it is right for Christians to hold political office,
to serve as judges, to judge matters by imperial laws and other exist-
ing laws, to impose just punishments, to engage in just wars, to serve
as soldiers, to make legal contracts, to hold property, to take oaths
when required by the magistrates, for a man to marry a wife, or a
woman to be given in marriage [Romans 13; 1 Corinthians 7:2]. (AC
XVI 1–2; *Concordia*, pp. 39–40)

This is why our teachers teach the churches about faith in this way.

First, they teach that our works cannot reconcile God to us or merit
forgiveness of sins, grace, and justification. We obtain reconciliation only by faith when we believe that we are received into favor
for Christ's sake. He alone has been set forth as the Mediator and

Atoning Sacrifice (1 Timothy 2:5), in order that the Father may be reconciled through Him. Therefore, whoever believes that he merits grace by works despises the merit and grace of Christ [Galatians 5:4]. In so doing, he is seeking a way to God without Christ, by human strength, although Christ Himself said, "I am the way, and the truth, and the life" (John 14:6). . . .

Furthermore, we teach that it is necessary to do good works. This does not mean that we merit grace by doing good works, but because it is God's will [Ephesians 2:10]. It is only by faith, and nothing else, that forgiveness of sins is apprehended. The Holy Spirit is received through faith, hearts are renewed and given new affections, and then they are able to bring forth good works. Ambrose says: "Faith is the mother of a good will and doing what is right." (AC XX 8–10, 27–30; *Concordia*, pp. 42, 43)

This entire topic about the distinction between the spiritual kingdom of Christ and a political kingdom has been explained in the literature of our writers. Christ's kingdom is spiritual [John 18:36]. This means that the knowledge of God, the fear of God and faith, eternal righteousness, and eternal life begin in the heart. Meanwhile, Christ's kingdom allows us outwardly to use legitimate political ordinances of every nation in which we live, just as it allows us to use medicine or the art of building, or food, drink, and air. Neither does the Gospel offer new laws about the public state, but commands that we obey present laws, whether they have been framed by heathens or by others. It commands that in this obedience we should exercise love. (Ap XVI 54–55; *Concordia*, pp. 194–95)

For Christ's Church always held that the forgiveness of sins is received freely. Indeed, the Pelagians were condemned. They argued that grace is given because of our works. Besides, we have shown above well enough that we hold that good works should follow faith. "Do we then overthrow the law?" asks Paul. "On the contrary, we uphold the law" (Romans 3:31), because when we have received the Holy Spirit through faith, the fulfilling of the Law necessarily follows. Patience, chastity, and other fruit of the Spirit gradually grow by this love. (Ap XX 91–92; *Concordia*, p. 201)

I do not know how to change in the least what I have previously and constantly taught about justification. Namely, that through faith, as St. Peter says, we have a new and clean heart [Acts 15:9–11], and God will and does account us entirely righteous and holy for the sake of Christ, our Mediator [1 Timothy 2:5]. Although sin in the flesh has not yet been completely removed or become dead [Romans 7:18], yet He will not punish or remember it.

Such faith, renewal, and forgiveness of sins are followed by good works [Ephesians 2:8–9]. What is still sinful or imperfect in them will not be counted as sin or defect, for Christ's sake [Psalm 32:1–2; Romans 4:7–8]. The entire individual, both his person and his works, is declared to be righteous and holy from pure grace and mercy, shed upon us and spread over us in Christ. Therefore, we cannot boast of many merits and works, if they are viewed apart from grace and mercy. As it is written, "Let the one who boasts, boast in the Lord" (1 Corinthians 1:31); namely, that he has a gracious God. For with that, all is well. We say, besides, that if good works do not follow, the faith is false and not true. (SA III XIII; *Concordia*, p. 283)

Affirmative Statements

The Pure Teaching of the Christian Churches about This Controversy

For the thorough statement and decision of this controversy, our doctrine, faith, and confession is as follows:

1. Good works certainly and without doubt follow true faith—if it is not a dead, but a living faith—just as fruit grows on a good tree [Matthew 7:17].

2. We believe, teach, and confess that good works should be entirely excluded from the question about salvation, just as they are excluded from the article of justification before God. The apostle testifies with clear words when he writes as follows, "Just as David also speaks of the blessing of the one to whom God counts righteousness apart from works: . . . 'Blessed is the man against whom the Lord will not count his sin' " (Romans 4:6–8). And again, "For by grace you have been saved through faith. And this is not your own doing; it is the gift of God, not a result of works, so that no one may boast" (Ephesians 2:8–9).

3. We also believe, teach, and confess that all people, but especially those who are born again and renewed by the Holy Spirit, are obligated to do good works [Ephesians 2:10].

4. In this sense the words *necessary*, *shall*, and *must* are used correctly and in a Christian way to describe the regenerate, and are in no way contrary to the form of sound words and speech.

5. Nevertheless, if the words mentioned (i.e., *necessity* and *necessary*) are used when talking about regenerate people, then only due obedience—not coercion—is to be understood. For the truly believing, so far as they are regenerate, do not offer obedience from coercion or

the driving of the Law, but from a voluntary spirit. For they are no more under the Law, but under grace (Romans 6:14; 7:6; 8:14).

6. We also believe, teach, and confess that when it is said, "The regenerate do good works from a free spirit," this is not to be understood as though it were an option for the regenerate person to do or not to do good when he wants, as though a person can still retain faith if he intentionally perseveres in sins [1 John 2:5–9].

7. This is not to be understood in any other way than as the Lord Christ and His apostles themselves declare. In other words, the free spirit does not obey from fear of punishment, like a servant, but from love of righteousness, like children (Romans 8:15).

8. However, this willingness (liberty of spirit) in God's elect children is not perfect. It is burdened with great weakness, as St. Paul complains about himself in Romans 7:14–25 and Galatians 5:17.

9. Nevertheless, for the sake of the Lord Christ, the Lord does not charge this weakness to His elect, as it is written, "There is therefore now no condemnation for those who are in Christ Jesus" (Romans 8:1).

10. We believe, teach, and confess also that works do not maintain faith and salvation in us, but God's Spirit alone does this, through faith. Good works are evidences of His presence and indwelling [Romans 8:5, 14]. (FC Ep IV 5–15; *Concordia*, p. 483)

COMMUNITY
We Are Not Alone[1]

I am a spiritual person, but I am not religious." Have you ever heard someone say something like this? Perhaps you have had the same thought yourself. Today, many people feel that no organized religion empowers them to be healthy, renewed, or growing human beings—or even Christians! To them, rituals and organizations found in churches are mere empty shells.

Such observations may be well-meant as one seeks a deeper relationship with God from our point of view. After all, human beings think of themselves as the center of the world. We all like to choose what is best for ourselves. So we tend to look for a "god" who may satisfy our desires and wishes. If the Christian God does not deliver or meet our specifications, we might seek another option to support and cultivate our own "spirituality." Further, in a religiously diverse environment, even Christians tend to switch denominational affiliations. They float around, attempting to find a place that they can call "home," at least temporarily.

Jesus says: "I came that they may have life and have it abundantly" (John 10:10). In this chapter, you will explore the Lutheran conviction that we do have abundant life given in the Church. Lutherans confess in Article VII of the Augsburg Confession that the Church is the assembly of all believers "in which the Gospel is purely taught and

---

1   Adapted from *The Lutheran Spirituality Series: Community*, written by Naomichi Masaki, edited by Robert C. Baker. Copyright © 2007 Concordia Publishing House.

the Sacraments are correctly administered."[2] It answers the questions "Where is the Church?" and "Where can I find a church home?" Lutherans confess that a true Church is not measured by personal taste or sincere spirituality; rather, the Church is where our crucified and risen Lord Jesus lives and gives His abundant gifts.

Jesus, who showed His love at Calvary, bids you come to His Church. Connected with Him, our lives will ever be "full of sap and green" (Psalm 92:14). Discover the richness and joy that is found in the Lord's Church alone and the life that is lived there together as Christians in community.

Where Christ Is, There Is the Church

I believe that I cannot by my own reason or strength believe in Jesus Christ, my Lord, or come to Him. But the Holy Spirit has called me by the Gospel, enlightened me with His gifts, sanctified and kept me in the true faith. In the same way He calls, gathers, enlightens, and sanctifies the whole Christian Church on earth and keeps it with Jesus Christ in the one true faith. In this Christian Church He daily and richly forgives all my sins and the sins of all believers. On the Last Day He will raise up me and all the dead and will give eternal life to me and to all believers in Christ. This is most certainly true. *Martin Luther*[3]

For some people, the Church is an institution with a certain hierarchy and distinguished buildings. For others, the Church is a gathering of like-minded religious people. For still others, the Church is a fellowship that works toward a common goal. The rise of the mega-church and mass marketing of religion has caused many to evaluate the Church or a specific gathering of believers as something designed primarily to meet their perceived needs. People seem to pick churches like they might pick restaurants. The problem with a focus on personal appeal and personal fulfillment is that our perceived "selves" change throughout our lives. The question becomes whether God's searchlight

---

2   *Concordia*, p. 34.
3   SC II; *Concordia*, p. 330.

of the Law can pierce the depths of our souls and whether we need a personal application of the Gospel that actually brings Christ's healing and renewal to us in a fundamental way. Luther confessed a Scripture-based "yes" on both counts. For him, the Church is believers who have been called, enlightened, and sanctified by the Holy Spirit through the Gospel, and the place where our sins are daily and richly forgiven.

JESUS CONTINUES HIS OWN MINISTRY _____

As a preparation for our inquiry into the New Testament Church, it may be helpful first to see the big picture. In Acts 1:1, Luke reminds his readers that he has written in his Gospel what Jesus "began to do and teach," and that his first book ended at the Lord's ascension. The form of the Greek word translated as "began" implies that what follows in the Book of Acts is what Jesus did and taught. A better title for *The Acts of the Apostles* might be *The Acts of the Lord Jesus*, because Jesus is the main figure in Acts. Another title could be *The Acts of the Word of the Lord*, because Luke tells of how "the word of the Lord" grew (Acts 6:7; 12:24; 19:20).

Luke presents the Book of Acts as a continuation of his Gospel. As the opening chapter unfolds, Luke summarizes the Lord's Passion, resurrection, and promise of the Holy Spirit (verses 3–5) before recounting again the ascension of the Lord (verses 6–11). The Book of Acts records the choice of Matthias to fill the apostolic office that was vacated by Judas (verses 12–26) before presenting the outpouring of the Holy Spirit on Pentecost (2:1–13). Luke includes the sermon Peter preaches on behalf of the Twelve (2:14–36) and identifies the results of Peter's sermon—the repentance and Baptism of three thousand people (verses 37–41)—before describing the life of the newly baptized disciples (2:42–47).

A particular feature of Luke's account of the ascension is the cloud that "took [Jesus] out of their sight" (Acts 1:9). In the Old Testament, clouds often indicate God's glory, holiness, and presence. There was the pillar of cloud during the exodus (Exodus 13:21–22; 14:19–25; 16:10; 19:9, 16; 24:15–18; 33:9–10; 40:34–38; Numbers 9:15–23; 10:11–35) and the cloud in and over the tabernacle (Exodus 40:36–37) and the temple (1 Kings 8:10–11; cf. John 12:41). Luke uses a similar expression of "overshadowing" by a cloud (see Exodus 40:35) at the conception of Jesus (Luke 1:35). Luke also records that a cloud overshadowed Jesus with Moses and Elijah on the mount of the transfiguration (Luke 9:34).

Along with the cloud, fire also indicated the glory and speech of the Lord (Exodus 3:2; 19:18; 24:17; Leviticus 9:24).

Jesus' bodily ascension into a cloud does not mean that He is no longer present and active upon the earth (see Ephesians 1:19b–23; 4:10).[4] The exalted Lord is actively and graciously present in His Means of Grace, as Acts 2:14–47 shows. In his *Lectures on Genesis,* Luther wrote: "But we see this glory [John 8:56] face to face. We hear God speaking with us and promising forgiveness of sins in Baptism, in the Supper of His Son, and in the true use of the keys. These Abraham did not have, but he saw in the spirit and believed. Therefore our glory is greater."[5]

More than half of Acts 1 is devoted to the story of Matthias (verses 12–26), who was selected to fill the apostolic office vacated by Judas, an office that could not be left empty. Thus before the events of the day of Pentecost, the Lord guided the selection of Matthias, who was nominated along with Barsabbas from the number of those who had accompanied Jesus and the disciples from the beginning. After prayer, "the lot fell on Matthias, and he was numbered with the eleven apostles" (Acts 1:26). But shortly after the events of Pentecost, the Twelve as a group disappeared. This is not surprising because the apostles are the ones who were *sent* by Jesus (John 20:21; Romans 10:15; Titus 1:5). As an ambassador speaks only what he is given by the sender to speak (John 8:28; 16:13; 15:26; 20:21–23), so the "apostles' teaching" (Acts 2:42) was heard and kept as the teaching, or doctrine, of Jesus (Matthew 28:20; Ephesians 4:11–13). What the Lord caused to grow, therefore, was not a special class of disciples called "apostles" or even the gathering of believers in terms of simple numbers, but He caused the words and doctrine of Jesus to grow—"the word of the Lord increased" (Acts 6:7; 12:24; 19:20).

THE HOLY SPIRIT AND JESUS' MINISTRY _____

In both his Gospel and the Book of Acts, Luke makes specific mention of the role of the Holy Spirit.[6] The Spirit came upon Mary at the conception of Jesus.[7] He descended on Jesus at His Baptism (Luke 3:22) as the voice from heaven declared that Jesus was the promised Suffering Servant who was sent by the Father to bear the sins of the whole world

---

4   See also FC SD VII 119; VIII 27–30 (*Concordia*, pp. 580, 586–87).
5   AE 2:353.
6   See Luke 1:35; 3:16 (cf. Acts 1:5; 2:1–4, 38); 3:22; 4:18; 24:49.
7   Luke 1:35; cf. AE 36:341 "through the Word."

and to answer for them on Calvary (Isaiah 42:1; 52:13–53:12; John 1:29–34). Luke records the words of John the Baptist concerning Jesus: "He will baptize you with the Holy Spirit and with fire" (Luke 3:16; cf. Acts 1:5; 2:1–4, 38), as well as Jesus' self-identification with the prophet Isaiah's statement that "the Spirit of the Lord is upon Me" (Luke 4:18). Before He left them, Jesus promised to send His disciples the Holy Spirit from the Father (Luke 24:49). In all of these passages, we observe that the Holy Spirit was active in what "Jesus began to do and teach" (Acts 1:1) in Luke's Gospel.

The apostle John tells us more about the works of the Holy Spirit. He records Jesus' statements that the Holy Spirit's office is to teach and bring to remembrance all that He has said (John 14:26), to bear witness about Jesus (15:26), to guide us to the truth (16:13), and to glorify Jesus (16:14). In other words, the Holy Spirit's job is to deliver Jesus. He distributes the benefits of the saving work of Jesus through the Means of Grace.

The ascension of Jesus and the sending of the Holy Spirit are followed by Peter's preaching on behalf of the Twelve. Peter's sermon as recorded in Acts 2:14–37 proclaimed Jesus of Nazareth—that He came from the Father, ministered among men, suffered, was crucified, rose, ascended, and poured out the promised Holy Spirit. But the clincher was that Peter rightly accused his hearers as those who had crucified this Jesus, who was made both Lord and Christ (Acts 2:36; cf. 1 Corinthians 1:18; 2:2). The hearers knew immediately that they were guilty, which prompted them to ask the disciples, "Brothers, what shall we do?" (Acts 2:37).

The preaching of Peter ended in water. Peter called for repentance and for Baptism for the forgiveness of sins (Acts 2:38). He also further taught and exhorted his listeners (Acts 2:40). In these verses, the passive voice dominates. Those who received the Word "were baptized"; they "were added" (Acts 2:41). In this way, what the Lord mandated and instituted was done: "repentance and forgiveness of sins should be proclaimed in [Jesus'] name" (Luke 24:47).

But what happened after Peter's sermon? The Pentecost congregation was gathered by preaching and Baptism, as we have seen, and those who were baptized held to the teaching of the apostles, fellowship, the breaking of the bread, and the prayers. "The teaching of the apostles" is the teaching of Jesus (John 14:26; 15:26; 16:13–14; Matthew 28:20). Fellowship (Greek: *koinonia*) embraces either the Lord's Supper (1 Corinthians 10:16–17), fellowship among the baptized through the love gifts (Romans 15:26; 2 Corinthians 8:9; 9:13; Hebrews 13:16), or both. The "breaking of the bread" is the celebration of the Lord's Supper (Acts 20:7–11). "Prayers" are answers to the gifts of God when they are received. Acts 2:43–47 further informs us about the life of this new congregation. The baptized were moved by the work of the apostles, they were ready to offer everything, they praised the Lord, they had favor with all the people, there was profound joy, and the Lord added to their number day by day.

FORGIVENESS ACHIEVED AND DISTRIBUTED

Luther wrote: "We treat of the forgiveness of sins in two ways. First, how it is achieved and won. Second, how it is distributed and given to us."[8] To see how this is accomplished, we look to the ascension of Christ, the descent of the Holy Spirit, and the life of the early Church.

The ascension of Christ and the sending of the Holy Spirit can never be separated. It is the ascended Lord Jesus (Acts 1:6–11) who continued His own ministry on earth (Acts 1:1) by sending the Holy Spirit (Acts 2:1–13; John 20:22–23). The Holy Spirit bound Himself to the Means of Grace (preaching, Baptism, the Lord's Supper) to do what He is given to do (John 14:26; 15:26; 16:7, 13–14). The Lord also gave the apostles to deliver these gifts; that was the reason for His *sending* them (Acts 1:12–26; John 20:21–23; Matthew 28:16–20; Mark 16:15; Luke 24:44–49; Ephesians 4:11–12; 2 Corinthians 5:17–21).

Recalling Luke 1:1, Acts 1:1–2:13 describes implicitly what Paul speaks about in 1 Corinthians 1:17–18 and Colossians 1:20 and 2:14, namely, how Jesus accomplished salvation for us (forgiveness achieved). Acts 2:14–47 shows how Jesus actually bestows the salvation upon us (forgiveness distributed) that He won on the cross. Luther helps us properly to distinguish between salvation achieved and salvation distributed. We confess that the Church's foundation is Jesus, our Lord. He builds His Church Himself through the work of the Holy Spirit in the Means of Grace. The Church is not built on the basis of the religious fellowship, the act of faith, the will of man, or the holiness of our lives. Neither is the Church found in our hearts and spirituality. The Church does not start with us; rather, it starts with Christ and His forgiveness.

---

8 AE 40:213.

WHERE CHRIST IS, THERE IS THE CHURCH ____

In Acts 2, the life of the congregation was characterized by the inexpressible joy of the newly baptized, the simplicity of faith clinging to the apostles' teaching, the awe of their hearts before the wonders of the Spirit, the brotherly love that was ready to offer everything, the prayers, the celebrations of the Sacrament of the Altar, and the praise of God. Today we see the same joy as we gather around Word and Sacrament in our congregations, repeating the same statements of invocation, confession, absolution, liturgical song, and great hymns that have been used for hundreds if not almost two thousand years. We also support one another, whether in prayer or through monetary or other physical means of action.

Ignatius of Antioch, a Christian pastor who lived immediately following the apostles, wrote: "Wherever the bishop [pastor] appears, there let the multitude [congregation] be; just as wherever Jesus Christ is, there is the catholic [universal] church."[9] According to Ignatius, the Church is where Christ is; Christ gives Himself in His Means of Grace. Therefore, if we want to see Jesus, we go to where a congregation is assembled in His name and is being served by His called and ordained servant distributing Jesus' gifts: the Gospel and the Sacraments.

SPIRITUAL EXERCISES _____

◇ Be comforted by the fact that even when we are tempted by Satan, the world, and our sinful flesh, we may still say with Luther: "Nevertheless, I am baptized."[10] Pray "God's Own Child, I Gladly Say It" (*LSB* 594) in thanksgiving to God for this precious gift.

◇ Luther wrote that the Church is like "the mother that conceives and bears every Christian through God's Word [Galatians 4:26]. Through the Word He reveals and preaches."[11] When you next attend church services, ponder how the Church cares for you through Word and Sacrament.

◇ Reflect on how Jesus as the Lord of the Church and the Giver of forgiveness and life may be reflected in other areas of congregational life, including the works of various congregational boards and committees. Also consider how this is true in your daily Christian life and in your family life.

---

9 Translated by the author of this chapter from vol. 1 of *The Apostolic Fathers*.
10 LC IV 44, 77–78; *Concordia*, pp. 427, 430.
11 LC II 42; *Concordia*, pp. 403–4.

POINT TO REMEMBER _____

So those who received his [Peter's] word were baptized, and there were added that day about three thousand souls. And they devoted themselves to the apostles' teaching and the fellowship, to the breaking of bread and the prayers. *Acts 2:41–42*

The Lord's Giving and Our Receiving

Our Lord speaks and we listen. His Word bestows what it says. Faith that is born from what is heard acknowledges the gifts received with eager thankfulness and praise. Music is drawn into this thankfulness and praise, enlarging and elevating the adoration of our gracious giver God. Saying back to him what he has said to us, we repeat what is most true and sure. Most true and sure is his name, which he put upon us with the water of our Baptism. We are his.[12]

Think about world religions that you may know or have studied, for example, Islam, Judaism, Hinduism, Buddhism, Confucianism, Shinto. You could also add to this list many groups that falsely claim to be Christian, such as the Latter-Day Saints (Mormons) or Jehovah's Witnesses. And of course there are the numerous cults and sects and groups that gather around charismatic leaders. Considering all these various groups, are there any common aspects to the purpose of worship?

In most religions, "worship" is humanity's approach to a deity or higher power. Even where worship is considered a two-way communication between the deity and human beings, many religions (including some bearing the name *Christian*) see people doing certain things (religious acts or rituals) to get God or the deity to perform some service for them. But this understanding of "worship" is quite different from what is described in the Bible. There, God shows us that He meets us on His own initiative and serves us not with what we want, but with what we truly need.

_____

12 *Lutheran Worship* (St. Louis: Concordia, 1982), p. 6.

THE LORD'S GIVING—OUR RECEIVING _____

When God finished creating the world, He saw everything that He had made and pronounced it "very good" (Genesis 1:31). Then, He kept a Sabbath (Genesis 2:1–3). In his *Lectures on Genesis*, Luther noted that "man was especially created for the knowledge and worship of God."[13] If we understand with Luther that the purpose of our creation was worship—that is, the Lord serving us with His Word as well as all His temporal (earthly) gifts—we may recognize such worship as a target of Satan. He seeks to attack "God's good will and makes it [his] business to prove from the prohibition of the tree that God's will toward man is not good. . . . The highest form of worship itself, which God had ordained, it tries to destroy."[14] Satan's specific target is our faith in God's Word. Luther continues: "For when the Gospel is preached in its purity, men have a sure guide for their faith and are able to avoid idolatry. But then Satan makes various efforts and trials in an effort either to draw men away from the Word or to corrupt it."[15]

Despite the fall into sin, God comforted Adam and Eve with the promise of a Messiah who would be born to crush the head of the serpent (Genesis 3:15). God then covered Adam and Eve with the skins of slain animals, whose blood had been spilled (Genesis 3:20–24). Luther notes that these skins served "as a reminder to them to give thought to their wretched fall from supreme happiness into the utmost misfortune and trouble" and "a sign that they are mortal and that they are living in certain death."[16] Because of humanity's fall into sin, God's atonement for our sin through "the Lamb of God, who takes away the sin of the world" (John 1:29) becomes the primary theme, common thread, and consistent focus running throughout all of Scripture (see Revelation 5:13; 21:22–23).

Even before Christ came into the world, God provided opportunities for His Old Testament people to receive His forgiveness of sins. Although there are many Old Testament passages that discuss the sacrificial services, in Exodus 29:38–46 we may discern the following four points:

1. Old Testament worship was not humanity doing something for God, but the Divine Service that God had instituted. While most English Bibles translate Exodus 29:38 as "This is what you shall *offer* on the

---

13 AE 1:80.
14 AE 1:146.
15 AE 1:146.
16 AE 1:221.

altar," the Hebrew text says, "This is what you are *to do* on the altar." "To offer" leaves an impression that the central point here is man's act of giving something to God. However, *to do* sounds strikingly similar to "*This do* in remembrance of Me," Christ's words instituting His Holy Supper (see Luke 22:19). In fact, in the Greek translation of the Old Testament (the Septuagint), the same Greek word is used in Exodus and in the accounts of the institution of the Lord's Supper.

2. The Old Testament services centered on the slaughtering and burning of the accepted animals, whose flesh and blood had been separated. The blood was used for purification (cf. Leviticus 4:14–16), and the flesh was burned. "A pleasing aroma" (Exodus 29:41) was a sign of God's acceptance of the sacrifice and of the people who brought the sacrificial animal, as well as of His withdrawal of wrath and judgment (cf. Genesis 8:21).

3. The purpose of such sacrificial service was for God to meet with His people at the sanctuary and to speak to them through Moses. The service was God's appointed meeting. The Hebrew used here indicates that it is not just people coming together as a congregation. The Lord draws His people by His appointment.

How does the worship of the early Christians correspond to the sacrificial worship of the Old Testament believers? In chapters 9 and 10, the writer to the Hebrews compares worship under the first covenant and under the new covenant (see also Matthew 28:19–20; Luke 24:46–47; 1 Corinthians 11:23–26).

1. Animal sacrifices were the chief part of the Old Testament Divine Service. However, these only pointed forward in time to the one perfect and final offering of Christ's body and blood on the cross (Hebrews 9:11–12). In the New Testament Divine Service, the chief parts of the Divine Service are preaching and the administration of the Lord's Supper.

2. While God mandated Old Testament ceremonial worship, which was also fulfilled in Christ, the New Testament Church centered its liturgy freely on the Service of the Word (taken from familiar synagogue worship) and the Service of the Sacrament (based on the Lord's institution of His Supper).

3. The Old Testament sacrifices, priesthood, tabernacle, and temple were all fulfilled in Christ; therefore their use ceased (Hebrews 10:8–10). In the New Testament, each believer is a priest having immediate access to God through Christ, who serves as High Priest over His Church (Hebrews 10:19–22).

4. As in the Old Testament, so also in the New: in worship, God takes an initiative in coming to serve His people with His grace. Luther writes: "For the Lord not only instituted it [the Lord's Supper], but also prepares and gives it himself, and is himself cook, butler, food, and drink."[17]

Christ's atoning sacrifice on Calvary and His resurrection are central to New Testament worship because "without the shedding of blood there is no forgiveness of sins" (Hebrews 9:22). All of Old Testament worship, ceremony, and Law pointed forward to the coming of Christ, who is their fulfillment. In the New Testament Church, the preaching of the Gospel and the administration of the Sacraments objectively deliver to their recipients the blessings and benefits of Christ's life, death, and resurrection. These can only be—and are—truly received through the gift of faith. Thus New Testament worship centers upon Christ: the salvation that He achieved for us and that He delivers to us even now through His Means of Grace.

FROM OUR RECEIVING TO OUR GIVING _____

Writing about Mary's song of praise in Luke 1:46–55, Luther noted: "For no one can praise God without first loving Him. No one can love Him unless He makes Himself known to him in the most lovable and intimate fashion. And He can make Himself known only through those works of His which He reveals in us, and which we feel and experience within ourselves."[18]

Mary loved and obeyed God because God first showed His love to her. She not only offered her praises to her gracious Lord, she offered her body and indeed her entire life to the Lord's service. She epitomizes total consecration, brought about by grace, to the Lord. Luther also writes on the Magnificat:

> "My soul magnifies God, the Lord." These words express the strong ardor and exuberant joy with which all her mind and life are inwardly exalted in the Spirit. Therefore she does not say, "I exalt the Lord," but, "My soul doth exalt Him." It is as if she said: "My life and all my senses float in the love and praise of God and in lofty pleasures, so that I am no longer mistress of myself; I am exalted, more than I exalt myself, to praise the Lord." . . . She is caught up, as it were, into Him and feels herself lifted up into His good and gracious will . . . . All words and thoughts fail us, and our whole life and soul must be set in

---

17 AE 37:142.
18 AE 21:300.

motion, as though all that lived within us wanted to break forth into praise and singing.[19]

The fruit of God's grace in our lives, as in the life of Mary, includes the confession of His name, both in the Divine Service and to our neighbor, and the good works or sacrifices we perform for our neighbor. Mundane tasks such as changing the baby's diaper take on a whole new meaning when it is understood that such is holy work when it is done by a believer trusting in Christ's merits. Our entire lives—including our bodies—are to be "living sacrifice[s]" (Romans 12:1) offered in faith to God and in service to our neighbor in love. Such good works, which the Lord both commands and enables, will be recognized on the Last Day (Matthew 25:31–46).

THE VITALITY OF FAITH

Luther noted: "It is a living, busy, active, mighty thing, this faith. It is impossible for it not to be doing good works incessantly. It does not ask whether good works are to be done, but before the question is asked, it has already done them, and is constantly doing them."[20]

The dynamic flow of the Gospel—the forgiveness of sins, life, and salvation—occurs in preaching, Absolution, Baptism, and the Lord's Supper. Luther writes:

> Wherever that Word is heard, where Baptism, the Sacrament of the Altar, and absolution are administered, there you must determine and conclude with certainty: "This is surely God's house; here heaven has been opened." . . . This is nothing else than calling it the kingdom of heaven and heaven itself, for the place where God dwells is the house of God. But where does God dwell? Does he not dwell in heaven? Therefore he joins the earth with heaven and heaven with the earth.[21]

After receiving the Lord's Supper, we ask God to strengthen us through this precious gift "in faith toward You and in fervent love toward one another."[22] God sends us back into our places in life, fed on His Word and on the Supper, eager to be of service to those in our congregation, our families, and our neighbors.

---

19 AE 21:302, 307.
20 AE 35:370.
21 AE 5:244.
22 From the collect penned by Luther for his German Mass of 1526; *LSB*, p. 183.

SPIRITUAL EXERCISES _____

❖ One result of the restoration of the Gospel at the Reformation was the participation of the congregation in the liturgy. Congregational participation means first and foremost hearing the words of the Lord and receiving His body and blood, because only then (as a result) do the gifts of the Lord flow into our lips and our works. Ask the Holy Spirit to make you a joyful recipient of the Lord's gifts.

❖ In preparation for receiving the Lord's Supper, meditate on the hymn "Thee We Adore, O Hidden Savior" (*LSB* 640).

❖ Using a Lutheran hymnal or service folder, distinguish between the sacrificial parts of worship (prayer, praise, thanksgiving) and the sacramental parts of worship (preaching, Baptism, the Lord's Supper).

POINT TO REMEMBER _____

Through Him [Jesus] then let us continually offer up a sacrifice of praise to God, that is, the fruit of lips that acknowledge His name. Do not neglect to do good and to share what you have, for such sacrifices are pleasing to God. *Hebrews 13:15–16*

Fellowship as Partaking

I believe in the Holy Spirit, the holy Christian Church, the communion of saints, the forgiveness of sins, the resurrection of the body, and the life ✝ everlasting. Amen. *Apostles' Creed*

Since we are gathered to hear God's Word, call upon Him in prayer and praise, and receive the body and blood of our Lord Jesus Christ in the fellowship of this altar, let us first consider our unworthiness and confess before God and one another that we have sinned in thought, word, and deed, and that we cannot free ourselves from our sinful condition. Together as His people let us take refuge in the infinite mercy of God, our heavenly Father, seeking His grace for the sake of Christ.[23]

As a community, the Lord has blessed us Christians with fellowship. Through Baptism, He incorporated us into His Body, the Church. We are not alone (see Ephesians 2:19–22). We recall what God said after

_____
23 *LSB*, p. 203.

the creation of Adam: "It is not good that the man should be alone" (Genesis 2:18). We were not created to live alone, nor are we re-created to live alone. Instead, God has planned that we are to live together in community.

FELLOWSHIP AS GIFT

In the first section of this chapter, we observed from Acts 2 that the fellowship God gives us in Christ is established by Baptism and culminates in the breaking of bread (the Lord's Supper). Paul, who addresses the church of God at Corinth as the saints who have been sanctified and called (1 Corinthians 1:2), declares that they have been called "into the fellowship [koinonia] of [God's] Son, Jesus Christ our Lord" (1:9). By the one Spirit, they were all baptized into one Body (1 Corinthians 12:13), the Body of Christ (verse 27). In Christ's Body, fellowship is not something that we do (active fellowship) but something that we receive (passive fellowship) as a gift. In his explanation of the Third Article of the Apostles' Creed, Luther notes that fellowship is received by the Spirit's grace through the Gospel, and not by our own doing.[24]

According to the apostle John, the proclamation of Jesus brings the hearers into fellowship (koinonia) with those who proclaim Him and into the fellowship (koinonia) with the Father and with His Son, Jesus Christ (1 John 1:3, 6, 7). In the apostolic benediction of 2 Corinthians 13:14, fellowship (koinonia) is associated with the Holy Spirit. Scholars discuss whether "the fellowship of the Holy Spirit" is to be understood either as a common participation in the Holy Spirit or the fellowship worked by the Holy Spirit. It should be both. Through the Means of Grace, we are brought into fellowship with the triune God. And it is the Holy Spirit who brings us into such fellowship by delivering Jesus to us through the Means of Grace.

In 1 Corinthians 10:16–17, Paul asks rhetorically whether the bread and wine that we bless in the Sacrament is a "participation" (ESV), "communion" (NKJV), or "sharing" (NASB) in Christ. All of these English words have been translated from koinonia, the same Greek word we find in 1 Corinthians 1:9. Why does Paul explain the Lord's Supper this way? In 1 Corinthians 10:16–17, those to whom our Lord gives His body and blood in the Lord's Supper are by that body and blood "fellowshiped." To be together at the Lord's Table is to be in the fellowship. The emphasis is not our being together at the table as brothers and

---

24 See SC II; *Concordia*, p. 330.

sisters in Christ, but what the body and blood of the Lord are doing to those who receive them. The fellowship does not come from us, but from the body and blood of Jesus.

The Greek word *koinonia* ("fellowship") comes from *koinon* ("the common thing"). Luther built upon this concept of "community" or "communion" that flows from the body and blood creating "fellowship" in 1 Corinthians 10:16–17 as follows: "Finally, 'participation' here means the common possession in which they all participate and share, viz. something which has been given to them all in common."[25] What we are given to eat and to drink at the Lord's Table is not faith in the heart but the body and blood of our Lord, as Luther says: "It cannot in this passage mean the fellowship of faith in the heart, for the text speaks here of a common possession which one may receive and enjoy, such as the bread and cup. . . . So it is now evident that *koinonia*, 'participation in the body of Christ,' is nothing else than the body of Christ as a common possession, distributed among many for them to partake."[26]

The usual interpretation of "communion of saints" (Latin: *sanctorum communio*) that is used in the Apostles' Creed of the Latin-speaking Christian tradition is a communion of holy persons, namely, the saints.[27] Some scholars argue that the phrase is better understood as a communion of *holy things* (the Lord's body and blood), a point that Greek-speaking Christianity has long emphasized in its liturgy.[28] At the very least, 1 Corinthians 10:16–17 does refer to the *koinonia* in the Lord's body and blood in His Supper and should at least leave room for understanding this phrase in the Creed as the communion of saints among whom the *holy things* (the body and blood of the Lord) are given and received.

In the New Testament, the word *koinonia* ("fellowship") also refers to the fellowship of believers arising from the fellowship that they have with their risen Lord. On the one hand, the preaching of the Gospel and

---

25 AE 37:353.

26 AE 37:353.

27 The Missouri Synod historically has focused on this as a reference to the Church. Most churches that come out of the Latin-speaking Christian tradition (medieval Catholicism) also stress this meaning.

28 See, for example, J. N. D. Kelly, *Early Christian Creeds*, 3rd ed. (London: Longman, 1972), 389–90. See also Hermann Sasse, "Sanctorum Communio," in *This Is My Body*, rev. ed. (Adelaide: Lutheran Publishing House, 1977), 351–70. Christians historically have interpreted *sanctorum communio* as a reference to both the Church and to the Sacraments, sometimes stressing one over the other. Lutherans and other Protestants rejected aspects of the phrase attached to Roman ideas of sainthood, saintly merits, and the cult of the saints, all of which are contrary to Scripture.

Baptism place the faithful into fellowship with the Lord and His body and blood. Such a fellowship then moves into love and work, among which the gifts for the bodily and spiritual needs of fellow believers are certainly first and foremost. On the other hand, the giver in giving and the receiver in receiving become united (2 Corinthians 8:13–15). According to Romans 12:12–13 and Hebrews 13:15–16, the praise and thanks sacrifices of the Christians are connected with prayer, love gifts, and works of charity. Intimate and personal experience with the temple sacrificial services, which continued in Jerusalem until AD 70, may have aided early Christians in interpreting love more sacrificially. Love gives all of itself, including the use of one's body (Romans 12:1).

The nineteenth-century theologian Friedrich Schleiermacher spoke of God contrary to Scripture as the "World Soul" that reveals itself within human hearts and minds throughout history. In this context, Schleiermacher wrote that the Church "is a fellowship created by the voluntary actions of men."[29] He also wrote: "The Christian church is formed by the coming together of regenerated individuals for ordered interaction and cooperation."[30] In stark contrast, we confess according to the Scriptures that our coming together does not constitute the Church, but that the Lord creates, nourishes, and maintains His Church through His Means of Grace (the Gospel and the Sacraments). The fellowship (*koinonia*) among believers is constituted not by our will or even by the common faith that we possess in our hearts, but solely by Christ.

THE LIFE OF FELLOWSHIP

A study of the Greek use of *fellowship* in the New Testament proves that God provides a unique, spiritual fellowship that is not derived from psychological, sociological, or common-cause convictions. Rather, it is a gift given to us by Christ to make us one with Him and with one another. When fellowship is confessed as something that flows from the Christian altar, we are prompted to treat one another not just as friends but as the ones into whose mouths are put the Lord's true body and true blood. In 1 Corinthians 10:16–17, Paul describes those who receive the body and blood of the Lord as one body (and perhaps also one blood). Christian fellowship goes beyond a fellowship hall; it

---

29 Translated by the author of this chapter from *Der christliche Glaube nach den Grund-sätzen der evangelischen Kirche*, 2nd ed. (Berlin: Reimer, 1830–31), section 2.2.

30 Translated by the author of this chapter from *Der christliche Glaube*, section 115.

flows from a Communion table (see Romans 14:9–10; Ephesians 5:21; Matthew 5:23–24).

As we saw earlier in the chapter, the Church's mission is Jesus' continual ministry on earth. Mission has as its purpose the fellowship/communion (*koinonia*) of the nations with their Lord (1 John 1:3; 1 Corinthians 1:9) in His body and blood (Acts 2:42; 1 Corinthians 10:16–17). Rather than following fundamental principles from therapeutic and social science models, the Church's evangelism and missions have at their center the proclamation of the Gospel and a vibrant sacramental life. Nevertheless, the Church can use helpful human observations to deal with communication and acts of mercy.

THE BLESSINGS OF FELLOWSHIP

Fellowship in the New Testament sense is much more than "the voluntary actions of men." While individual members serve one another in holy love, a Christian congregation is far different from a support group or a special-interest group. Left to ourselves, most of us search out community with people who are just like us or who share similar joys or concerns. But God loves us too much to abandon us to our own inclinations. He provides us with a deeper fellowship. Christian fellowship is unique because it is rooted in the cross where our Lord bore all of our sins. We experience both the fellowship of His sufferings (Philippians 3:10) and the power of His resurrection, because in Holy Baptism we have been united with Him in His death and resurrection (Romans 6:3–4). Because of Christ's strength, shared with us in Word and Sacrament, we are enabled to attend to the needs of our neighbors (Galatians 6:2), serving them in Christian love.

In our Christian fellowship, the Lord supplies us with a family of faith that transcends race, culture, political persuasion, nationality, and even time and space because the Christian community is united to the God-man, Jesus Christ. We hear in the liturgy: "Therefore with angels and archangels and with all the company of heaven we laud and magnify Your glorious name."[31] Similarly, Paul writes: "I therefore, a prisoner for the Lord, urge you to walk in a manner worthy of the calling to which you have been called . . . . There is one body and one Spirit—just as you were called to the one hope that belongs to your call—one Lord, one faith, one baptism, one God and Father of all, who is over all and through all and in all" (Ephesians 4:1, 4–6).

---

31   *LSB*, p. 208.

SPIRITUAL EXERCISES _____

◈ Today, North American culture emphasizes the desires and demands of the individual, often at the expense of or to the detriment of the community as a whole. In prayer, ask the Lord to help you to discern how you, your family, and your congregation might become more aware of and active in caring for the physical and spiritual needs of your community.

◈ Commit to memory Luther's explanation of the Third Article of the Apostles' Creed (*Concordia*, p. 330).

◈ Give thanks to God for Christian community by meditating on the hymn "The Church's One Foundation" (*LSB* 644).

POINT TO REMEMBER _____

The cup of blessing that we bless, is it not a participation in the blood of Christ? The bread that we break, is it not a participation in the body of Christ? Because there is one bread, we who are many are one body, for we all partake of the one bread. *1 Corinthians 10:16–17*

The Gift and Service of the Pastor

So that we may obtain this faith, the ministry of teaching the Gospel and administering the Sacraments was instituted. Through the Word and Sacraments, as through instruments, the Holy Spirit is given [John 20:22]. He works faith, when and where it pleases God [John 3:8], in those who hear the good news. *Augsburg Confession*[32]

Our churches teach that no one should publicly teach in the Church, or administer the Sacraments, without a rightly ordered call. *Augsburg Confession*[33]

Jesus continues His own ministry on earth through the Church that preaches, baptizes, absolves, administers His body and blood, encourages, comforts, exhorts, and sustains. What, then, of pastors? This is what God's Word says about this precious gift:

You are fellow citizens with the saints and members of the household of God, built on the foundation of the apostles and prophets, Christ Jesus Himself being the cornerstone. *Ephesians 2:19–20*

---

32 AC V 1–2; *Concordia*, p. 33.
33 AC XIV; *Concordia*, p. 39.

How then will they call on Him in whom they have not believed? And how are they to believe in Him of whom they have never heard? And how are they to hear without someone preaching? *Romans 10:14*

And He gave the apostles, the prophets, the evangelists, the shepherds and teachers, to equip the saints for the work of ministry, for building up the body of Christ. *Ephesians 4:11–12*

So often we hear about the power struggle between a pastor and a congregation. "Who is the boss?" "Who is in charge?" Martin Chemnitz, an important Lutheran theologian after Luther and Philip Melanchthon, taught that the Church consists of both teachers (pastors) and hearers (laypersons). The pastor is not there for himself but to serve the congregation. People are not left alone to serve the Gospel to themselves but are given the instrumental service of the pastor. The sound understanding of the pastoral office starts with the recognition that the Lord of the Church is Jesus, and that Jesus continues to serve His people with the Gospel in His Church.

THE OFFICE THAT DELIVERS THE MEANS OF GRACE

The Lutheran Confessions note several passages of Scripture pertaining to the doctrine of the Office of the Holy Ministry. The chief passage is John 20:21–23, which recounts one of Jesus' appearances to His disciples after the resurrection. According to Article XXVIII of the Augsburg Confession, the authority of the Keys or of the bishops (pastors)

is a power or commandment of God, to preach the Gospel, to forgive and retain sins, and to administer Sacraments. Christ sends out His apostles with this command, "As the Father has sent Me, even so I am sending you. . . . Receive the Holy Spirit. If you forgive the sins of anyone, they are forgiven; if you withhold forgiveness from any, it is withheld" (John 20:21–22).[34]

Immediately preceding this command from Jesus, He has given His peace to His disciples (John 20:19, 21). To the weak, vulnerable, and fearful disciples, Jesus comes not with a word of judgment, but of peace. But Jesus' statement of "Peace to you" is no mere greeting. This peace is different than the peace the world gives (John 14:27). With His words, Jesus bestows the peace that His blood on Calvary accomplished for us all (Ephesians 2:13–14). To make this greeting more unique, Jesus

---

34 *Concordia*, p. 58.

breathes on His disciples as He gives the Holy Spirit. This reminds us of the creation account, where God breathed into man's nostrils the breath of life, and man became a living being (Genesis 2:7). It also brings to mind the story of the valley of dry bones in Ezekiel 37. In the Nicene Creed, we confess the Holy Spirit as "the giver of life." Here, Jesus is doing what only God can do: He gives life to the dead. He gives to His disciples His breath, His Spirit, and His words. These are one gift, which should not be broken into pieces. Jesus' words, alive with His breath and His Spirit, bring the forgiveness by which we dead sinners are brought back to life.

The Lutheran Confessions also refer to Matthew 28:19–20[35] as the Lord's mandate and institution of the Office of the Holy Ministry.[36] In Greek, the first words that Jesus speaks to the Eleven are "given to Me" (Matthew 28:18). The "authority" Jesus has is a gift from the Father. The Greek word for "authority" (*exousia*) is the noun form of a common impersonal verb meaning "it is permitted, allowed." The significant point is that the apostleship is not an office of crude power. Neither does Jesus pass on "all authority" to the Eleven. All authority continues to stay with Jesus even as He commands the Eleven to carry out certain tasks (going, baptizing, teaching).

The duties Jesus assigns to the Eleven have nothing to do with the power and governance of the world or worldly things. He gives the mandate to the Eleven to make disciples by baptizing and teaching in the place(s) where the Lord would have them go, until the consummation of time. This mission would extend to all the Gentiles. The apostles do not float about, "going," with nothing given them from the Lord to do, nor do Baptism and teaching float around as abstract functions seeking someone to carry them out. The mandate does not end with the original apostles. The apostles' ministry will continue through their successors as the apostolic ministry. Matthew, like Luke, presents the ministry and office of Jesus through the instrumentality of the apostolic office.

Still another passage the Confessions use to confess the Holy Ministry is 2 Corinthians 5:17–21.[37] According to the apostle Paul, Christ gave to the Church the "ministry of reconciliation" (2 Corinthians 5:18), entrusting to the Church "the message [word] of reconciliation"

---

35 Together with the Jesus' words in John 20, this passage from Matthew's Gospel account has always been heard in the Church's ordination rite for pastors.

36 See Tr 31; *Concordia*, p. 298.

37 See Ap XXIV (XII) 79–81; *Concordia*, pp. 232–33.

(verse 19). Thus the apostles speak "on behalf of [in the place of] Christ" (verse 20) as the authorized sent-ones, as the "ambassadors for [in the stead of] Christ" (verse 20). Paul's statement that "in Christ God was reconciling the world to Himself" (verse 19) becomes the proclamation: "Be reconciled to God" (verse 20). The reconciliation of God in Christ takes place subjectively (in those who hear the message) in the very proclamation of the messengers of God. "When they[38] offer God's Word, when they offer the Sacraments, they offer them in the stead and place of Christ."[39]

Martin Chemnitz comments on this passage from 2 Corinthians:

> . . . as Paul asserts, that in the preaching of the Gospel Christ Himself speaks through the mouth of the ministers (Rom. 15:18–19; 2 Cor. 13:3) and that God is "making His appeal through us" (2 Cor. 5:20). So in the action of the Eucharist the minister acts as an ambassador in the place of Christ, who is Himself there present, and through the ministers pronounces these words: "This is My body; this do," etc., and for this reason His Word is efficacious. Therefore it is not a man, the minister, who by his consecration and blessing makes bread and wine into the body and blood of Christ, but Christ Himself, by means of His Word, is present in this action, and by means of the Word of His institution, which is spoken through the mouth of the minister, He brings it about that the bread is His body and the cup His blood, clearly in the same manner as it is He Himself who baptizes, though it be through the minister, and through His Word brings it about that Baptism is a washing of regeneration and renewal.[40]

Christians can take great comfort in knowing that it is Christ Himself who operates on their behalf where the Gospel is proclaimed in its purity and the Sacraments are administered according to His institution. Our salvation is dependent upon and is delivered to us by Christ through the office that He Himself instituted to serve out the Means of Grace.

MISUSE OF THE OFFICE

Jesus has mandated and instituted the Office of the Holy Ministry to deliver the forgiveness of sins that He won on the cross. Attention is

---

38 Ministers, that is, those who represent the person of Christ on account of the call of the Church.

39 Ap VII and VIII 28; *Concordia*, p. 148. The phrase in Latin is: *Cum verbum Christi cum sacramenta porrigunt, Christi vice et loco porrigunt.*

40 Martin Chemnitz, *Examination of the Council of Trent*, trans. Fred Kramer, Chemnitz's Works 2 (St. Louis: Concordia, 1978), 229.

not directed to the pastor; there is no scriptural ground to claim that a pastor has an indelible character. A pastor is not a better-sanctified person. He is not in a higher class within the Lord's Church. Any such talk can only invite the power talk of the world into the Church, which may prompt the questions "Who is the boss?" and "Who is in charge?" Lutherans rejoice in the doctrine of the Holy Ministry as the Lord's arrangement for the dynamic flow of the Gospel. The focus is not on the pastor, but on the words and actions he delivers: the preaching of the Gospel and the administration of the Sacraments. It is not a case of the pastoral office versus the royal priesthood of believers.

As Article XIV of the Augsburg Confession states—and reflecting "the sending" of John 20, Matthew 28, 2 Corinthians 5, and Romans 10—no one steps into the preaching office; instead, men are put into it. The call does not come immediately, but mediately through the Church. If a man puts himself into the Office of the Holy Ministry, even though the content of his message may be sound, it causes doubts in the minds of hearers because, as Chemnitz says, "the real heart of the ministry is that God by His Spirit and His grace wants to be present with the ministry and through it work efficaciously."[41] Jesus instituted not only functions of the Means of Grace but also the office of preaching, which is to be filled by a man whom He sends. If a man is given profound understanding of the sound doctrine and the ability to teach it, then the right attitude, according to Chemnitz, is not to teach without a call but to seek a legitimate call.[42]

THE OFFICE, NOT PERSONS

When we look to our pastors, we look to the office that they hold and not to them as persons. Recognizing that they are forgiven sinners just like us, overlooking their petty faults, and forgiving them their sins, we support them as they serve us. This is both our job and our joy as Christians.

According to Paul, pastors have the right to expect that their services for Christ's flock will be fairly remunerated (see 1 Corinthians 9:14 and 1 Timothy 5:17–18; Paul often did not demand his rights, however). Of course, "how" and "how much" and other such questions are answered at the congregational (or institutional) level. Nevertheless,

---

41 Martin Chemnitz, *Loci Theologici*, trans. J. A. O. Preus, Chemnitz's Works 8 (St. Louis: Concordia, 2008), 1315.

42 Chemnitz, *Loci Theologici*, 8:1316–18.

church members should see to it that their pastors (and all called workers and staff) are adequately cared for. In addition to living expenses, insurance, and retirement plans, this includes prayer, moral support, and encouragement for those who preach, teach, and serve us in the name of Christ.

Pastors who abuse their authority, who persistently teach false doctrine, or whose lifestyle betrays their confession of Christ should not be tolerated as spiritual leaders within the Church. However, those pastors who serve faithfully and selflessly should be duly honored as God's servants, loved, and, when it comes to preaching God's Word faithfully, obeyed, so that their work might be a joy (Hebrews 13:17).

SPIRITUAL EXERCISES

◈ Meditate upon the hymn " 'As Surely as I Live,' God Said" (*LSB* 614) as you give thanks to God for the gift of your pastor(s).

◈ Pray for your pastor(s), as well as all called and contract staff, other employees, officers, and volunteers in your congregation. Ask them personally if they have any special needs to which you could attend.

◈ Support the livelihood of your pastor(s) and other church workers through your sacrificial gifts and offerings of money, talents, and time.

POINT TO REMEMBER

Jesus said to them again, "Peace be with you. As the Father has sent Me, even so I am sending you." And when He had said this, He breathed on them and said to them, "Receive the Holy Spirit. If you forgive the sins of any, they are forgiven them; if you withhold forgiveness from any, it is withheld." *John 20:21–23*

We Are Not Alone

A Priest is not identical with Presbyter or Minister—for one is born to be priest, one becomes a minister. . . . We neither can nor ought to give the name priest to those who are in charge of Word and sacrament among the people. *Martin Luther*[43]

---

43 AE 40:18, 35.

The Church does not depend on the faith of individuals but on the preaching of the Gospel and the administration of the Sacraments. Through these means, God creates faith. However, faith is never autonomous. As Lutherans rejoice in the preaching office that delivers the Means of Grace, they also treasure the precious doctrine of the priesthood of believers.

THE ROYAL PRIESTHOOD AS THE LORD'S GIFT

The most frequently cited passage of Scripture addressing the "priesthood of believers" is 1 Peter 2:9–10. However, this passage draws on the account of the Israelite exodus out of Egypt and the giving of the Law at Mount Sinai.

In Exodus 19:5–6, most English translations render verse 5 in terms of obedience ("if you will indeed obey My voice" [ESV]; "if you obey Me fully" [NIV]; etc.). But the Hebrew text reads: "if you really hear My voice" or "if you listen closely to My voice." What difference does this make in our understanding of Exodus 19:5? By designating Israel as His possession, God proclaimed His gracious election of Israel and its treasured status before Him. God is not talking about the duties of Israel in the world but about Israel's special relationship with Him.

In Exodus 19:6 ("you shall be to Me a kingdom of priests and a holy nation"), the word *priests* modifies *kingdom* in the same way that the word *holy* modifies *nation*. The priesthood as an office had not yet been instituted by God (see Exodus 28). The priestly imagery would have come from the priestly service of the patriarchs (the heads of households) (see Genesis 4:3; 8:20; 12:8) or those who functioned as *priests* already. The priestly service was characterized by consecration to the Lord (Exodus 19:22), the privilege to draw near to God (Exodus 19:22, 24), and possibly the responsibility of sacrifice. Since the Aaronic priesthood had not yet been instituted, and since all were not required to serve as official priests even then, here in Exodus 19:6 the phrase "of priests" is a figure of speech, a metaphor. It denotes a dignity and privilege that come from a special relationship with God. Thus God established a relationship with His chosen and delivered people, who were to Him like unto priests, that is, wholly consecrated to Him. They are His "treasured possession" through hearing His Word.

Even before the Aaronic priesthood was established, some served in a special official priestly capacity (see Exodus 19:22, 24). Perhaps this is in anticipation of the service Aaron and his sons would provide later. However, this would indicate a distinction between the "priestly kingdom" and the "office" of priest, which would develop later.

In the first chapter of his first Epistle, Peter presents strong baptismal imagery (verses 3–5). In chapter 2, Peter carries the rebirth imagery forward, creating "milk" imagery based on the "rebirth" of Baptism that he discusses in chapter 1. Like newborns, believers should "long for the pure spiritual milk" (verse 2) of God's Word, which gives growth. By remaining in the Word (i.e., milk, see 1 Peter 1:22–25), which in Baptism translated them into the kingdom, they will "grow up into salvation" (1 Peter 2:2).

Peter explains that the result of the election into the kingdom is "being built up" (1 Peter 2:5). The work is God's, and He does it through Baptism. The use of the word *spiritual* throughout these chapters does not mean nonmaterial, but that which is caused by the Holy Spirit, something that comes to us as a gift, that which belongs to the sphere of the Holy Spirit. Thus a "spiritual house" is a house in which the Spirit dwells, where He does His work and bestows His gifts. We are reminded of the Spirit descending on Jesus at His Baptism. In our Baptism, we become temples of the Holy Spirit. He placed His name on us as God's chosen children. Only in 1 Peter are we told of the "priesthood." In Greek, it includes action, actor, and community. A better translation would be "a body of functioning priests." Peter is speaking of the priesthood as a community, a people of God. They are given something to do: "to offer spiritual sacrifices acceptable to God through Jesus Christ" (1 Peter 2:5). "Spiritual sacrifices" are works done in and by the Holy Spirit. Because the Holy Spirit dwells in the body of priests through Baptism, such sacrifices flow from them.

Peter borrows from Isaiah 43:20 when he writes: "But you are a chosen race" (1 Peter 2:9). The one who does the electing is exclusively God (Jesus). Jesus is Himself "the Chosen One" (Luke 9:35; 23:35). The chosen-ness of Christ (1 Peter 2:4, 6) is now explicitly given to the baptized. The election of God's people is founded on and derived from the election of Jesus as the Messiah.

THE ROYAL PRIESTHOOD IN LUTHER _____

Luther spoke of the royal priesthood primarily as a defense against the Roman Church and its concept of priesthood. While Luther never used the term "the priesthood of believers," in *The Babylonian Captivity of the Church* he pointed to 1 Peter 2 as proof that all Christians are priests.[44] Luther also cited 1 Corinthians 4 when discussing the Office of the Holy Ministry, whose officeholders are priests according to their Baptism and ministers according to their call.

In his Epistles, Paul speaks to equality of all believers before Christ and with one another (see Galatians 3:26–29). However, among those who are equal "sons of God through faith" in Christ Jesus are those whom God, through His call, has officially set apart to serve His Church with His Means of Grace. These ministers are servants of the Body of Christ (see 1 Corinthians 4:1).

A proper distinction between the Office of the Holy Ministry and the priesthood of believers provides the laity a sense of freedom. While all believers are equally "priests" in the sense of 1 Peter 2, within the Body of Christ, the Church, we serve one another through our particular station of life. Thus the unity and equality of the individual members of Christ's Body does not mean uniformity of action. Each is called to serve within his and her distinctive vocation, using his or her own God-given gifts. One does not invade, so to speak, another's office and its duties and responsibilities. Congregational leaders do not belong in the pulpit; the pastor should not "run the show." All in all, the doctrine of the priesthood of believers confesses Jesus as the Lord and Head of the Church, for cut off from the High Priest (Christ), priests would lose their priesthood.

THE JOY OF LIVING
AS THE ROYAL PRIESTHOOD

In his *Retraction*, Luther wrote: "In all my writings I never wanted more than that all Christians should be priests; yet not all should be consecrated by bishops, not all should preach, celebrate mass, and exercise the priestly office unless they have been appointed and called to do so. This was my final intention."[45]

What may we make of the fact that 1 Peter 2:9 is referenced only once in the Lutheran Confessions, and then only to point out that the Church cannot be deprived of pastors, as Rome wanted?[46] The doctrine of the priesthood of believers was never intended to support the practice that all Christians should preach and administer the Sacraments.

44 See AE 36:112–13.
45 AE 39:233.
46 See Tr 69; *Concordia*, p. 304.

Rather, it was to defend the Church from any kind of displacement of Christ as the Giver of all His gifts. This teaching serves to defend the Church against unfaithful and legalistic pastors. It teaches pastors to be faithful to their calls even as it teaches believers to be faithful in their vocations. Therefore, in citing 1 Peter 2:9 in the Treatise on the Power and Primacy of the Pope, Philip Melanchthon does not suggest that every baptized person should publicly preach, teach, and administer the Sacraments. His concern was that the baptized should never be deprived of the service of a faithful pastor of the Gospel.

In 1 Peter 2, we hear such phrases as "newborn infants," "living stones," "a chosen race, a royal priesthood, a holy nation," and "God's people" (verses 2, 5, 9–10). The gifts of the Lord continue to flow into the royal priesthood to enliven, energize, and shape our lives. What a privilege! What a joy! It is no wonder that Lutherans have always rejoiced in the teaching of the priesthood of believers. The royal priesthood originates in Baptism. The Church is made up of people elected from every nation, a chosen crowd gathered by the Holy Spirit, assembled under Christ the Head. The Church is not just an assembly of like-minded individuals coming together. The Church is the Body of Christ, in which all the individual members are incorporated and where all members form one body. The baptized are the priests who praise the wonderful deeds of Christ for our salvation and serve one another with His love. We are not alone. We are connected with Christ; we are also connected with all His people—those who are alive here on earth as well as those who are alive with Christ in heaven.

SPIRITUAL EXERCISES

◈ Read and reflect on 1 Peter 2:1–10. Say a prayer or sing a praise to the Lord as these words of the Lord guide you.

◈ Meditate on the following hymns as you consider your various callings as God's royal priest:

"All Christians Who Have Been Baptized" (*LSB* 596)
"The Gifts Christ Freely Gives" (*LSB* 602)
" 'Come, Follow Me,' the Savior Spake" (*LSB* 688)
"Not for Tongues of Heaven's Angels" (*LSB* 695)
"May We Thy Precepts, Lord, Fulfill" (*LSB* 698)

◈ Apply the doctrine of the priesthood of believers to the life of your congregation. Think about how this doctrine may be a great blessing in our Church.

POINT TO REMEMBER

> But you are a chosen race, a royal priesthood, a holy nation, a people for His own possession, that you may proclaim the excellencies of Him who called you out of darkness into His marvelous light. Once you were not a people, but now you are God's people; once you had not received mercy, but now you have received mercy. *1 Peter 2:9–10*

Church, Family, and the World

> All fathers and mothers who regulate their household wisely and bring up their children to the service of God are engaged in pure holiness, in a holy work and a holy order. . . . Above these three institutions and orders [church, family, government] is the common order of Christian love, in which one serves not only the three orders, but also serves every needy person in general with all kinds of benevolent deeds, such as feeding the hungry, giving drink to the thirsty, forgiving enemies, praying for all men on earth, suffering all kinds of evil on earth, etc. Behold, all of these are called good and holy works. However, none of these orders is a means of salvation. There remains only one way above them all, viz. faith in Jesus Christ. *Martin Luther*[47]

The Lord of the Church is Jesus. He is our Savior both in terms of His going to the cross for us and His bringing His gifts from the cross to us here and now. When we have received His gifts, He continues to give us more. His giving is abundant (John 3:34; 10:10). But His giving does not stop with our receiving. When the people of God have been enlivened by His gifts, they bear fruit in their lives.

CHRISTIAN VOCATION

When we hear the word *vocation*, we usually think only in terms of an occupation or a job (counselor, civil servant, electrician, mother). However, the functions we perform are only part of our vocation. Vocation means "calling," and this calling embraces the whole of our lives. In our vocations, we serve others in the relationships to which God has called us.

47   AE 37:364, 365.

In Ephesians 4:1 and 2 Thessalonians 2:13–14, Paul uses the word *calling* to refer to the salvation we have received by God's grace through the Gospel of Jesus Christ. But this calling to the salvation we have received in Christ, our calling to eternal life, moves us out into our earthly callings, our vocations. Luther writes: "We conclude, therefore, that a Christian lives not in himself, but in Christ and in his neighbor. Otherwise he is not a Christian. He lives in Christ through faith, in his neighbor through love. By faith he is caught up beyond himself into God. By love he descends beneath himself into his neighbor."[48] Luther's remarks detract from self-made "spiritualities" that would be self-seeking or self-serving. Faith is directed toward Christ, who strengthens us by His grace. Love is directed toward our neighbor. Faithful attendance at the Divine Service, caring for an ill loved one, Bible reading, daily prayer at home, and maintaining faithful work habits on the job are all examples of the numerous, interconnected daily ways in which we live out our calling to salvation.

The service of God's royal priests takes place not only within the congregation but also in the world where God has placed us—in our families, in our daily work, and with our friends. The Lord does not need our service, but He directs us to the people who need our service of Christian love. Luther's vibrant understanding of vocation as the context for the life of the royal priesthood is seen vividly in his Small Catechism. Particularly in the Table of Duties, Luther describes the priestly sacrifices of believers without even once mentioning the word *priest*. Yet they are priestly sacrifices offered as to the Lord, priestly because of the sacrifices believers make as they serve their neighbor in his or her need, there where the Lord puts Himself to receive our service.

While individual Christians are called to specific vocations, the Church is called to a common mission of edification (teaching) and mission. We, as the royal priesthood, engage in the works of edification and mission because we cannot do otherwise. The direction of both edification and mission is toward the conversion of the sinner, his or her incorporation into the Body of Christ in Baptism, and his or her reception of the body and the blood of our Lord in Holy Communion. Luther writes:

> He leads us first into His holy congregation and places us in the bosom of the Church. Through the Church He preaches to us and brings us to Christ. . . . The Spirit has His own congregation in the

---

48 AE 31:371.

world, which is the mother that conceives and bears every Christian through God's Word [Galatians 4:26]. Through the Word He reveals and preaches . . . . We further believe that in this Christian Church we have forgiveness of sin, which is wrought through the holy Sacraments and Absolution [Matthew 26:28; Mark 1:4; John 20:23] and through all kinds of comforting promises from the entire Gospel. . . . Everything, therefore, in the Christian Church is ordered toward this goal: we shall daily receive in the Church nothing but the forgiveness of sin through the Word and signs . . . . There is nothing but ‹continuous, uninterrupted› forgiveness of sin. This is because God forgives us and because we forgive, bear with, and help one another.[49]

Rather than following therapeutic and social science models, the Church's edification and mission are centered around proclamation of the Gospel and a vibrant sacramental life.

God's royal priests go about their daily affairs and business, doing their work as wives or mothers, husbands or fathers, sons or daughters, employers or employees, and so on. In various stations inside and outside the home, they are urged to lead "beautiful" lives, doing "beautiful" works, as Matthew 5:16 and 1 Peter 2:11–12 and 3:1, 15 tell us (the Greek word translated as good literally reads "beautiful" or "noble" works, deeds, and conduct). By these good works, believers attract unbelievers to the faith that they hold and confess and of which they speak as opportunities arise. Such evangelism and mission may be said to be the highest expression of priestly love for the neighbor. As only good trees bear good fruit (Matthew 5:13–16), and a branch bears fruit only when it is connected to the vine (John 15:5), the key here is to continue to be at the receiving end of the Lord's gifts. In other words, we are encouraged to be the people of God, the royal priesthood, and to let the vitality of the Lord flow in our daily living in service to our neighbors, both for their temporal needs and their eternal salvation.

SPOUSE AND FAMILY

Marriage and family cannot be separated from our life in the priesthood of believers. Marriage is holy ground and sacred space. In the New Testament, "to marry" means "to fit together" or "to pair." Jesus says, "What therefore God has joined together [which literally means yoked together or paired together], let not man separate" (Matthew 19:6). Marriage is where the Lord Himself fits and fastens two persons to each other. Life *together* is a gift, just as life itself is a gift (Genesis 2:23;

---

49 LC II 37, 42, 54, 55; *Concordia*, pp. 403, 404, 405.

2:7). Adam ruined the glorious life in the presence of God and in the world. But the Second Adam redeemed us (1 Corinthians 15:22, 45; Romans 5:12–19). Marriage is the Lord's work. A Christian husband and a Christian wife have first been fitted to Christ, and then they fit with each other. Therefore as Christian marriage, begun by God, begins with the forgiveness of sins by Christ, so it continues, grows, and flourishes within His forgiveness of sins. Husband and wife live in the water of Baptism, feed upon the body and the blood of the Lord's Supper, speak Absolution as they forgive each other in the name of Christ, hear and read the Word of the Lord in the home, and pray together as coequal children of the same heavenly Father. Such a marriage, in which both a husband and a wife look to the Lord and His gifts, is very different from the one in which they look at each other to try to hold their marriage together with their own love.

In the same way that marriage is best when lived in the Lord, so the best thing that Christian parents can do to and for their children is to continue to bring them to Jesus (Matthew 19:14) through Bible stories; through prayers at table and before bed; teaching them the Scriptures, the Small Catechism, and Christian hymns; by bringing them regularly to the Divine Service and to other services and instructional settings such as Sunday school; and by modeling before them a life of continual repentance and the forgiveness of sins. The best way parents can serve their children is by being people of God, by continuing to receive His gifts in the context of a life lived out not merely with our lips but also with our lives. Children will see, remember, and, with God's grace, put into practice our daily course of living and our faithfulness to the Lord and His Means of Grace.

FOR HIS CHURCH, JESUS PRAYS _____

Jesus' preservation of His Church is no smaller miracle than His founding of it, just as His preservation of the world is no smaller miracle than His creation of it. The Church can no more be destroyed than Christ can be destroyed. For His Church, Christ prays.

In John 17, especially verses 9–11, 20, Jesus moves from His farewell discourse to His disciples to His farewell prayer. He speaks to the Father, but this is not a mere man who is praying. Here prays the eternal Son. All other prayers are prayers of creatures to their Creator, but this prayer is prayed by the Son to the Father. Jesus, the only Priest in the New Testament in the proper sense of the word, prays for His Church as the High Priest. The one who is on the way to the cross prays for His disciples: "Holy Father, keep them in Your name, which You have given Me, that they may be one, even as We are one. . . . Sanctify them in the truth; Your word is truth" (John 17:11, 17). Jesus does not think only of His apostles. Rather, He looks further than the farthest times of the Church's history, over all generations, over all the centuries to the end of the world. He prays: "I do not ask for these only, but also for those who will believe in Me through their word" (John 17:20). Jesus prays for the preservation of the Church. And His prayer is heard. This is why we confess in the words of the Augsburg Confession that "one holy church is to remain forever."[50] What a joy and comfort for us to know that Jesus, the Lord and the Head of the Church, prays for His members, His Church!

There is nothing that more deeply binds parents and children together then the intercession we make for each other. There would be far less anxiety about our children if we would lay all our cares for them on the fatherly heart of God. There is nothing that so binds husband and wife together, that so helps them bear each other's burdens, as the intercessions they make for each other. There also is nothing in the Church that so binds its members together as interceding for one another. Paul wrote: "For this reason I bow my knees before the Father, from whom every family in heaven and on earth is named" (Ephesians 3:14–15). We are reminded of a scene from Bo Giertz's novel *The Hammer of God* in which a dying father responds to his daughter when she urged him to think about Jesus: "I am not able to, Lena. I can't think any longer. But I know that Jesus is thinking of me."[51] What holds sure and certain is not what we do to God or to each other. The most certain ground of our confidence is that we are God's. The Lord gave us an eternal home and an everlasting destiny through Baptism. He gives us abundant life in His Church by continuing to serve us with the forgiveness of sins won by Christ on the cross and delivered in preaching and the Lord's Supper. Jesus is continually thinking of us. He continually prays for His Church. He prays for you! His Church will live forever!

---

50 AC VII 1; *Concordia*, p. 34.
51 Bo Giertz, *The Hammer of God* (Minneapolis: Augsburg, 1973), 165.

SPIRITUAL EXERCISES _____

◈ Meditate on the Table of Duties in the Small Catechism (*Concordia*, pp. 346–48). Reflect on the Scripture passages that apply to the stations in your life.

◈ We have discussed the common vocation of the royal priesthood in the Church, which has to do with edification (teaching) and mission. Consider how you may contribute to these two areas of our life together as baptized people.

◈ The vitality in our daily calling, whether it may be found in our church or family or world, comes from the Lord's gifts. Seek the opportunities to receive the comfort, strength, and vitality that come through the forgiveness of sins in faithful hearing of preaching, daily remembrance of your Baptism, humble reception of the Lord's body and blood, and the hidden treasure of private Confession and Absolution.

POINT TO REMEMBER _____

And they devoted themselves to the apostles' teaching and the fellowship, to the breaking of bread and the prayers . . . praising God and having favor with all the people. And the Lord added to their number day by day those who were being saved. *Acts 2:42, 47*

Lutheran Teaching on Community

Our churches teach that one holy Church is to remain forever. The Church is the congregation of saints [Psalm 149:1] in which the Gospel is purely taught and the Sacraments are correctly administered. For the true unity of the Church it is enough to agree about the doctrine of the Gospel and the administration of the Sacraments. It is not necessary that human traditions, that is, rites or ceremonies instituted by men, should be the same everywhere. As Paul says, "One Lord, one faith, one baptism, one God and Father of all" (Ephesians 4:5–6). (AC VII; *Concordia*, p. 34)

Strictly speaking, the Church is the congregation of saints and true believers. However, because many hypocrites and evil persons are mingled within them in this life [Matthew 13:24–30], it is lawful to use Sacraments administered by evil men, according to the saying of

Christ, "The scribes and the Pharisees sit on Moses' seat" (Matthew 23:2). Both the Sacraments and Word are effective because of Christ's institution and command, even if they are administered by evil men.

Our churches condemn the Donatists, and others like them, who deny that it is lawful to use the ministry of evil men in the Church, and who think that the ministry of evil men is not useful and is ineffective. (AC VIII; *Concordia*, p. 34)

Our churches teach that no one should publicly teach in the Church, or administer the Sacraments, without a rightly ordered call. (AC XIV; *Concordia*, p. 39)

We do not agree with them [the Roman Church] that they are the Church. They are not the Church. Nor will we listen to those things that, under the name of Church, they command or forbid. Thank God, ‹today› a seven-year-old child knows what the Church is, namely, the holy believers and lambs who hear the voice of their Shepherd [John 10:11–16]. For the children pray, "I believe in one holy Christian Church." This holiness does not come from albs, tonsures, long gowns, and other ceremonies they made up without Holy Scripture, but from God's Word and true faith. (SA III XII; *Concordia*, p. 283)

I believe in the Holy Spirit, the holy Christian Church, the communion of saints, the forgiveness of sins, the resurrection of the body, and the life everlasting. Amen.

What does this mean?

Answer: I believe that I cannot by my own reason or strength believe in Jesus Christ, my Lord, or come to Him. But the Holy Spirit has called me by the Gospel, enlightened me with His gifts, sanctified and kept me in the true faith. In the same way He calls, gathers, enlightens, and sanctifies the whole Christian Church on earth and keeps it with Jesus Christ in the one true faith. In this Christian Church He daily and richly forgives all my sins and the sins of all believers. On the Last Day He will raise up me and all the dead and will give eternal life to me and to all believers in Christ. This is most certainly true. (SC II; *Concordia*, p. 330)

I believe in the Holy Spirit, the holy Christian Church, the communion of saints, the forgiveness of sins, the resurrection of the body, and the life everlasting. Amen.

I cannot connect this article (as I have said) to anything better than Sanctification. Through this article the Holy Spirit, with His office, is declared and shown: He makes people holy [1 Corinthians 6:11]. Therefore, we must take our stand upon the term *Holy Spirit*, because it is so precise and complete that we cannot find another. For there are many kinds of spirits mentioned in the Holy Scriptures, such as the spirit of man [1 Corinthians 2:11], heavenly spirits [Hebrews 12:23], and evil spirits [Luke 7:21]. But God's Spirit alone is called the Holy Spirit, that is, He who has sanctified and still sanctifies us. For just as the Father is called "Creator" and the Son is called "Redeemer," so the Holy Spirit, from His work, must be called "Sanctifier," or "One who makes holy."

"But how is such sanctifying done?"

Answer, "The Son receives dominion, by which He wins us, through His birth, death, resurrection, and so on. In a similar way, the Holy Spirit causes our sanctification by the following: the communion of saints or the Christian Church, the forgiveness of sins, the resurrection of the body, and the life everlasting. That means He leads us first into His holy congregation and places us in the bosom of the Church. Through the Church He preaches to us and brings us to Christ." (LC II 34–37; *Concordia*, p. 403)

PROMISE
God Is for Us[1]

The Lord is a promise maker and a promise keeper. The Bible records God's first promise in Genesis in which He promises to crush the head of the serpent-deceiver (Genesis 3:15). It also records God's last promise in Revelation, in which the crucified, risen, and reigning Christ promises, "Surely I am coming soon" (Revelation 22:20). The Bible is the written record of God's promise making and promise keeping.

The life of faith is lived trusting in God's promises, which all find their "yes" and "amen" in Jesus Christ (2 Corinthians 1:20). Faith clings to God's promises and calls upon them in every facet of life. A genuine Christian spirituality—that is, a life shaped by the Holy Spirit working through the Word—is centered and focused on God's promises in Jesus Christ. These promises are worked out in Jesus' death on the cross, His resurrection from the dead, and His ascension to the right hand of the Father. Christian spirituality is a trinitarian spirituality flowing from the Father through the Son by the Holy Spirit, and it flows from God to us and returns from us to God.

In our consumer-oriented society, God's promises are obscured by promises of an easy life filled with material abundance, perfect health, and self-centered peace. The emphasis of much of modern Christian spirituality is the promise of the self-actualized individual whose private relationship with God provides an insider's advantage for victorious, purpose-filled living. The spirituality of the Scriptures is quite the

---

1 Adapted from *The Lutheran Spirituality Series: Promise*, written by William M. Cwirla, edited by Robert C. Baker. Copyright © 2007 Concordia Publishing House.

opposite. The Christian disciple is called each day to lose one's life, to take up one's cross, and to follow Jesus in the way of death and resurrection. This may seem counterintuitive to today's notion of spirituality, but the spiritual life lived in, with, and under God's promises is lived outside of one's self—in Christ by faith and in the neighbor by love.

This chapter will explore God's promises for us with a particular emphasis on how these play out in our daily lives of prayer and vocation.

God Keeps His Promises

My eyes are awake before the watches of the night, that I may meditate on Your promise. *Psalm 119:148*

Promises, promises. We make them all the time; we also break them more often than we would care to admit. Husbands and wives promise to live together "until death do us part." Baptismal sponsors and parents promise that the newly baptized infant will be taught the faith into which he or she has been baptized. Children promise to be home on time or to do better in school. Employers promise raises and benefits to their employees, who, in turn, promise to work hard. Our trust in promises affects our actions and attitudes toward those making and breaking their promises to us.

WE HAVE GOD'S WORD ON IT _____

As introduced above, the Bible is filled with God's promises. Those promises in Scripture are fulfilled in the world and in our lives—from His promise of a Savior to our first parents, to the promises of deliverance from this world, to the promise given to the apostle John of eternal life in the new earth and new heaven. As we review these promises, consider the many ways God has given, kept, and continues to keep His words of promise.

Genesis 3:15 records God's first promise of the Savior. It is often called the "first Gospel" (*proto-evangelium*) in the Scriptures, but Genesis 3:14–15 is actually a threat to the devil that God would work enmity between the devil and the woman, though at that specific moment there had developed an alliance of sin. Ultimately, Jesus Christ, born of a woman, came to crush the devil by His own death on the cross.

Adam, who had heard God's promise to the devil, apparently trusted the promise, because even under the sentence of death he named his wife "Eve," which is the Hebrew word for "life" (Genesis 3:20). And this name was fitting for she would become the mother of all the living, and Adam trusted that he would live even though he was sentenced to die. Eve likewise believed God's promise, because she said at the birth of her firstborn son, "I have gotten a man with the help of the LORD" (Genesis 4:1), thinking that she had conceived the Promise.[2]

God promised that He would never again destroy the whole earth with water (Genesis 9:11).[3] The visible sign of this promise to creation was the rainbow, which is appropriate because it is water in the air that refracts the light of the sun into the colors of the prism. Thus the means of destruction (water) becomes the sign of salvation (rainbow). The promise to Noah was kept in Christ by the Baptism that joins us to His death and resurrection. In Baptism, water drowns the old nature but gives birth to the new person in Christ.

God promised that Abraham would be the father of many, that his offspring would inherit the land, and that through his promised Seed all nations of the earth would be blessed (see Genesis 15:9–21; 17:1–27). Abraham believed God's promise, and God credited Abraham's faith as righteousness before Him (Genesis 15:6). In Christ, the promised Offspring and Seed of Abraham, Abraham has many children who share his faith, and we inherit, literally, an entire re-created universe along with eternal life with God. Through Jesus, the Son of Abraham, all nations of the world are blessed through His death and resurrection.

Through Nathan, God promised David that he would have a son to succeed him who would establish his throne and kingdom and build a house for the Lord's name (2 Samuel 7:5–16). Solomon did indeed establish David's kingdom and build the temple in Jerusalem. Jesus, David's greater Son, established David's throne forever at the right hand of God and made His own flesh God's eternal temple, the dwelling place of God with man (see John 2:21).

The prophet Isaiah depicted salvation on the "mountain of the LORD" (Zion) as a feast of fatted meats and fine wines, similar to the "marriage supper of the Lamb" (Isaiah 25:6; cf. Revelation 19:6–10). Feasting and table fellowship with God is a major theme in the Scriptures. Here in Isaiah, God promises that at this feast, the shroud of death

---

2   See the note for Genesis 4:1 in *The Lutheran Study Bible* (St. Louis: Concordia, 2009), p. 21.

3   The next time it will be fire! See 2 Peter 3:7, 12.

that is spread over all nations will be lifted, death will be swallowed up forever, and the tears of grief will be wiped away (Isaiah 25:7–8). The assurance for this is the Word of the Lord: "the LORD has spoken" (verse 8). When God says something, it is as good as done. As a funeral text, this section of Scripture reminds those who grieve that God has the last word over death. In His Son, Jesus, and the mountain of His cross, He has once and for all rolled up the shroud of death.

Through Jeremiah, God promises a new covenant in which God Himself will write His Torah (Word) on the hearts and minds of the people. Then they will all know God and His promise to forgive and forget their sins (see Jeremiah 31:31–34). Jesus brings the new covenant with His own blood ("this cup is the new covenant in My blood" [1 Corinthians 11:25]) and by His death takes up our sins so that they are forgiven and forgotten, buried in His death. He also sends the Holy Spirit to renew our hearts and minds and keep us with Him. The Spirit reveals Christ to us and grants us faith in Him so that we might "know Him."

JUST AS HE PROMISED

The conception and birth of Jesus marked the fulfillment of God's promises to Old Testament Israel concerning the long-promised Messiah. Repeatedly, the evangelists, particularly Matthew and John, emphasize that these things happened "in order to fulfill the Scriptures." Of particular note are the New Testament psalms in which God's faithfulness is the basis of prayer and praise. Zechariah's Benedictus (Luke 1:68–79) and Mary's Magnificat (Luke 1:47–55) are two such texts.

In the Benedictus, Zechariah recounts the promises of God even as he celebrates the circumcision and naming of his son, John. Zechariah rejoices that God has "raised up a horn of salvation" in this child (Luke 1:69), promising salvation (verse 71), mercy based on God's covenant to Abraham (verse 72), deliverance from enemies (verse 74), and freedom to serve without fear (verse 74). Zechariah proclaims that the child John "will be called the prophet of the Most High, for you will go before the Lord to prepare His ways, to give knowledge of salvation to His people in the forgiveness of sins" (verses 76–77). John's coming fulfills the promise of the messenger who prepares the way for the coming of the Lord (see Malachi 3:1; 4:5).

In the words of the Magnificat (Luke 1:46–55), Mary also recalls God's many promises to His Old Testament people. There are also parallels to the song of Hannah (1 Samuel 2:1–10). Both women gave birth to children of promise. Both women speak of God's undeserved goodness and of the great reversal of fortunes by which the humbled are exalted and the exalted are humbled. Hannah's song in particular states: "The LORD kills and brings to life; He brings down to Sheol and raises up" (1 Samuel 2:6). The extraordinary pregnancies of both these women bear witness to the fact that with God nothing is impossible and that God keeps His promises.

FULFILLED IN JESUS

The Good News of Jesus is the news of God's promises kept. God promised salvation through Israel, and God made good on His promise in the sending of His Son, Jesus, the Messiah, whose death atoned for the sin of the world and whose resurrection provided the hard evidence that God's Word is sure.

Acts 13:16–48 records Paul's sermon in the synagogue of Pisidian Antioch, a sermon that gives a dramatic overview of God's promises to Israel and their fulfillment in Jesus. In seemingly one breath, Paul takes the hearers through a recitation of what would have been familiar material: Israel, the exodus, Samuel, Saul, David, and Abraham. Then Paul proclaims: "And we bring you the good news that what God promised to the fathers, this He has fulfilled to us their children by raising Jesus" (Acts 13:32–33). The bodily resurrection of Jesus is held up as evidence that God keeps His Word. Thus the promise spoken to David, who died and was buried, was fulfilled in the Son of David who rose from the dead (see verses 36–37). This is a key point in the New Testament: if Christ was not raised from the dead, there is no reason to trust in God's promises (see 1 Corinthians 15).

The Father always deals with us through His Son, Jesus, in whom all of God's promises find their fullest expression and fulfillment (see 2 Corinthians 1:18–22). Since Jesus is the fulfillment of God's promises, it is proper to speak of the certainty of trust "through Jesus Christ," recognizing that only in Christ are we able to say our "amen" to God. Jesus is God's promise incarnate, because by His coming in the flesh and entering our history in order to redeem it, all the promises that God had in mind from all eternity are brought to bear on us. Through the same flesh of Jesus, God fulfills His promise of salvation to us in Holy Baptism, the Lord's Supper, and the spoken Word of forgiveness.

SPIRITUAL EXERCISES

◈ Recall the promises of God and apply them to your own life as a baptized believer. You may wish to record your insights in a journal.

◈ Pray meditatively on the promises of God. Luther taught a simple fourfold way of prayer that begins with a Bible text. Reflect on one or several passages from the previous pages that particularly caught your attention. First, tell God what you learned about His promises. Second, confess how those promises have not had their way with you and how you have not always trusted them. Third, ask God to deepen and widen your knowledge and trust in His promises. Fourth, thank God for fulfilling His every promise to you in Jesus.

◈ Sing or say the hymn "I Know My Faith Is Founded" (*LSB* 587).

POINT TO REMEMBER

For all the promises of God find their Yes in [Christ]. That is why it is through Him that we utter our Amen to God for His glory. *2 Corinthians 1:20*

Children of the Promise

Let Your steadfast love come to me, O LORD, Your salvation according to Your promise. *Psalm 119:41*

Children live on promises, and they trust wholeheartedly that promises made to them will be kept. The father who promises a toy to his child will be sure to hear, "Dad, you promised." No wonder Jesus compared the life of faith to that of a little child! Faith clings to God's promises. The promise of forgiveness, life, and salvation in the death and resurrection of Jesus creates and enlivens this childlike faith. As baptized believers, we are truly "children of the promise."

GOD'S LAST LAUGH

God promised Abraham that his offspring would be like the stars (Genesis 12:2; cf. Genesis 15:5), but after years of waiting, Sarah and Abraham still had no children. So Sarah followed the local custom and sent her maidservant Hagar to Abraham so they might have a child.

Thus Abraham listened to his wife instead of trusting the promise of God, and Ishmael became Abraham's firstborn son (Genesis 15:15).

Genesis 18:1–15 records a third promise of a child for Abraham and Sarah. Three visitors arrive at Abraham's tent, and one, who is really the Lord, says, "I will surely return to you about this time next year, and Sarah your wife shall have a son" (verse 10). Overhearing the conversation from the entrance to the tent, Sarah laughed audibly, but denied her laughter when confronted. A year later, Sarah did indeed conceive and bear a son just as God had promised. His name, *Isaac*, means "he laughs," reflecting Sarah's doubting laughter and God's last laugh (see Genesis 21:1–7).

Of Abraham's two sons, Ishmael, though Abraham's lawful son and firstborn, was not the son of the promise because he was born out of Abraham's unbelief. Isaac is the son of the promise because he was conceived and born according to the promise of God.

In many ways, the genealogy of Jesus recorded by Matthew in the opening verses of his Gospel is a list of "children of promise." Patterned after the lists of Genesis, the names indicate that God's promise of a Savior is carried forward through the birth of the promised child. And behind this list are often colorful stories, as the presence of the four exceptional women in Jesus' genealogy indicate. Tamar conceived by her father-in-law Judah while posing as a prostitute (Matthew 1:3; cf. Genesis 38). Rahab, a prostitute in the city of Jericho, nevertheless trusted the promise of God and was saved from destruction (Matthew 1:5; cf. Joshua 6:25). Ruth was an "outsider" to Israel, a woman of Moab, a traditional enemy of Israel. However, she promised to live as an Israelite under Yahweh, the God of Israel (Matthew 1:5; cf. Ruth 1–4). Bathsheba is not named, but is called "the wife of Uriah," reminding us of David's adultery and act of murder (Matthew 1:6; cf. 2 Samuel 11–12). These four women, each in her own way, remind us that God's promise of grace in Christ is unmerited grace toward sinners that extends to all. God works His promise "in, with, and under" the ordinary flow of history, which is riddled with sin.

The apostle Paul identifies those who truly are the children of Abraham, the children of promise: "The Spirit Himself bears witness with our spirit that we are children of God, and if children, then heirs" (Romans 8:16–17). The true children of Abraham are those who have faith in the promise as Abraham did when he believed God (see Romans 9:6–9). We know we are the children of God because the Spirit of God testifies with our spirit and enables us to say, "Abba, Father" (Romans

8:15). A true Israelite, in New Testament terms, is one who trusts in the promises of God fulfilled in Jesus, the Messiah of Israel. The Israel of the New Testament is the Church, not a specific people or parcel of land.

Paul also discusses the true offspring of Abraham in Galatians 4:22–23, 31:

> For it is written that Abraham had two sons, one by a slave woman and one by a free woman. But the son of the slave was born according to the flesh, while the son of the free woman was born through promise. . . . Brothers, we are not children of the slave but of the free woman.

The "children of the slave woman" are those who live under the Law, particularly the Law of Sinai. The "children of the free woman" are those who have been born from above from their free mother, the Church, a reference to Baptism. In Baptism we are conceived and born as children of the promise.

CHILDREN OF GOD

Children are conceived and born. That may seem obvious, but it needs to be said. The image of new birth and new creation is a strong one in John's Gospel, and in the prologue, John uses such imagery to set the tone leading up to the incarnation. God the Father has only one Child, namely, the only-begotten Son, Jesus Christ (John 1:14). All God's other children are those who are born "anew" and "from above." The baptized believer is a child of God because he or she is in Christ, God's Son. As children of God in Christ, baptized believers receive all the promises of the sons of God.

In John 1:10–13 we are reminded that all who receive Christ, that is, who believe in His name (trust His person and work), are given the right to become children of God. This is a new and heavenly birth—not a birth out of descent, decision, or by natural conception. We are born of God (John 1:12). When Jesus speaks with Nicodemus, He further clarifies that this birth is a new birth "from above" (the Greek word in John 3:3 means both "again" and "from above"). It is a new creation by water and Spirit (see Genesis 1:2). The allusion is obviously to Baptism.

In Baptism every person is treated exactly the same, whether circumcised or uncircumcised, slave or free, male or female (see Galatians 3:26–29). Despite our contemporary need for gender neutrality, Galatians 3:26 is better translated as "you are all *sons* of God" (emphasis added), even when referring to females. The point of comparison in this passage is inheritance. All are equally heirs according to the promise fulfilled in Abraham's Seed (that is, Christ), whether they are Jew or Gentile by birth, slave or free in status, male or female. Paul does not seek to obliterate these distinctions; in this world, we continue to live in the various orderings into which God has placed us. However, Paul states that in Christ these distinctions have no validity. The two gifts of Baptism in this passage are

1. We are Abraham's offspring (even if we are not related by blood to Abraham)
2. We are heirs according to the promise

Women also are "sons" in the sense that they are coequal heirs of eternal life and connection to a father or husband is not a requirement for salvation.

A NEW IDENTITY

Children draw their primary identity from their family, especially from their father, mother, and siblings. As children of God, baptized believers draw their identity from their heavenly Father; from their Brother, Jesus the Son; and from the Holy Spirit, their guardian and guide. When children act contrary to their family identity, fathers are quick to point out, "That is not who you are!" Baptism gives us a new identity in Christ Jesus as children of God. Sin is no longer who we are; that belongs to old, dead Adam. Who we are is determined by who God says we are, namely, His children (1 John 3:1).

According to Paul's words in 1 Corinthians 6:9–11, some members of the congregation in Corinth apparently had quite a past. But their former sins do not define their present identity. Despite their sinful past, the Corinthians' identity comes from what God has done for them in Christ. Paul writes: "But you were washed [baptized], you were sanctified [made holy], you were justified [declared righteous] in the name of the Lord Jesus Christ and by the Spirit of God" (1 Corinthians 6:11). That is their identity over and against their past. The future of the members of the Corinthian congregation is that they will inherit eternal life, even though those who commit such sins do not. Our baptismal identity causes us to identify with Christ rather than with our sins and to disown our sins because they are not "who we are" in Christ.

In Ephesians 5, Paul exhorts the members of that church to "be imitators of God, as beloved children" (verse 1), walking in love, "a fragrant offering and sacrifice to God" (verse 2). The apostle further clarifies that the Ephesian Christians are to avoid becoming partners with the "sons of disobedience" who walk in darkness, but they are to "walk as children of light" (verses 6–8). Paul's exhortation to holiness is not a command to shape up or ship out; rather, it is a call to be who we already are as God's children. God's children are "imitators of God," living lives of love, maintaining sexual purity, and edifying speech. As "children of light," they do not participate in the works of darkness but expose them for what they are. Instead of drunkenness, they are filled with the Spirit and address each other with psalms, hymns, and spiritual songs, giving thanks to the Father through the Son (Ephesians 5:18–20). Repentance and forgiveness is a continual call out of darkness into light, returning to our Baptism and our baptismal identity as God's children of the promise.

SPIRITUAL EXERCISES

◈ Your fellow members of the Body of Christ are brothers and sisters through Holy Baptism. As you are aware, record special needs of your baptismal brothers and sisters. As you are able, try to meet these needs. It may be as simple as a phone call or visit or sharing a meal with someone who is alone.

◈ Pray the Third Article of the Apostles' Creed together with its meaning from Luther's Small Catechism (*Concordia*, p. 330).

◈ Say or sing the hymn "God's Own Child, I Gladly Say It" (*LSB* 594). Meditate on each stanza by saying it aloud and remembering that the words apply to you in your Baptism.

POINT TO REMEMBER

See what kind of love the Father has given to us, that we should be called children of God; and so we are. The reason why the world does not know us is that it did not know Him. *1 John 3:1*

The Promise of Baptism

We must think this way about Baptism and make it profitable for ourselves. So when our sins and conscience oppress us, we strengthen ourselves and take comfort and say, "Nevertheless, I am baptized. And if I am baptized, it is promised to me that I shall be saved and have eternal life, both in soul and body." *Martin Luther*[4]

"Nevertheless, I am baptized!" was Luther's retort to the accusations of sin and conscience. This is the promise of God trusted in faith and put to use. We sometimes hear people speak of the promises we make in Baptism. The real promises in Baptism are made by God to us. In this Sacrament, all that Christ accomplished by His incarnation, His perfect life, His sacrificial death on the cross, His resurrection, and His ascension are revealed, offered, and applied to us personally in the name of God. To be baptized is to have the personal assurance of the triune God Himself that we are His children. With God's testimony comes many wonderful promises—sure as God's name is sure.

THROUGH WATER AND SPIRIT

According to the account of the creation in Genesis 1, the earth was covered with water and the Spirit of God hovered over the waters (see Genesis 1:1–3). Then God speaks into the creation to call forth life and bring order out of chaos. All life has its basis in "water and Spirit with the Word" according to Genesis.

The flood (see Genesis 6:1–8:22) returned the earth to its state in Genesis 1:2. In this sense, the flood was a type of baptism of the earth, a death of the creation and most of the world's inhabitants and a resurrection of Noah and the representatives of the creation kept in safety in the ark. Curiously, the ark was first opened on Noah's 601st birthday! It was a kind of new birth for Noah and those under him. The apostle Peter links the flood and the ark to Baptism, "which now saves you" (1 Peter 3:21). The promise in Baptism in 1 Peter 3 is that of a clear conscience before God through the resurrection of Jesus.

Another type of Baptism is the crossing of the Red Sea by the children of Israel. This event marked Israel's birth as a nation and the drowning of Israel's enemy, the army of Pharaoh (Exodus 13:17–14:31). Notice that a great east wind blew across the sea as it parted (Exodus 14:21). The Hebrew word for *spirit* and *wind* are the same, as is also the word for *breath*. At Pentecost, the Holy Spirit was manifested as a rushing wind (see Acts 2:2). In crossing the parted sea, Israel emerged as God's own people (compare Exodus 19:6 and 1 Peter 2:9), baptized into Moses (see 1 Corinthians 10:2).

---

4   LC IV 44; *Concordia*, p. 427.

The Sacrament of Baptism has also been identified with the healing of Naaman, which was accomplished when he washed in the Jordan River (see 2 Kings 5:1–15). Through the prophet Elisha, God spoke His promise of physical healing to Naaman. The actual healing took place when Naaman entered the waters of the Jordan. The text notes that the healing was so extensive or significant that Naaman's skin was renewed like that of a young boy (verse 14). So, in a sense, God's healing of Naaman served like a physical "rebirth."

After His Baptism in the Jordan, God the Father openly declared Jesus to be His beloved Son (Matthew 3:17; cf. Isaiah 42:1). The Holy Spirit descended visibly in the form of a dove (Matthew 3:16). As Jesus told John, who had objected to the arrangement, "It is fitting for us to fulfill all righteousness" (verse 15). In His Baptism, Jesus identified Himself with us sinners, so that in our Baptism we might receive His righteousness (see 2 Corinthians 5:21).

Among His final words to His disciples is Jesus' Great Commission (Matthew 28:16–20). The only imperative in this passage is "make disciples," which may be translated as "disciple the nations" (verse 19). Disciples are made by baptizing in the triune name of God and teaching them everything Christ has mandated. There is no temporal sequence implied in the text. One can be baptized into teaching or taught into Baptism; either way, the result is the same—a disciple. Jesus promises to be with His followers in this "discipling" activity until the end of the age. When they baptize, He is the one who is baptizing; when they teach, He is the Teacher. The disciples, as ministers, are Christ's instruments.

FOR YOU AND FOR YOUR CHILDREN _____

In Baptism, God's promises fulfilled in Jesus are made our own in a personal way. Every person is baptized individually, by name. On the cross, God saved the world and all of humanity in the death of Jesus, His Son. In Baptism, God saves a particular person and calls him or her to be His own child of His promise. From the time of the apostles, children were baptized because they, too, were included in the promise of salvation. In fact, you might say that adults are baptized as though they were children. Regardless of age, everyone is born anew from above (John 3:3) in the water of Baptism.

In his Pentecost sermon, Peter promises the forgiveness of sins and the Holy Spirit (see Acts 2:38). He says this promise is not only to those who are present to hear it "and for your children [but] for all who are far off, everyone whom the Lord our God calls to Himself" (verse 39). Paul also applied the promise of Baptism to the Philippian jailer and his household (Acts 16:33), which would have included not only his own children but also his servants and their children. The promise of Baptism applied to children is nothing else than to say that (1) children are born in sin and in need of salvation, and (2) Jesus died for all—including children. There are no limits to the Gospel, including age limits.

In his Epistle to the Romans, Paul emphasizes that "all of us who have been baptized . . . were buried therefore with Him by baptism into death, in order that, just as Christ was raised from the dead by the glory of the Father, we too might walk in newness of life" (6:3–4). Since children are born into the sin and death of Adam, which is proven by the fact that they can die, it would make sense that they should be united with Christ in His death and life as soon as possible. Parents would want the greatest possible confidence that their child is in Christ and therefore a child of the promise. This is not to say that those who are not baptized cannot be saved, but God gives us the gift of Baptism for the certainty of salvation in Christ.

THE PROMISES OVERFLOW

Baptism is like a deep, underground aquifer that springs up and overflows with promises and blessings. One of our problems is that we are not aware of all that God does in Baptism. Another problem is that we fail to draw on Baptism. It is like having a large bank account but never drawing any money from it and living as though we were poor. The baptismal font brings promises overflowing. Consider the following gifts and promises of Baptism:

Scripture	Gift or Promise of Baptism
Mark 16:16	Salvation to those who believe and are baptized
Galatians 3:27	Clothed in Christ★
Colossians 2:12	Burial and resurrection in Christ
1 Peter 3:21	Salvation
Titus 3:5	Rebirth and renewal by the Holy Spirit

★It is better to translate this in the passive: "For as many of you as *were baptized* into Christ *have been clothed* with Christ." The white robe sometimes given to the newly baptized in the rite of Baptism is symbolic of being clothed with Christ.

Paul says that God has "put His seal on us" (2 Corinthians 1:22), which He does in Holy Baptism. A seal (Greek: *sphragis*) is a mark of ownership. Soldiers in Caesar's army received such a mark on their foreheads to show their allegiance to Caesar. In Revelation 7 (based on Ezekiel 9), those who are marked by the Lamb are safe from the destruction of the final judgment. In placing His mark of ownership on us, God is making a promise that we belong to Him. In Ephesians 1:14, Paul discusses this seal in terms of a down payment or guarantee of our redemption and the inheritance of eternal life.

SPIRITUAL EXERCISES

◈ Celebrate the anniversary of your Baptism.

◈ Pray the Small Catechism on Holy Baptism (*Concordia*, pp. 339–40). Say each of the four parts aloud and concentrate on the words. Thank God for the water and Spirit that have given you a new birth and life in Jesus.

◈ Sing or speak the hymn "All Christians Who Have Been Baptized" (*LSB* 596).

POINT TO REMEMBER

We were buried therefore with Him by baptism into death, in order that, just as Christ was raised from the dead by the glory of the Father, we too might walk in newness of life. *Romans 6:4*

The Promise of Absolution

But we should hold in high and great esteem God's Word in the Absolution part of Confession. We should not proceed as if we intended to perform and offer Him a splendid work, but simply to accept and receive something from Him.

When I urge you to go to Confession, I am doing nothing else than urging you to be a Christian. *Martin Luther*[5]

---

5   Brief Exhortation to Confession 18 and 32; *Concordia*, pp. 651, 653.

Baptism is but once in a lifetime. Just as we are born once, so we are reborn once. Yet Baptism has daily impact and promises. We are clothed with Christ's righteousness and are covered with His forgiveness. Sin, guilt, and shame make it easy for us to forget who we are as God's children. We may fall into despair and doubt—even doubting that we are truly saved in Christ. Although we receive Baptism once in our lives, the gifts of Baptism are renewed every time we hear the Word of God forgiving our sins. Just as we were washed with water and the Word in Baptism (Ephesians 5:26), so in Holy Absolution we are washed with the Word of forgiveness, returning us again to the promises God made to us in the water of Holy Baptism. Forgiveness frees us from the past to live freely in the present with the promise of a bright future.

A CLEANSING WORD

In 2 Samuel 12, the prophet Nathan shared with King David a story about a rich man who kills the only lamb of his poor neighbor to provide a meal for a traveler. David became very angry after hearing Nathan's tale. David pronounced sentence, saying, "The man who has done this deserves to die" (2 Samuel 12:5). Then Nathan turned the tables on David. He declared: "You are the man!" (verse 7). Despite all that the Lord had given to David, David had committed adultery, then conspired to kill the man to take his wife. In doing so, David had despised the Lord Himself. David confessed, "I have sinned against the LORD" (verse 13). All sin, no matter how great or small, is a sin against God. Nathan responded to David's confession with words of absolution: "The LORD also has put away your sin." But God imposed a discipline: the son born to David by Bathsheba would die. David is forgiven but he is still disciplined by the Lord, as we all are. Although God forgives, and we do not die as sinners, He nevertheless imposes temporal disciplines to teach and admonish us and others (see Hebrews 12:5–11).

According to Scripture, David's son became ill after his birth. For six days and nights, David fasted and prayed to the Lord for his son's life. But David's son died on the seventh day (2 Samuel 12:18) without name or circumcision, which would have occurred on the eighth day. After David was told of the death, he cleaned himself up, worshiped God, and went home—actions that troubled his servants. But David said, "While the child was alive, I fasted and wept, for I said, 'Who knows whether the LORD will be gracious to me, that the child may live?' But now he is dead. Why should I fast? Can I bring him back again? I shall go to him" (2 Samuel 12:22–23). God remembered the promise he had made to David through Nathan concerning a son who would follow him (see 2 Samuel 7:1–17) and gives David a son, Solomon, by Bathsheba. Solomon succeeded David in office as king and was an ancestor of Jesus.

After Jesus' arrest, trial, and death on the cross, the disciples were afraid of the Jews. They feared they were next. So the disciples gathered behind locked doors. But Jesus appears and proclaims, "Peace be with you" (John 20:19). Then He shows His disciples the wounds in His hands and side. Again, He says, "Peace be with you," but He follows it by giving His Holy Spirit to His disciples and sending them as apostles and ministers with the authority to forgive sins (John 20:21–23). With the same Spirit and words, we hear the words of forgiveness from Christ through His authorized representatives in the Office of the Holy Ministry, trusting that we are hearing forgiveness from the Lord Himself. Pastors extend God's forgiveness in Christ on behalf of the Church.

However, Absolution is the prerogative of every Christian. Jesus' words in Matthew 18:15–18 give us an action plan for confronting someone concerning sin. When someone sins against us, we are to go to that person alone. If the person will not acknowledge the sin, then we are to take one or two others as witnesses. Finally, when all else fails, we are to bring the matter to the whole congregation. Every avenue for forgiveness and reconciliation is used. Within the community of believers, there is the authority to bind and loose, to free people from the chains of sin, guilt, and shame and bring them into the freedom of forgiveness. Luther called the Church a "mouth-house of forgiveness," that is, a place where forgiveness is spoken. This is the true and proper work of the Church. As Luther writes: "In this Christian Church [the Holy Spirit] daily and richly forgives all my sins and the sins of all believers."[6]

Psalm 32 is one of the seven penitential psalms that deal with the personal side of confession and forgiveness. The psalmist David speaks of his bones wasting away and his strength being sapped as on a hot day (verses 3–4). He feels the heavy hand of the Lord upon him. There are physical as well as spiritual effects to sin. In confessing his sin, David finds release. God forgives the guilt of his sin. Instead of wasting his energy covering up his sin, David is now free to rejoice and be glad and sing, as well as to teach others in the way they should go (see verse 11). In James 5, the sick are ministered to with prayer, anointing, and also

6   SC II; *Concordia*, p. 330.

confession in the same recognition that what is good for the soul is also good for the body.

At what point does a congregation need to reach out in forgiveness to one who is under discipline? In 2 Corinthians 2:5–11, Paul discusses a man who has been excommunicated from the congregation. The man has repented and desires to be readmitted, and Paul encourages the congregation to reach out to him. Paul does not desire that he be overwhelmed by excessive sorrow. The ultimate goal of any church discipline is the repentance and restoration of the sinner to the life of forgiveness.

JOY RESTORED

Sin that has not been confessed is like a festering wound. The infection spreads from the original site and gradually affects the whole body. It holds the sinner captive in a prison of secrecy. Absolution provides the healing balm of the Gospel on the specific place where sin has done its damage. Specific forgiveness spoken to specific sins breaks the cycle of secrecy and floods the wound with the healing blood of Jesus.

Psalm 51 is traditionally ascribed to David as his response to the confession elicited by the prophet Nathan concerning his adultery with Bathsheba and the murder of Uriah. David states that he has done "what is evil in [God's] sight" (verse 4). Sin always has a vertical component—it is always before the Lord. David recognizes that sin has been his condition from the very moment of his own conception (Psalm 51:5). Even the developing child in the womb is sinful in the sense that he or she is conceived in the same hereditary guilt from Adam. We sin because we are sinful; the sins that we do are the result of our sinful condition. This is why even a tiny baby who is not capable of much action or speech is still considered sinful. It is a condition of natural-born man.

Sin always robs us of joy, whether we are wallowing in guilt and shame, hiding from others, or are anxious over getting caught. In fact, getting caught is the first step toward freedom. When our sin becomes public, the silence of the secret has been broken, and now a word of forgiveness can be spoken and heard. Having been forgiven, David is now in a position to teach others as well (Psalm 51:13). As long as we are bound up in sin, we will attempt to justify ourselves and futilely try to atone for our sins. Such sacrifices God does not desire. He desires instead broken and contrite hearts (verse 17). Having been forgiven and set free, we are then in a position to offer right and pleasing offerings of thanks to God.

AN EMBASSY OF RECONCILIATION _____

The apostle Paul calls his ministry a "ministry of reconciliation," and he sees himself as an "ambassador for Christ" (2 Corinthians 5:18, 20). That makes the Church an embassy of reconciliation where the Prince of Peace brings a peace that surpasses our understanding by His own dying and rising. As an embassy of peace, the Christian congregation both hears and speaks peace.

Those who are in Christ have already died and have become a "new creation. The old has passed away; behold, the new has come" (2 Corinthians 5:17). The certainty that we are "in Christ" comes not from within us, but from God in our Baptism and in the word of forgiveness (Absolution) that restores us (see Ephesians 1:13–14). In the death of Christ, God the Father reconciled the world to Himself, which means that in Christ He no longer counts people's sins against them. They are justified in Jesus, who took on humanity's sin in His innocence, so that we might receive His righteousness as a gift. This is what Luther called a "sweet swap"—our sin for Jesus' righteousness.

Are there any practical limits to forgiveness? Jesus provides the answer as He so often does by way of a parable. In Matthew 18:21–35, He tells of two servants who must make account to their king. The first servant owes a huge amount and cannot pay what he owes. The king is prepared to sell the servant and his family into slavery to take care of the debt. But the servant pleads, "Have patience with me, and I will pay you everything" (verse 26). The king relents and even forgives the debt. However, upon leaving the court of the king, this same man meets up with a fellow servant who owes him a relatively small amount. He calls in the debt, and when the other servant cannot pay, he has him thrown in prison. His actions are reported to the king, who reinstates the verdict of punishment. The king imprisons the unforgiving servant until he should pay his debt, which this loveless servant will never be able to do. The point Jesus seeks to make with this parable is that forgiveness is without limits or boundaries. Jesus makes this same point in the prayer He taught us: "Forgive us our debts as we also have forgiven our debtors" (Matthew 6:12).

In the parable, the first servant is forgiven an outrageous debt by the king. The expectation is that the second servant will also be forgiven his petty debt. Jesus amplifies the difference to remind us of how great God's forgiveness is to each of us. When we forgive one another, we are drawing upon the infinite resource of God's forgiveness in Jesus. Therefore, there can be no limits to forgiveness, whether by the congregation or by the individual. Refusal to forgive implies limits on God's forgiveness and is a denial of the atoning sacrifice of Jesus. The Christian and the Christian congregation will always look for opportunities to forgive and restore the sinner to a right relationship with God and with fellow members of the Body of Christ.

SPIRITUAL EXERCISES

◈ Meditate prayerfully on the penitential psalms (Psalms 6; 32; 38; 51; 102; 130; 143). Look for the blessings and promises of forgiveness in these psalms. Sing or speak the hymn " 'As Surely as I Live,' God Said" (*LSB* 614).

◈ If your conscience is troubling you, make arrangements with your pastor to use Individual Confession and Absolution (see *LSB*, pp. 292–93). Use the Ten Commandments as a template for your confession.

◈ Intentionally seek the forgiveness of someone against whom you have sinned—a family member, a congregation member, a friend, a co-worker. Intentionally seek to forgive someone who has sinned against you.

POINT TO REMEMBER

Blessed is the one whose transgression is forgiven, whose sin is covered. *Psalm 32:1*

The Promise of the Lord's Supper

Therefore, the Sacrament is given as a daily pasture and sustenance, that faith may refresh and strengthen itself [Psalm 23:1–3] so that it will not fall back in such a battle, but become ever stronger and stronger. *Martin Luther* [7]

---

7   LC V 24; *Concordia*, p. 434.

The Lord's Supper is a meal filled with promise—the promise of forgiveness, life, and salvation. Jesus established this Supper of His body and blood on the very night He was betrayed unto death, literally on the same day He gave His body and blood as an atoning sacrifice for the life of the world. In this Holy Supper, as in Baptism and Absolution, God's promises fulfilled in Christ are made personally our own. God speaks them to us as we hear the words of Jesus "given and shed for you" and we receive with our own mouths the gifts of Jesus' sacrifice on the cross—His body and blood.

EATING AND DRINKING WITH GOD _____

The Passover meal united every Israelite with the event of the exodus. For centuries and generations following the events in Egypt, every Israelite family participated in the observance of the Passover. At the Passover table, children learned from their fathers as they told the narrative of God's deliverance. In taking the bread and cup of the Passover, Jesus did something new, yet the Supper remains deeply connected to the Passover observance. In the Lord's Supper, we are united with Christ in His exodus through death to life and also with one another as fellow Israelites of the new covenant in Christ's shed blood.

After Moses met with God on Mount Sinai, he read the Law to the Israelites. After the people said they would be obedient, Moses took half of the blood from the sacrifice "and threw it on the people and said, 'Behold the blood of the covenant' " (Exodus 24:8). As sure as the blood landed on someone and stained his or her robe, so sure was this person's participation in the covenant. The Israelites heard the Word of God and they saw the blood of the covenant. After this, Moses and Aaron, Nadab and Abihu, and the seventy elders of Israel ate and drank with God on His mountain (verses 9–11). Although no one may see God and live to tell about it, these men ate and drank in God's presence and were not harmed. In the same way, we eat and drink in the presence of God at the Lord's Supper, and, under bread and wine, Christ gives us forgiveness, life, and salvation with His body and blood by the creation of the sacramental union through His words.

Many years later, Elijah was sustained in his wilderness journey by bread and water supplied by an angel (see 1 Kings 19:1–9). This hearkened back to Israel being sustained by bread (manna) and water in the wilderness. The angel tells Elijah that the journey is too long and arduous for him without this food and drink. In the same way, our life of faith is too long and demanding without the sustenance of Jesus' body and blood. Notice that the strength of the food God gave him enabled Elijah to complete the forty-day trek to Sinai.

In John 6, Jesus preaches a sermon in the Capernaum synagogue that outraged even His own disciples. He begins by calling Himself the "living bread" and saying that He is greater than Moses and the manna eaten by Israel. To believe in Jesus is to eat of this "living bread" that came down from heaven. As He continues, Jesus intensifies the eating of Him by faith to a scandalous eating of Him with the mouth. While Jesus is not speaking directly about the Lord's Supper as He does in the Words of Institution, nevertheless, His words are clearly an allusion to the Lord's Supper just as His words in John 3:5 are a clear allusion to Baptism. In John 6, Jesus promises that those who believe in Him and who eat His flesh and drink His blood have life in them, and He will raise them up on the Last Day. When we read this account and the question of the outraged hearers in the Capernaum synagogue, we know the answer. How can Jesus give us His flesh to eat and His blood to drink? In the bread and wine of the Lord's Supper, of course!

Each account of the institution of the Lord's Supper provides some unique details. Matthew mentions that it is for the "forgiveness of sins" (26:28). Matthew and Mark place an emphasis on blood while Luke accents the "new covenant." Luke also has the command "Do this in remembrance of Me" (22:19). Luke also gives us more details concerning the Passover meal. When Paul discusses the institution of this meal, the cup of the Lord's Supper is the "cup of blessing" (1 Corinthians 10:16), the third cup of the Passover meal, which immediately followed the supper. Luke also mentions a cup before the meal began.

The account in 1 Corinthians is an account of the Lord's Supper given to Paul "from the Lord." It reflects the ongoing nature of the Lord's Supper as a liturgical act in the Church. There is a mandate to "do this" both for the bread and for the cup. Paul also specifies that this is to continue until the Lord comes, that is, until the Last Day (1 Corinthians 11:26). This account provides the confidence that the Lord intended this meal to continue in His Church until the end of days. It also demonstrates the centrality of the Lord's Supper in the life of the Church. In addition, Paul provides some instructions concerning the right use of the Holy Supper in verses 27–32.

THE BREAKING OF THE BREAD _____

From the very beginning of the New Testament Church, the Lord's Supper has been a central element of Christian worship. This should not be surprising to anyone familiar with the Scriptures. Table fellowship with God is a major theme throughout the Old and New Testaments. Jesus Himself taught and ate with people constantly. On two occasions, He fed large crowds with multiplied bread and fish. Two incidents in particular profoundly shaped Christian worship and liturgy and illustrate how central the Lord's Supper is in Christian spirituality.

In Jesus' encounter with the two disciples on the Emmaus road, He first taught them from the Scriptures (the Old Testament) about His suffering, death, and resurrection, and upon reaching their destination, He revealed Himself in the breaking of the bread (see Luke 24:13–35). It was a "Word and Sacrament" event. Jesus teaches that the main point of the Scriptures is Himself—His death and resurrection. Although the disciples were prevented from recognizing Jesus (it was not their fault), He revealed Himself as He broke the bread at the table. The story indicates that Jesus would be present in His Church in a new way—not visibly and locally as the disciples had experienced Him, but He would be recognized in the "breaking of the bread," that is, in His Supper.

The first believers gathered daily in the temple for the morning and evening offices of prayer. They also gathered in private homes to celebrate the Lord's Supper in fellowship with one another (Acts 2:46). As a fellowship, they had all their possessions in common (verse 44). Luke tells us that they were devoted to the doctrine of the apostles; the communion or fellowship, which is the "breaking of the bread"; and to the prayers (verse 42). (The syntax of this sentence in the Greek text favors three distinct elements—doctrine, communion, prayer.) This is the outline of the Divine Service as we know it—the Service of the Word, in which the doctrine of the apostles is preached, and the Service of the Sacrament, in which the Lord Jesus makes Himself known to us in the breaking of the bread.

ONE BREAD, ONE BODY _____

The promise of forgiveness of sins in the Lord's Supper is also a promise of life and salvation. In eating the one bread, the body of Christ, we are the Body of Christ. You might say that the Church is what she eats! This unity in the body of Christ means that we are in communion not only with God but also with our fellow baptized believers in a "communion of saints"—holy things uniting a holy people. Here is a community that can be found nowhere else on earth, a community that mystically includes "the angels, archangels, and all the company of heaven." Holy Communion always happens with peripheral vision—with eyes fixed on Jesus and His gifts to us, in view of our fellow baptized believers with whom we are one Body in Christ.

The apostle Paul states that we are one body because we eat of one bread (1 Corinthians 10:17). We also drink of one cup. Since the same body and blood are given to and received by all communicants, we share or have these things in common. This is what the word *communion* or *fellowship* means—to have something in common. In the Sacrament, our unity in Christ is revealed and manifested. Therefore, it is vitally important that there be no divisions among us (as there were in Corinth, against which Paul warned). Our communion is not only with Christ, but it is also with one another as the Body of Christ.

Paul's discussion of the Lord's Supper takes place because of his concerns for how the Corinthians are celebrating the meal. The members of the congregation were getting drunk at their fellowship meal and despising the poor and hungry within their group (1 Corinthians 11:17–22). Both of these things were denials of their unity in Christ. In failing to discern the body of the Lord in the Supper and their unity together as the Body of Christ, the Corinthians incurred God's temporal judgment—some became ill and some even died. To avoid this, Paul says that they are to examine themselves in light of the gift that is being given and, in this way, eat of the bread and drink of the cup.

The greeting of peace is an ancient sign of our peace and reconciliation in Christ. The actual style of the greeting has varied. In the early Church it was a kiss. Later, everyone kissed a cross. In our culture, it is a handshake and verbal greeting. All of these things show our unity in the Body of Christ. Luther's 1526 post-Communion prayer asks that the gifts received would work faith toward God and love toward the neighbor. Faith and love are the two ways that Christians live outside of themselves. This is precisely what is lacking in the Corinthian congregation—faith and love. These two are also inseparable—there can be no faith in Christ without love for the neighbor; there can be no God-pleasing love for the neighbor without faith in Christ.

SPIRITUAL EXERCISES

◈ Make self-examination a regular, intentional part of your preparation to receive the Lord's Supper. Read "Christian Questions with Their Answers" (*LSB*, pp. 329–30).

◈ Pray the Small Catechism on the Lord's Supper (*Concordia*, p. 343). Acknowledge the gift of Christ's body and blood as food and drink together with the blessings and benefits that go with the Sacrament.

◈ Meditate prayerfully on the Nunc Dimittis (Luke 2:29–32). Consider it both as a post-Communion hymn and a hymn in the hour of one's death. Speak or sing the hymn "O Lord, We Praise Thee" (*LSB* 617).

◈ Visit someone who is alone, whether at home, in the hospital, or in a nursing home. Offer to accompany your pastor on a shut-in call and bring the comfort of your presence to another member of the Body of Christ.

POINT TO REMEMBER

For as often as you eat this bread and drink this cup, you proclaim the Lord's death until He comes. *1 Corinthians 11:26*

The Promise of Life

Where there is forgiveness of sins, there is also life and salvation.
Martin Luther [8]

"Get a life." You have likely heard that line at one time or another. Perhaps you have said it yourself, or someone has said it to you. The great news of Jesus is that in Him you already have a life! Here is the "secret" of the spiritual life: It is not centered in you but in Jesus Christ, who is your life. The promise of eternal life is not simply a promise of life in heaven one day, but it is a promise of eternal life here and now. God gave you new life in your Baptism, a life that is renewed in the forgiveness of your sins, a life that flows from Jesus to you in the Supper of His body and blood, a life that is lived now by faith in the Son of God who loved you and gave Himself up for you. As we live in Christ by faith and He lives in us, we discover a life we cannot have any other way. Jesus said, "I came that they may have life and have it abundantly" (John 10:10).

---

8   SC VI; *Concordia*, p. 343.

ABUNDANT LIFE

The image of Jesus as our Good Shepherd teaches us much about the promise of life (see John 10:1–18). We know that the Good Shepherd gives life to His sheep. He protects them from robbers and wolves. His voice is the means by which His sheep recognize and follow Him. He lays down His life for the sheep. When read in light of Jesus' words, Psalm 23 provides a wonderful job description of the Good Shepherd:

1. He leads the sheep to quiet waters and green pasture.
2. He restores them when they fall down.
3. He leads them through the threatening dark valley of death, going before them.
4. He anoints their wounds with oil.
5. He prepares a feast for them in the presence of their enemies.

Good Shepherd Jesus leads us through death to resurrection, having followed that path ahead of us. He baptizes us in the quiet waters of Baptism. He anoints us with the healing balm of forgiveness in Absolution. He grants us a place at His table where He feeds us His own body and blood in the presence of our enemies: sin, death, devil, our sinful nature, and the Law that condemns us.

In John 15, Jesus describes our relationship to Him as that of the relationship between the vine and the branch. The branch draws its life from the vine and is nourished by it. We abide in Christ, and Christ abides in us. His life is our life, and His life is fruitful. The Father "prunes" (disciplines) us, not to punish us as our sins deserve but that we might be even more fruitful. This pruning occurs in the day-to-day encounter with God's Law that kills us in order that we may be raised to life in Christ. Jesus promises that we will receive whatever we ask, provided that we abide in Him through faith and He abides in us through His Word. This is not a carte blanche promising an affirmative answer to every prayer, but rather the promise that, as the life of Christ flows through us, our will and Christ's will are one, so that our requests are shaped to His will. In the Lord's Supper, the death and life of Christ literally flow into us as His body and blood. It is no accident that the illustration of the vine was used in the Upper Room on the night Jesus instituted the Lord's Supper!

Philip Melanchthon recorded the words of Church father Cyril of Alexandria on this topic as part of the Apology of the Augsburg Confession:

> For who has doubted that Christ is in this manner a vine, and we the branches, deriving life for ourselves from this? Hear Paul saying, "For you are all one in Christ Jesus; so we, though many, are one body in Christ; for we all partake of the one bread" (Galatians 3:28; Romans 12:5; 1 Corinthians 10:17). Does he perhaps think that the virtue of the mystical benediction is unknown to us? Since this is in us, does it not also, by the communication of Christ's flesh, cause Christ to dwell in us bodily?[9]

By observing how God cares for His creatures, we can realize that we need not be anxious about this life. Instead, we can be joyous about our participation in the Body of Christ. Neither the birds nor the lilies are anxious for anything in their lives, yet God provides abundantly for them (Matthew 6:26, 28–29). God values us so greatly that He declares us to be worth the price of God's Son, Jesus, and His holy, precious blood shed on the cross for our redemption. By worrying, we are deprived of rest and often fail to see what God has already provided us without our asking. In Philippians 4, Paul says, "Do not be anxious about anything, but in everything by prayer and supplication with thanksgiving let your requests be made known to God" (verse 6). The phrase "with thanksgiving" indicates that we are to ask our petitions while thanking God for the circumstances and need that brought us to prayer in the first place. (Remember, Paul was in prison when he wrote the joyful Epistle to the Philippians!) The promise of prayer is not that we will get whatever we ask for, but that the peace of God that surpasses our understanding will keep our hearts and minds where they belong and where our life is—in Christ Jesus, our Lord (see Philippians 4:7).

In many places, Jesus promises the Holy Spirit, "another Helper," to His disciples (for example, John 14:16; 16:13). In sending the Spirit from the Father, Jesus Himself will be with His disciples so that they will never be alone in this life. The spiritual life is life in the Holy Spirit, whose work is to convict and convince the world of sin, righteousness, and judgment. He is the "delivery man" of the Trinity, taking from what Jesus has and delivering it to us through the Word and Sacraments.

In the third part of His High Priestly Prayer, Jesus prays for all who would believe through the apostolic Word (John 17:20–25). That includes all believers, including us. He prays that believers may be

---

9   Ap X 56; *Concordia*, p. 154.

brought to complete unity in Him, just as He and the Father are one (verse 22). This is not, as some believe, an external or institutional unity of the churches, but our mystical, hidden union with Christ as our life is in Him. He prays also that we would be with Him and see His glory that He eternally has from the Father (verse 24). This is Jesus' abiding prayer for us and for the whole Church. What a comfort to know that Jesus is continually interceding for us as our own High Priest and that we need no other mediator save Jesus.

And this is clearly exemplified in the account of the thief on the cross. The penitent thief prayed, "Jesus, remember me when You come into Your kingdom" (Luke 23:42). He did not pray to be saved or to be spared his cross; he recognized that his death sentence was well deserved but that Jesus was innocent of any wrongdoing. In turn, Jesus promised the dying thief: "Today you will be with Me in Paradise" (verse 43). Although the thief was about to die, his life was held safely in the Man dying next to him who promised him heaven. This is Jesus' promise to all who trust in Him as that thief did, a promise we can take to our deathbeds: "Today you will be with Me in Paradise."

NOW HEARD, NOT YET SEEN

Perhaps the greatest "mystery" of the Christian life of promise is that we have already died, risen, and now reign with Christ even as we live out our lives on earth. While this may seem confusing, it follows a consistent pattern. God never does things in bits and pieces. He gives us the whole lot in Jesus—then He gives a whole lot more. Now we are the children of God, and there is still more to come. The abundant life of promise is living in the promise, knowing that when God speaks it is done and that in Christ a promise made is a promise kept by God. Now we must hear and trust; soon we will see.

Ephesians 1:3–14 is a marvelous run-on sentence in Greek, emphasizing that one thing cannot be isolated from the next. At least ten times in this passage, Paul underscores the fact that all our spiritual blessings are in Christ. In Christ we are chosen, predestined, adopted, redeemed, and forgiven. The plan and purpose of God's eternal will is to unite (the Greek word means "recapitulate" or "bring together under one head") all things in heaven and earth in Christ. We were included in Christ when we first heard the Word of the Gospel and were baptized (marked) with the seal of "the promised Holy Spirit, who is the guarantee of our inheritance" (verse 14), which will be fulfilled in the resurrection.

According to Hebrews 11:1, faith is certainty in a promise: "the assurance of things hoped for, the conviction of things not seen." The writer to the Hebrews gives a kind of hall of fame of the faithful: Abel, Enoch, Noah, Abraham, Isaac, Jacob, Joseph, Moses, Rahab, Gideon, David, and a host of others (Hebrews 11:4–40). Thus we see how others have lived by faith and not by sight, trusting the promises of God over and against what they saw and experienced in their own lives. Their abundant life in Christ was lived in hopeful expectation of our union together with Him. The spiritual life of faith is one of hearing the Word of God and trusting in His promises, not in receiving and seeing the fulfillment of every promise in this life.

GOD'S LAST PROMISE AND HIS FIRST _____

The Bible begins and ends with a promise. Most people do not think of the Book of Revelation as a book of promises, but it is. It is God's last word on His promises. Revelation was written at a time of great struggle and persecution for the Church, especially the congregations of Asia Minor. Things seemed to be going from bad to worse, and many believers despaired that what they believed might not come to pass. Revelation provides an image book of promises kept: the crucified Lamb lives and reigns, His city comes down from heaven as a bride on her wedding day, and her saints and martyrs are eternally blessed—just as Jesus promised.

The seven churches of Asia Minor to whom John was writing the account of this vision were real congregations living in an actual time in history. They also provide a cross section of the Church as it is through-out all time—faithful, conflicted, heterodox, complacent, poor, strug-gling. Yet to each of the churches there is a specific promise of life and salvation from Christ, the Lord of the Church.

1. To doctrinally pure though loveless Ephesus: the right to eat from the tree of life (2:1–7).

2. To poor and faithful Smyrna: the crown of life (2:8–11).

3. To steadfast though immoral Pergamum: a new name (2:12–17).

4. To persevering though heterodox Thyatira: authority over the nations (2:18–29).

5. To sleepy Sardis: unsoiled clothing and names not blotted out of the Book of Life (3:1–6).

6. To weak but faithful Philadelphia: the name of God and of His city (3:7–13).

7. To complacent, lukewarm Laodicea: new clothes, salve for their eyes, and table fellowship with Christ (3:14–22).

As we have seen, water and Spirit always go together in the Scriptures (see John 3:5). The river of the water of life described in Revelation 22:1–5 is a picture of the Holy Spirit flowing from the throne of God (the Father) and the Lamb (the Son) down the center of the city. The tree of life (Genesis 3:24) straddles the river (the Spirit is the Lord and Giver of life), and it is once again accessible to the nations. It bears fruit twelve months in the year, and its leaves are a healing medicine for the nations. What began in a garden ends with the tree of life in a kind of central park within the glorious heavenly city of God. The promise of enmity with the devil has come to its fulfillment, and he who by a tree once overcame now has been overcome by the tree of the cross. The result is that we may once again eat from the tree of life and live forever. The final promise of Scripture is the fervent prayer of the Church as she lives in the watchful waiting of the end times. Jesus promises, "I am coming soon" (this can also be translated, "I come quickly"). And the Church prays, "Amen. Come, Lord Jesus!" (Revelation 22:20).

This is the prayer of the spiritual life of promise, a life of hopeful expectation, lived in the "now" of new life in Christ and in the hope of eternal life to come in the resurrection. Each and every day of a baptized believer's life is lived in the hope of this prayer: "Amen. Come, Lord Jesus."

SPIRITUAL EXERCISES

◈ Meditate prayerfully on Psalm 27. Note especially the promises of God and the psalmist's trust in God's Word of promise. Speak or sing the hymn "O God, O Lord of Heaven and Earth" (*LSB* 834).

◈ Each day pray one petition of the Lord's Prayer and its explanation from the Small Catechism (*Concordia*, pp. 331–38).

◈ Intentionally seek opportunities to speak of life in Christ to another person. Begin with a fellow believer in your congregation, and then speak to someone who does not know of God's love in Christ.

POINT TO REMEMBER

I have been crucified with Christ. It is no longer I who live, but Christ who lives in me. And the life I now live in the flesh I live by

faith in the Son of God, who loved me and gave Himself for me.
Galatians 2:20

Lutheran Teaching on Promise

JUSTIFYING FAITH IS TRUST IN THE PROMISE

Faith means not only a knowledge of the history, but the kind of faith that believes in the promise. Paul plainly testifies about this when he says in Romans 4:16, "That is why it depends on faith, in order that the promise may rest on grace and be guaranteed." He judges that the promise cannot be received unless it comes through faith. Therefore, he puts them together as things that belong to one another. He connects the promise and faith. It will be easy to decide what faith is if we consider the Creed, where this article certainly stands: the forgiveness of sins. It is not enough to believe that Christ was born, suffered, was raised again, unless we add also this article, which is the purpose of the history: the forgiveness of sins. To this article the rest must be referred, namely, that for Christ's sake, and not because of our merits, forgiveness of sins is given to us. For what need was there that Christ was given for our sins if our merits can make satisfaction for our sins? (Ap IV [II] 50–52; *Concordia*, p. 89)

THE PROMISE MUST ALWAYS BE IN VIEW OF FAITH

The promise should always be in sight. Because of His promise, God wishes to be gracious and to justify for Christ's sake, not because of the Law or our works. In this promise timid consciences should seek reconciliation and justification. By this promise they should sustain themselves and be confident that they have a gracious God for Christ's sake, because of His promise. So works can never make a conscience peaceful. Only the promise can. If justification and peace of conscience must be sought in something other than love and works, then love and works do not justify. This is true even though they are virtues and belong to the righteousness of the Law, insofar as they are a fulfilling of the Law. Obedience to the Law justifies by the righteousness of the Law—if a person fulfills it. But imperfect righteousness of the Law is not accepted by God unless it is accepted because of faith. So legal righteousness does not justify, that is, it neither reconciles nor regenerates nor by itself makes us acceptable before God. (Ap V [III] 59–60 [180–181]; *Concordia*, p. 109)

JUSTIFICATION GAINED THROUGH FAITH IN THE PROMISE

Since justification is gained through the free promise, it follows that we cannot justify ourselves. Otherwise, why would there be a need to promise? Since the promise can only be received by faith, the Gospel (which is properly the promise of forgiveness of sins and of justification for Christ's sake) proclaims the righteousness of faith in Christ. The Law does not teach this, nor is this the righteousness of the Law. For the Law demands our works and our perfection. But, for Christ's sake, the Gospel freely offers reconciliation to us, who have been vanquished by sin and death. This is received not by works, but by faith alone. This faith does not bring to God confidence in one's own merits, but only confidence in the promise, or the mercy promised in Christ. This special faith (by which an individual believes that for Christ's sake his sins are forgiven him, and that for Christ's sake God is reconciled and sees us favorably) gains forgiveness of sins and justifies us. In repentance, namely, in terrors, this faith comforts and encourages hearts. It regenerates us and brings the Holy Spirit so that we may be able to fulfill God's Law: to love God, truly fear God, truly be confident that God hears prayer, and obey God in all afflictions. This faith puts to death concupiscence and the like. So faith freely receives forgiveness of sins. It sets Christ, the Mediator and Atoning Sacrifice, against God's wrath. It does not present our merits or our love. This faith is the true knowledge of Christ and helps itself to the benefits of Christ. This faith regenerates hearts and comes before the fulfilling of the Law. Not a syllable exists about this faith in the teaching of our adversaries. Therefore, we find equal fault with the adversaries because (a) they teach only the righteousness of the Law, and (b) they do not teach the righteousness of the Gospel, which proclaims the righteousness of faith in Christ. (Ap IV [II] 43–47; *Concordia*, p. 88)

THE PROMISE OF BAPTISM

Therefore, every Christian has enough in Baptism to learn and to do all his life. For he has always enough to do by believing firmly what Baptism promises and brings: victory over death and the devil [Romans 6:3–6], forgiveness of sin [Acts 2:38], God's grace [Titus 3:5–6], the entire Christ, and the Holy Spirit with His gifts [1 Corinthians 6:11]. In short, Baptism is so far beyond us that if timid nature could realize this, it might well doubt whether it could be true. Think about it. Imagine there was a doctor somewhere who understood the art of saving people from death or, even though they died, could restore them quickly to life so that they would afterward live forever. Oh, how the world would pour in money like snow and rain. No one could find access to him because of the throng of the rich! But here in Baptism there is freely brought to everyone's door such a treasure and medicine that it utterly destroys death and preserves all people alive. (LC IV 41–43; *Concordia*, p. 427)

THE PROMISE OF ABSOLUTION

Here you see that Baptism, both in its power and meaning, includes also the third Sacrament, which has been called repentance. It is really nothing other than Baptism. What else is repentance but a serious attack on the old man‹, that his lusts be restrained,› and an entering into a new life? Therefore, if you live in repentance, you walk in Baptism. For Baptism not only illustrates such a new life, but also produces, begins, and exercises it. For in Baptism are given grace, the Spirit, and power to suppress the old man, so that the new man may come forth and become strong [Romans 6:3–6]. (LC IV 74–76; *Concordia*, p. 430)

THE PROMISE OF THE LORD'S SUPPER

Therefore also, it is useless talk when they say that Christ's body and blood are not given and shed for us in the Lord's Supper, so we could not have forgiveness of sins in the Sacrament. Although the work is done and the forgiveness of sins is secured by the cross [John 19:30], it cannot come to us in any other way than through the Word. How would we know about it otherwise, that such a thing was accomplished or was to be given to us, unless it were presented by preaching or the oral Word [Romans 10:17; 1 Corinthians 1:21]? How do they know about it? Or how can they receive and make the forgiveness their own, unless they lay hold of and believe the Scriptures and the Gospel? But now the entire Gospel and the article of the Creed—I believe in . . . the holy Christian Church, . . . the forgiveness of sins, and so on—are embodied by the Word in this Sacrament and presented to us. Why, then, should we let this treasure be torn from the Sacrament when the fanatics must confess that these are the very words we hear everywhere in the Gospel? They cannot say that these words in the Sacrament are of no use, just as they dare not say that the entire Gospel or God's Word, apart from the Sacrament, is of no use. (LC V 31–32; *Concordia*, p. 435)

Glossary

Absolution. Literally, "set free." The application of the forgiveness of sins in Christ by means of the spoken word.

Anfechtung. Luther used this German word to describe the all-consuming fear for one's life and salvation in light of God's right to condemn all sinners and in light of the unceasing attacks of the devil, the world, and the sinful flesh. Without the Gospel, someone experiencing this fear has no way of escape from certain doom and no hope. The only answer for *Anfechtung* is Absolution.

anti-authoritarianism. Narrowly defined, anti-authoritarianism is the rejection of any form of coercion or abuse of power, whether political, social, or economic. Broadly, anti-authoritarianism is the rejection of power held or used by another, whether an individual, group, or institution. *See also* **individualism.**

Antinomianism. Adherents maintained that a Christian is free from all moral law and that the Gospel causes knowledge of sin and repentance. Some in this movement denied the third use of the Law and the role of the Law in good works. John Agricola championed this view at the time of the Reformation. Both Luther and the Lutheran Confessions rejected it because it ultimately turned the Gospel into a new Law.

Cafeterianism. An attempt to create one's own worldview by selecting, cafeteria-style, religious or moral concepts, ideas, and practices from a variety of sources. A person who attends a Christian church on Sunday while believing in reincarnation might be viewed as a "cafeterian," for example, since bodily resurrection and reincarnation are inherently incompatible.

clarity of the Scriptures. While not all texts in the Scriptures are equally clear, the heart and center of Scripture is Jesus Christ, who is the light of the world and makes the whole of the Bible lucid. Obscure passages are interpreted and understood in the light of those texts that are clear.

285

confession. Has two general meanings: (1) Acknowledgment, admission, or disclosure of one's own sins. Confession is beneficial and should be embraced as an opportunity to renew the rejection of Satan made at Baptism and to receive forgiveness in Christ through the Gospel. Confession is necessary when a believer has committed a coarse, premeditated sin. The Lutheran Confessions reject both the requirement and even the possibility of enumerating all sins in confession (AC XI; Ap XI; SA III III) but insist on retaining private confession, though they grant that it is a human establishment of the Church. The Absolution that follows confession is the "living voice of the Gospel" (Ap XI; SC V). (2) Speaking in unity with others of the same faith (John 9:22; Romans 10:9; Philippians 2:11; 1 Timothy 3:16; 1 John 4:3; 2 John 7; Revelation 3:5).

contrition. Movement of the heart prior to conversion, namely, that "the heart must perceive sin, [and] dread God's wrath" (FC SD II 70; *Concordia*, p. 533). Scripture teaches two truths about contrition: (1) Contrition always precedes genuine conversion (FC SD II 70). Fear of God's wrath and damnation always precedes faith (Joel 2:12; Mark 1:15; Luke 15:18; 18:13; 24:47; Acts 2:37; 16:29; FC SD II 54, 70). True contrition is not active, that is, fabricated remorse, but passive, that is, true sorrow of the heart, suffering, and pain of death (SA III III 2). It should not be concluded from this that contrition is a cause of forgiveness (Romans 3:28). (2) Contrition in no way brings about, implements, or occasions justification through faith (FC SD II 30–31).

coram Deo. Before God.

Darwinian evolution. Sometimes referred to as organic or macroevolution. This view is currently represented by "neo-Darwinism" and maintains, as corollary theories, that a spiritual realm does not exist (philosophical materialism) and that everything exists by natural causes alone (naturalism). Modern science is proving some Darwinian beliefs less and less tenable.

Darwinism. An explanation for the existence and diversity of life on earth, attributed to Charles Darwin, which includes such concepts as Darwinian evolution and other related concepts of how living organisms change and either thrive or die out. Influential thinkers such as Herbert Spencer developed Darwin's ideas into a social theory that promoted "survival of the fittest" and formed part of Nazi thought regarding the Holocaust.

Deus absconditus. The hidden God, or God as He hides Himself.

Deus revelatus. The revealed God, or God as He reveals Himself in Christ.

doxology. In the context of worship, a statement proclaiming God's glory. Although not appearing in the text of the Lord's Prayer, a traditional doxological ending is recited at the prayer's conclusion: "For Thine is the kingdom and the power and the glory forever and ever."

efficacy of the Word. The power of God's Word to effect or accomplish its divine purpose.

enthusiasts. The word describes a person so taken by his views that he uses violence or radical separation from society to enforce those views—actions typical of religious cults. The Lutheran Confessions use the word to describe fanatics who believed that God spoke to them directly without Holy Scripture and would save them without the Means of Grace.

Evangelicalism. In North America, "evangelical" is used to describe Protestant churches that generally stem from the Reformed, Baptist, and Wesleyan denominational families rooted in the American revivalist movements of the eighteenth and nineteenth centuries. Modern Evangelicalism is typified by a strong belief in biblical inerrancy, Christ's work on the cross as the only means of man's forgiveness, an emphasis on personal conversion, and the centrality of evangelism in congregational and personal life.

exegesis. Literally "to lead or draw out" of the biblical text, to say what the text says by careful study using the original languages.

external Word. An expression used by Luther to describe the Bible and biblical teaching. Luther contrasted the external Word with the internal word or feelings sought by people who believed that the Spirit guided them directly, apart from the Bible.

extra nos. Outside of us. Used to refer to the external character of the Gospel and Sacraments.

faith. God-given trust in the promise of forgiveness, life, and salvation on account of Jesus' life, death, and resurrection.

forensic justification. The central way the Bible speaks of our justification before God is in a forensic, or judicial, way. God declares us sinners righteous in His sight through faith in His Son, Jesus Christ.

fundamentalism. A reactionary movement against liberalism and modernism that focuses on certain cardinal tenets of the Christian faith—biblical inerrancy among them—often to the exclusion of other beliefs. Liberal Christians often accuse those believing in biblical inerrancy of being "fundamentalists."

Gospel reductionism. Using the Gospel to suggest considerable latitude in faith and life not explicitly detailed in the Gospel. Associated with liberal Christianity, Gospel reductionism is closely aligned with Antinomianism and partial inspiration.

grace. The undeserved kindness of God to forgive and save the sinner for Jesus' sake.

Heilsgewissheit. German for "assurance of salvation."

heterodox. A mixture of truth and error. A church is said to be "heterodox" when it holds to the central truth of the Gospel yet teaches errors that contradict the Gospel.

historical critical method. An approach to the study of the Scriptures shaped by Enlightenment presuppositions regarding history and the accessibility of historical events to the interpreter. Those who practiced this method more often than not denied the divine character of the Scriptures.

hours of prayer. Set times and customs of prayer rooted in early Christian practice: Matins, Lauds, Prime, Terce, Sext, None, Vespers, Compline. (Matins and Lauds were combined in some traditions.) Lutheran hymnals often contain services for Matins (morning service) and Vespers (evening service).

humanism. A broad range of philosophies that emphasize human dignity and worth and recognize a common morality based on universal, rational human nature. Humanists who deny the possibility of any supernatural involvement in human affairs are sometimes called secular humanists.

incarnate. To be "enfleshed," referring to the Second Person of the Trinity becoming a human being in the womb of the Virgin Mary. "The Word became flesh and dwelt among us" (John 1:14).

individualism. A worldview emphasizing self-reliance and the achievement of personal goals or desires without the interference of society, the state, or other institutions. Individualism has been described by some philosophers, including Alexis de Tocqueville, as influencing a decline of society.

inerrancy. The teaching that the Bible, as originally inspired by the Holy Spirit and recorded by the prophets, apostles, and evangelists, did not contain errors. Churches teaching biblical inerrancy recognize that scribes and translators may have erred in copying the Bible over the centuries.

intercession. Prayer offered on behalf of another person or persons.

justification. God declares sinners to be just or righteous for Christ's sake; that is, God has imputed or charged our sins to Christ and He imputes or credits Christ's righteousness to us.

koinonia. The Greek term commonly translated in the Bible as communion, participation, sharing, or fellowship. Koinonia expresses a deep fellowship by faith between believers and their risen Lord, with His body and blood in the Lord's Supper, in His sufferings, death, and resurrection, and between believers and each other. This koinonia, beginning in Christ, expresses itself in concrete actions of charity and service for one's neighbor.

larvae Dei. Literally, the "masks" God wears to serve us. Through vocation, or calling, God serves us while concealing Himself behind the masks of our spouse, employer, family member, public servant, or neighbor.

lectionary. From the Latin word for "reading." A collection of texts for public reading for each Sunday and festival in the Church Year.

liturgical prayer. Prayers offered in the sacrificial part of the Church's public worship (hymns, collects, prayers, Preface, Sanctus, Lord's Prayer, Agnus Dei, canticles, etc.).

Lord's Prayer. Prayer taught by Jesus (see Matthew 6:9–13; Luke 11:2–4). In some Christian traditions, also called the "Our Father," after the prayer's introduction.

modernism. A cultural movement emerging in the late 1800s and later emphasizing the inevitability of human achievement (especially through science and technology) and a positive view of human reason, particularly in its ability to determine the truth.

mysticism. While mysticism itself is a broad form of spirituality with distinct nuances, it is best characterized by the movement to transcend or move above the earthly through inward experience.

norma normans. Literally "norming norm." This Latin term is used to describe the function of the Bible as absolutely normative in the life of the Church.

norma normata. Literally, "normed norm." This Latin term is used to describe the Lutheran Confessions as authoritative because they are derived from the Bible.

Office of the Keys. The peculiar, special, unique spiritual authority given by Christ to the whole Church to forgive the sins of repentant sinners but to withhold forgiveness from the unrepentant as long as they do not repent (John 20:22–23; Matthew 16:19; 18:15–20; Revelation 1:18). In particular, the Office of the Keys, administered by pastors (AC V) by the call of the Church (AC XIV), is the office Christ has given to His Church to administer forgiveness and discipline by rightly distinguishing Law and Gospel. The Christian congregation, by the command of Christ, calls pastors to carry out the Office of the Keys publicly in His name and on behalf of the congregation.

opinio legis. The "opinion of the Law" that God deals with us on the basis of our works, which must have value or merit in the scheme of salvation.

oratio, meditatio, tentatio. Prayer, meditation, and trial. Luther said that theologians (students of God's Word) are made by *prayer, meditation,* and the *trial* of life under the cross.

particularism. Used here negatively to describe the understanding of a group of people that sees God's activity solely tied to them and that therefore seek to preserve their own identity at the expense of reaching out to others and incorporating them into their midst.

penance. In Roman Catholic theology, the third sacrament, consisting of three parts: contrition, confession to the priest, and works of satisfaction. Also in Eastern Orthodoxy and Roman Catholicism, the actions assigned by the priest as an aid to repentance and amendment of life.

Pietism. A post-Reformation religious movement associated with Philip Spener (1635–1705) that was characterized by a shift from the objective reality of Christ's gifts to the subjective appropriation of the Gospel and the subsequent renewal of the believer's life personally and socially. Its main features include (1) Church based on small-group Bible studies; (2) governing right of the universal priesthood of believers; (3) essential requirement of both Christian knowledge and its practice; (4) sympathetic attitude to those adhering to false doctrine; (5) centrality of the devotional life in Christian university training; (6) preaching style that emphasized conversion, implanting doctrine into the new man, and reaping the fruit of faith.

postmodernism. Refers to a cluster of themes that are somewhat interconnected in their opposition to the attempts to establish truthfulness which characterized the period of modernity. The focus of postmodernism is characterized by pluralism and the rejection of claims to absolute truth.

Rationalism. The Enlightenment movement that saw human reason as the ultimate criterion for reality.

reductionism. A modern concept focusing on the human ability to reduce complex ideas or things to simple or more fundamental ideas or things. Fundamentalism exhibits reductionism in its attempt to reduce the Christian faith to very few "key" concepts or teachings. Gospel reductionism makes a similar error by devaluing or outright rejecting God's Law in the life of the believer. *See also* **antinomianism.**

revelation. God's act of making His will manifest in both Law and Gospel to human beings. The instrument of God's revelation is the prophetic and apostolic Scriptures.

righteousness. God's perfection and holiness. The righteousness of the Christian is the righteousness of Jesus Christ applied through faith in Christ.

sola scriptura. Scripture alone. Scripture is the unique fountain of Christian teaching and the final rule by which to evaluate all proclamation in the Church.

sufficiency of Scripture. The Scriptures are sufficient for the purpose that God gave them, namely, to impart saving knowledge of Jesus Christ.

theology of glory. Theology of mystic and scholastic speculation, which holds that true knowledge of God derives from the study of nature, which reflects God's glory. A theology of glory focuses on human reason, mysticism, or morality.

theology of the cross. A term gleaned from Luther's Heidelberg Disputation of 1518, referring to a theology that is derived from the study of the humiliation, sufferings, and death of Christ.

type. A person, place, or event in the Old Testament that prefigures or pictures the person and work of Christ or the Church in the New Testament.

verbal inspiration. The Holy Spirit guided the prophets, evangelists, and apostles in writing the books of the Bible, inspiring their very words while using their particular styles of expression. Conservative Christian churches hold that the Bible's words are God's Word and that the original manuscripts of Scripture were without error, but some mistakes may have entered the text as it was copied, edited, or translated over the centuries.

vicarious atonement. This refers to the entire ministry of Christ, His obedience to the will of God, His death, and His resurrection. He did it all on our behalf or in our stead—that is, vicariously.

Scripture Index